THE DEVIL AND THE
SACRED IN ENGLISH DRAMA, 1350–1642

John Cox tells the intriguing story of stage devils from their earliest appearance in English plays to the closing of the theatres by parliamentary order in 1642. The book represents a major revision of E. K. Chambers' ideas of stage devils in *The Medieval Stage* (1903), arguing that this is not a history of gradual secularization, as scholarship has maintained for the last century, but rather that stage devils were profoundly shaped from the outset by the assumptions of sacred drama and retained this shape virtually unchanged until the advent of permanent commercial theatres near London.

The book spans both medieval and Renaissance drama including the medieval Mystery cycles on the one hand, through to plays by Greene, Marlowe, Shakespeare (*1* and *2 Henry VI*), Jonson, Middleton and Davenant. An appendix lists devil plays in English from the beginning to 1642.

JOHN D. COX is Professor of English at Hope College, Michigan. He has taught at Westmont College, the University of Victoria B.C., Harvard University, Calvin College and the University of California at Berkeley. His books include *Shakespeare and the Dramaturgy of Power* (1989) and *A New History of Early English Drama*, co-edited with David Scott Kastan, which was chosen as the winner of the 1997 Best Book of the Year Award by the American Association for Theatre in Higher Education.

THE DEVIL AND THE
SACRED IN ENGLISH
DRAMA, 1350–1642

JOHN D. COX

CAMBRIDGE
UNIVERSITY PRESS

PUBLISHED BY THE PRESS SYNDICATE OF THE UNIVERSITY OF CAMBRIDGE
The Pitt Building, Trumpington Street, Cambridge, United Kingdom

CAMBRIDGE UNIVERSITY PRESS
The Edinburgh Building, Cambridge CB2 2RU, UK www.cup.cam.ac.uk
40 West 20th Street, New York, NY 10011-4211, USA www.cup.org
10 Stamford Road, Oakleigh, Melbourne 3166, Australia
Ruiz de Alarcón 13, 28014 Madrid, Spain

First published 2000

Printed in the United Kingdom at the University Press, Cambridge

Typeface Monotype Baskerville 11/12¼ pt.   *System* QuarkXPress™ [SE]

A catalogue record for this book is available from the British Library

Library of Congress cataloguing-in-publication data
Cox, John D., 1945–
The devil and the sacred in English drama, 1350–1642/John D. Cox.
p. cm.
Includes index.
ISBN 0 521 79090 5 (hb)
1. English drama – Early modern and Elizabethan, 1500–1600 – History
and criticism.   2. Devil in literature.   3. English drama – 17th century –
History and criticism.   4. English drama – To 1500 – History and criticism.
5. Christian drama, English – History and criticism.   6. Christianity and
literature – England – History.   7. Good and evil in literature. 8. Holy, The,
in literature.   9. Evil in literature.   I. Title.

PR635.D48 C69 2001
822.009'351 – dc21   00-036290

ISBN 0 521 79090 5 hardback

In memory of
Muriel Clara Bradbrook
and
Mabelle DuMez Frei

Contents

Illustrations

Acknowledgments

I am grateful to Andrew Gurr for an invitation to present preliminary research about early stage devils to a seminar I had joined at the Folger Shakespeare Library in the spring of 1990. My interest in the subject grew when I taught an upper-division seminar at Hope College in the spring of 1992, and began to take serious shape in 1993, when I had a sabbatical leave in the spring and the support of a Summer Stipend from the National Endowment for the Humanities. Further and invaluable support was provided by the Pew Charitable Trusts, enabling me to spend the academic year 1995–96 at the Cambridge University Library. Able librarians have also assisted me at Hope College's Van Wylen Library, the University of Chicago's Regenstein Library, the University of Michigan's Hatcher Library, Harvard University's Widener Library, and the Folger Shakespeare Library.

Portions of the book have appeared as journal articles: chapter 1 in *The American Benedictine Review* (1994), chapters 2, 3, and 5 in *Comparative Drama* (1994–95, 1996, 1998), and parts of chapters 6 and 7 in *The Yearbook of English Studies* (1993). I am grateful to the editors of these journals for their support in publishing these essays and for permitting them to reappear, now much revised and sometimes rearranged, in the pages that follow. I am also grateful to Cambridge University Library and the Regenstein Library for permission to reprint the plates that appear in chapter 5.

I have incurred many debts to individuals in the process of writing this book. Colleagues at Hope College have been generous with time, financial assistance, encouraging words, and ideas. I wish particularly to mention Presidents John Jacobson and James Bultman, Provost Jacob E. Nyenhuis, Dean William Reynolds, the chair of my department, Peter J. Schakel, John Quinn, who assisted with Latin translations, and Kate Maybury, who came to my rescue numerous times when I was baffled by details of computerized composition. Sarah Stanton represented

Cambridge University Press with patience, tact, timely responses, and unfailingly good suggestions. Anne Lancashire read both a preliminary draft and a completed version of the book for the Press, responding fully and helpfully to both. Janette Dillon read the later version and also provided careful and productive comments. David Bevington has promptly read everything I've sent him, including most of what follows, even in the roughest of rough drafts, and his responses have invariably encouraged, enriched, and corrected what I've thought and written. I am especially grateful to him for his patience and generosity in responding to issues on which we differ. During the time of the book's gestation, my three children all attended college, and all contributed generously with tactful listening, challenging questions, and memorable conversation. For support, encouragement, patience, infinite good sense, and beyond that more than I could ever say, I am grateful to my wife, Karen.

The book is dedicated to the memory of two remarkable women whose only connection with each other is their support, in different ways, for this project, though I am sorry to say that neither lived to see its completion. The eminent Shakespearean, M. C. Bradbrook, was retired when I first met her, but I had many good and bracing conversations with her, and her encouragement at a difficult time in the life of my family made me realize that she was as good a person as she was a scholar. Though I never met Mabelle DuMez Frei, her generosity to Hope College made possible the endowed chair that the college bestowed on me in 1996, along with research support that contributed substantially to the completion of this book, and I maintained regular correspondence with her for two years. Mrs. Frei was a 1926 graduate of Hope College but lived most of her life in North Carolina. After offering to endow the DuMez Chair, she drove by herself to Holland, Michigan, in personal possession of the funds "in various forms" as someone told me, to give them to the college. She was ninety-one years old at the time.

Introduction

Histories of the devil abound, and I do not claim to be familiar with more than a fraction of them. Histories of stage devils in English drama, however, are more manageable. The earliest are nineteenth-century dissertations in German, which is the model adopted by the first study of the subject in English, L. W. Cushman's *The Devil and the Vice in the English Dramatic Literature before Shakespeare.* Cushman's book in fact originated as a doctoral dissertation at Goettingen in 1899 and was published the following year by Max Niemeyer in Halle, when Cushman was teaching English at the University of Nevada. I have often wondered if Cushman's going from Goettingen to Reno in 1900 was not, perhaps, a little like meeting the subject of his book in person.

In any case, previous histories of the devil in English drama were swept aside by the magisterial work of E. K. Chambers' *The Medieval Stage,* published in 1903. Chambers read Cushman and dismissed him. What Chambers offered for the first time was a narrative so coherent and persuasive that it continues to influence critical thinking about early English drama, even though Chambers' assumptions have long since been recognized and dismissed in their own turn. One task of the present book is to retell the story of English stage devils for the first time since Chambers but with different assumptions. The first chapter explains what those assumptions are and how they affect the interpretation of stage devils, but the issue is important throughout and accounts for this study's engagement with other critics of early drama who have been influenced in one way or another by Chambers, even when they set out to revise his work.

Chambers began with an oppositional scheme that interpreted stage devils in a narrative of teleological secularization. In this scheme, enlightened secularity was bound to flourish in the long run in its opposition to benighted superstition. Chambers saw the introduction of devils into vernacular drama in the fifteenth century as early evidence of

1

drama's gradual evolution toward its brilliant secular flowering in the work of Shakespeare. In other words, though devils would, in the long run, be recognized and discarded as part of the religious superstructure that drama eventually outgrew, Chambers argued that they were themselves, at first, a secular incursion in sacred drama.

The assumptions that govern this book are also oppositional, but they are derived from what Stuart Clark calls "the mental world" of demonology, not from social Darwinism (*Thinking with Demons: The Idea of Witchcraft in Early Modern Europe* [Oxford, 1997]). Demons were inherently oppositional, Clark argues, because they were constructed as the subordinate term in a hierarchical polarity. This binary distinction between God and the devil became the model for a series of parallel oppositions that profoundly influenced thinking about science, history, religion, and politics. In similar terms, I argue that the role of stage devils in pre-Reformation drama was to enact whatever opposed individual wellbeing and the sacramental community. Far from being a secular innovation, devils were a way of imagining how and why the sacred needed to function redemptively in the life of the individual and the community. Chapters 2 to 4 make this argument in detail for pre-Reformation drama, noting continuity across dramatic genres (mystery, morality, and saints' plays), and accounting for the origin of dramatic social satire in recognition of the gap between moral affirmation and practice.

The first major change from traditional oppositional thinking about stage devils comes with the Protestant Reformation, as I argue in chapter 5. Reformers continued to think in dichotomies, but they substituted new terms for both the positive and negative poles of their world. The Christian community was thus conceived anew as the reformed church, with the king at its head, while the traditional church, with the pope at its head, was identified with the devil, along with its sacramental system. Chapter 6 argues that the second major change in stage devils came with the establishment of commercial theatres near London and the advent of Christopher Marlowe, who is the first playwright to exploit, in *Dr. Faustus*, the instability of traditional polarized thinking about devils. In this, he was not influential; in fact, chapter 7 discusses several devil plays from around the turn of the seventeenth century that react to his radicalism by reasserting familiar values, ultimately derived from drama before the Reformation.

One of the major benefits of looking at stage devils in light of traditional demonological assumptions is that it enables the recognition of continuity and specific difference in early Stuart drama, as I argue in chapters 8, 9, and 10. About forty new plays that we know of put devils on stage between Marlowe's *Faustus* and the closing of the theatres in 1642, with the last of them being performed for the first time as late as 1641. This is not what one would expect, given Chambers' secular teleology. Even Cushman terminates his discussion before the advent of the commercial theatres near London. Moreover, early seventeenth-century stage devils are more continuous with the formative tradition than is usually recognized. Despite rising skepticism and the advent of widespread metadramatic irony, as in Fletcherian tragicomedy, devils continue to bring with them a number of traditional oppositional assumptions. New directions for stage devils are explored in chapter 10, most remarkable being their social function: the traditional association of devils with pride, and therefore with the highest social classes, increasingly gives way to a prevailing association of devils with the lower social classes.

In making this argument, I have deliberately limited my discussion to plays that stage devils, thus excepting those that stage only witches, the Vice, or Vice-derived human beings, like Richard III, Iago, or Deflores in *The Changeling*. My reason for this limitation is to sharpen the focus and keep the study, already long, within reasonable bounds. But I make one exception. In pre-Reformation morality plays, I treat personified vices as devils, because I argue that playwrights made no distinction between them. The seven deadly sins, which are personified abstractions, are often called devils, they behave like devils, they are costumed like devils, and I argue that they have the same derivation as devils. That is why Medwall's *Nature* and Skelton's *Magnificence* receive detailed attention here, even though they stage personified vices, not literal devils. In popular Tudor plays, the character called "the Vice" appears for the first time, and playwrights distinguish him from stage devils. I do not, therefore, deal with Reformation plays that stage the Vice alone or Vice-derived human beings, but I do discuss plays, including a number of Tudor morality plays, that stage the devil and the Vice together.

Shakespeare does not figure very largely in this book, because he included devils in only two plays, *1* and *2 Henry VI*, both discussed in chapter 7. When referring to these plays and others on occasion, I cite David Bevington's *Complete Works of Shakespeare*, 4th edn. (New York: Longman, 1997). I have included dates for all the plays referred to, both in the text and the appendix. For nearly all of them, however, dating is uncertain, and for the earliest plays it is sometimes little more than a scholarly guess. That is why the beginning date is 1350: though the earliest texts are fifteenth-century, the York mystery plays were certainly being performed in the second half of the fourteenth century, and *The Castle of Perseverance* may be as early as 1382, but nothing more precise than that can be said about the originating dates of these plays. For consistency, I have relied principally on Sylvia Wagonheim's revision of *Annals of English Drama, 975–1700* (Routledge, 1989), originally compiled by Alfred Harbage and revised by S. Schoenbaum, though occasionally I have used dates suggested in recent editions of particular plays. In any case, one of the salutary benefits of abandoning an evolutionary and teleological scheme is that dating becomes less important to the argument.

CHAPTER ONE

Stage devils and oppositional thinking

Aside from human beings, nothing was staged more continuously in early English drama than the devil and his minions. For about 300 years – from the late fourteenth century to the late seventeenth – playwrights regularly put devils on stage in every kind of English play for every kind of audience, whether aristocratic, popular, or commercial. Long after they stopped seeing God and the angels, audiences continued to see devils on stage, and there was no appreciable decline in opportunities to do so on the London commercial stage before the closing of the theatres in 1642. That devils should have so long outlived other characters produced by traditional dramaturgy has neither been noticed nor explained in the critical record, yet it is a singular fact. This book explores both questions: why devils are the last explicit remnant of continuous traditions in staging the sacred, and why no one has recognized that they are.

One reason devils endured on stage was that the material base of culture changed very little throughout the time they were popular: the slow pace of economic and technological change meant that costumes and the materials for assembling them remained the same.[1] "The devill in his fethers" (presumably black feathers) appears in costuming lists from Chester, both for the mystery plays and for the annual Midsummer Show, which reputedly endured from 1499 to the 1670s.[2] At Coventry a charge is recorded "for making ye demones head" in 1543 and "for a yard of canvas for ye devylles mall [maul]" in 1544.[3] "The dymons cote" (p. 240), "the devells hose" (p. 246), "pwyntes [points (for attaching the hose to the doublet)] for the deman" (p. 218), and "a stafe for the deman" (p. 238) add details to the picture at Coventry. The St. John's College Cambridge Register of Inventories lists "ij blak develles cootes with hornes" in 1548–49.[4] A dangerous variation on the devil's canvas maul is recorded at Tamworth on Corpus Christi Day, 1536, where "an actor playing the Devil . . . came with his chain by one of the spectators, Sir Humfrey Ferrers, the lord of Tamworth Castle, and unwittingly broke his shins with it."[5] The earliest reference to devils' costumes discovered so far is from York in 1433, where "garmentes," "faces," and "Vesernes [visors]" for devils are listed;[6] the latest before the closing of the theatres is from Thomas Nabbes' masque, *Microcosmus* in 1637, where a stage direction specifies "A divell in a black robe: haire, wreath and wings black."[7] The wings were presumably made of black feathers.

This relatively stable material base of costuming and props was less important in perpetuating stage devils, however, than the mental world that originated them in the first place. The outlook in which demonology flourished has recently been described in detail by Stuart Clark as it affected science, history, religion, and politics throughout the sixteenth and seventeenth centuries.[8] Clark comments that demonology "was construed dialectically in terms of what it was not; what was significant about it was not its substance but the system of oppositions that it established and fulfilled" (p. 9). These oppositions, moreover, were hierarchical, beginning with God and the devil, and embracing a series of parallels: good and evil, truth and illusion, community and chaos, baptized and non-baptized, belief and heresy. The flexibility of binary thinking was both its strength and its greatest weakness, Clark argues: while almost anything could be made to fit the model of hierarchical polar oppositions, their infinite confirmability made them unstable. Traditional oppositional thinking therefore endured an extended crisis in the sixteenth and seventeenth centuries:

In the case of demonology, the dominance of privileged first terms set in hierarchical opposition to their contraries was for a long time successful in yielding coherent and persuasive arguments. However, once the two reformations were under way the very enthusiasm with which writers of different religious persuasions gave authenticating roles to devils betrayed the instability of the logic involved. (p. 147)

What was true of devils per se was equally true, as we shall see, of devils on the stage.

Recognizing the crisis caused by the Protestant and Counter Reformations as *extended*, however, is important. The habit of oppositional thinking did not collapse as soon as Protestants turned the tables on traditional religion by identifying it as idolatrous and demonic. Thinking in opposed hierarchical polarities was so deeply ingrained that it characterized both sides of the religious divide for a long time, with almost no recognition of the incongruities involved. Though virtually all the devil plays discussed in the following pages invite deconstructive analysis by virtue of their oppositional thinking, only Marlowe's *Dr. Faustus* deliberately exploits the resulting instability.

One of the principal reasons for the failure of modern criticism to recognize and explain the durability of stage devils has been the misreading
of traditional assumptions about a polarized world. Primary credit for
this failure belongs to E. K. Chambers, who first read early drama
according to a different model altogether – a teleological pattern of
gradually developing secularization.[9] Stage devils were important for
Chambers, because they were a key element in his theory. The earlier he
could find evidence of secularization, the more credible was his claim
that change was incremental, progressive, and aimed where he thought
it was. He therefore regarded the "relaxing of the close bonds between
the nascent drama and religious worship" as the earliest form of secularization, and he found this "relaxation" in the expansion of early liturgical tropes to include other biblical material, the movement of the plays
out of the church, the innovation of lay control and financing, the
replacement of Latin with the vernacular, and the appearance of folk-
play elements – especially devils – in the biblical stories told by vernacular drama:

For your horned and blackened devil is the same personage, with the same
vague tradition of the ancient heathen festival about him, whether he riots it
through the cathedral aisles in the Feast of Fools, or hales the Fathers to limbo
and harries the forward spectators in the marketplace of Beverley or
Wakefield.[10]

Chambers' belief that devils were among the first indications of the
secular in early English drama made him incapable of seeing them as
one of the last vestiges of traditional sacred dramaturgy in the seventeenth century.

More than thirty years ago, O. B. Hardison pointed out that
Chambers' assumptions about early drama derived from social
Darwinism and its evolutionary preoccupations.[11] Chambers regarded
secularization as progressive, Hardison argued, because "he lived in an
age when Christianity was suspect" (p. 14). A romantic conception of vital
but repressed pagan folk culture informed Chambers' view of stage devils
(they are vestiges of "the ancient heathen festival"), and the reassertion
of this culture against oppressive pre-Reformation Christianity was, for
Chambers, one of the first signs of healthy secularization in drama.
Chambers' thinking is thus marked by a "strong polarity," as Hardison
points out (p. 15), that is foreign to the drama he was trying to understand.
The primary terms in Chambers' hierarchical binary rhetoric are not
God and the devil, but pagan (the favored term) and Christian, followed
closely by a series of supporting terms: "braved," "won," "sportive," and

"deep-rooted instinct" on the positive side, opposing "bishops," "barbar-ians," "gaolers," "ban," "triumphed," and "barred," on the side of the church.[12]

Chambers did not invent the oppositional system that Hardison identifies; rather, Chambers inherited it as a derivative from the very system he failed to recognize in the early drama he studied. For binary thinking did not collapse in the eighteenth century, as Clark suggests.[13] Instead, the deep-rooted sense of certainty that it had provided was transmuted into a new system, in which the favored terms were "secular," "progressive," "rational," "modern," and the like, in opposi-tion to "religious," "backward," "enthusiastic," "medieval." We can see these two incommensurate binary systems in transition and in collision with one another in the eighteenth century.[14] James Sharpe recounts a trial in Hertfordshire in 1751, when Thomas Colley was found guilty and hanged for seizing and drowning Ruth Osborne on suspicion of witch-craft.[15] Before his execution, Colley was visited in prison by one who sought to persuade him that "witches had no manner of existence but in the minds of poor infatuated people, in which they had been confirm'd by the tradition of their ancestors, as foolish and crazy as themselves" (p. 3). Colley's well-meaning visitor speaks from within the new system of oppositional thinking, dividing the world along lines of reason and enlightenment, seeking to dispel centuries of infatuated folly and craziness. On the other hand, after Colley's hanging, many who heard of it, believed "it was a very hard case, that a man shold be hang'd for destroying an old wicked woman, who had done so much mischief by her abominable charms and witchcraft" (p. 4). These people viewed Colley's execution from within the old system, dividing the world between God and the devil.

Chambers' binary thinking descends, then, from the Enlightenment, where it developed as a way of grounding rational confidence against the archaic polarities it replaced. Secular knowledge based on reason and experiment came to oppose sacred ignorance, as illustrated in the deists' rejection of "priestcraft," a rejection which was itself a legacy of radical Protestant anticlericalism in the seventeenth century and of the early Protestant Reformers' rejection of traditional clergy and ritual as "superstitious." For Chambers, the added feature is that Darwin and the social Darwinists had transferred the teleology of sacred history (already secularized in Hegel's historical "spirit") into biological and social evolu-tion, in such a way that the hierarchical superior in the Enlightenment binary system seemed bound to flourish in the long run. Reason would inevitably defeat ignorance; the secular would inevitably defeat "other-worldliness" and superstition. Writing from the heart of the British Empire at the height of its success, the social evolutionary assumption that the fittest survive seemed obvious to Chambers, and it was apparent that the fittest culture had evolved along with enlightened English Protestantism: anti-Catholic, secularized, and favorable to individual freedom of conscience.

In short, Chambers' inability to understand traditional oppositional thinking was due to the Enlightenment transformation of an earlier mental world into a new set of binary assumptions. Moreover the latter have remained active in assessments of early drama, even though Chambers' argument has been repudiated. Chambers' continuing influence is due, in part, to the inspiration (complementing that of Darwin and Herbert Spencer) of Jules Michelet, who first proposed in *La Sorcière* (1862) that vestigial pagan folk customs were the focus of peasant revolt against ecclesiastical and feudal authority.[16] The Romantic basis of Michelet's thesis needs no emphasis, and its debt to Enlightenment binary thinking in the French Revolution is clear. Michelet's influence has been considerable in modern attempts to understand witchcraft, especially when witchcraft has been interpreted romantically as a form of populist or feminist resistance, but Michelet has not been adequately recognized as a factor in the study of early drama.

Despite Hardison's critique, Chambers' legacy with regard to stage devils remains largely unquestioned. The first broad challenge to Chambers came in the important revisionist work of Bernard Spivack and David Bevington, writing just after the middle of the century, yet both retained a narrative of organic incremental development with secularization as its goal.[17] The concept of the "hybrid morality," for example, is important to Spivack and Bevington as a mid-sixteenth-century phase in the gradual development of dramatic characterization, from the personified abstractions inspired by Christian morality to the represented human beings inspired by secular observation.

Most striking is the perpetuation of Chambers' Victorian and Whig liberal assumptions in the neo-Marxist criticism of Robert Weimann, who has been a Trojan horse for Enlightenment antinomies within the ramparts of postmodernism. Weimann is most responsive to Michelet, arguing that a vestigial pagan folk tradition found expression in clowns, Vices, stage devils, the doctor of St. George plays, and the gargantuan feasts of shepherd plays in the mystery cycles as various expressions of peasant resistance to high culture. Weimann sees devils' and personified vices' proximity to the audience as encouraging subversive identification and sympathy with ostensibly anti-social behavior, blasphemy, and heterodoxy. For heresy was "inevitably and inextricably entangled with attempts on the social order, always anarchic, always political."[18] The soliloquies, knowing asides, and down-stage comic antics of demonic figures were all means of taking auditors into the confidence of an anti-establishment viewpoint, engaging them on its side and creating distance from the more formal, "correct," and socially elevated characters of the main action. In Weimann's view, the social function of devils is to provide a subversive expression for class frustration and protest – a function closely analogous to the one described by Chambers and ultimately indebted to Michelet. Also influential in some postmodern criticism has been the historical work of Keith Thomas, who identifies the purpose of pre-Reformation ritual with that of magic and compares magic unfavorably with science and technology, thus offering another version of the Enlightenment polarity exhibited in Chambers.[19] Thomas' influence on Stephen Greenblatt is explicit, and Greenblatt's ideas about exorcism are considered below in chapter 8.[20]

My purpose in what follows is not to argue that secularization had no effect on the history of early drama, and particularly on stage devils. Rather, what I propose is a way of conceptualizing secularization that recovers some sense of traditional oppositional thinking without falling into the polarization and tendentiousness of Enlightenment and Romantic assumptions. John Sommerville's argument for a nuanced and sociologically informed theory of secularization is helpful. He contrasts "a people whose religious rituals are so woven into the fabric of their life that they could not separate religion from the rest of their activities" with "a society in which religion is a matter of conscious beliefs, important primarily for the times of one's most philosophical and poetic solitude."[21] The first is a "sacred" culture; the second, "secular."[22] Looked at this way, the story of English secularization effectively begins with Henry VIII, because Henry originated a process that formally defined the power and influence of religion apart from the influence of other social and political institutions (especially the monarchy) and eventually separated them. Where secularization is concerned, Henry's declaring himself the head of the church was not a uniting of monarchy and church but a delimiting of religion from its traditional permeation of cultural life, a subordination of this newly distinct entity under the crown, a consequent redefinition of the church in national terms, and a promotion of a non-ecclesiastical office (the monarchy) to unprecedented charismatic ascendancy. The material impact of this process was immediate and dramatic, beginning with the transfer of ecclesiastical real estate to Henry's "new men" and proceeding with the way people refashioned their worship spaces, spent their money, distributed largesse to the poor (or sought relief, if they were poor), lived virtually every facet of their daily lives, and died.[23] But eventually the impact was intellectual and psychological as well, and it is the latter effect that we see at work in the secularization of early English drama and particularly in the secularization of stage devils.[24]

To see Henry VIII as the effective originator of secularization in English life is to see the situation before him very differently from the way Chambers does. Viewing stage devils as a separation of the sacred from the secular is understandable from an evolutionary and secularized Protestant perspective, but as Sommerville points out,

the devil is as much a part of the realm of the supernatural as is God. The secular or profane realm contains only everyday beings, not those remarkable for their diabolic character. An inversion of religion in sacrilege, desecration, or sorcery is not evidence of secularization, however bad-mannered. In medieval England, hostility toward some aspect of religion was often expressed in religious terms. The evidence of thorough-going secularization, on the other hand, is to be found in indifference, even though it might be respectful to the Church. (p. 10)

Technically, as we shall see, the devil was not supernatural; he was merely superhuman. In pre-Reformation England, however, he was indeed as much a part of the sacred outlook as God was. He was ubiquitous, because his opposition to God accounted for everything that was wrong, not merely in obvious moral or religious terms (committing the seven deadly sins or sacrilege) but in sickness, death, accidents, crop failure, and social conflict. One of the major purposes of religious activity throughout one's life, from baptism to the last rites, was therefore to reject and defeat the devil, and innumerable liturgical celebrations in the course of every year performed the same purpose for the community. In the traditional society that produced early religious drama, encounters with the devil were deeply involved in the ritual life of the community.[25] Indeed, everyone first encountered the devil without being aware of it and without being able to do anything about it. The doctrine of original sin was construed to mean that newborns literally belonged to the devil, and the baptismal rite therefore involved an exorcism that was designed to expel the devil from the infant to be baptized, whom the rite claimed, instead, for Christ and the Christian community: "Taken together, the rituals of expulsion, repudiation, and prophylaxis or apotropaism formed a series of ceremonies that dramatized in a striking way the very real struggle that every Christian waged with the devil."[26] Every infant had to be reclaimed for Christ from God's opposite, a cosmic and personal enemy who was malign and dangerous, the source of childhood illness, accidents, death, and deformity, dramatically apostrophized by the presiding priest at baptism as "cursed devil."[27]

The dramatic encounter at baptism, marking the beginning of the Christian life, was repeated even more forcefully at the end of life, on everyone's deathbed, especially in the late Middle Ages. This culture's preoccupation with death is well known, evident in the flourishing of the *ars moriendi*, the dance of death, and the intense interest in purgatory and indulgences. Such a preoccupation was doubtless fostered by the Black Death and recurring bouts of the plague, but it may also have been encouraged by the explosion of wealth, which preachers denounced at every social level, reminding their charges of life's brevity and the consequent obligation to prepare well for their end.[28] That members of the clergy were themselves, in many cases, prime beneficiaries of the new wealth obviates neither the force of moral admonitions that came from the church nor of its provisions for everyone at the end of life.

What was true at baptism was also true in dying, when the preserving power of Christ was pitted against the fearful onslaught of Satan and his followers, which was stronger in one's ultimate weakness than at any previous time of life. This was because the approach of death was accompanied by strong temptation to doubt the efficacy of the Christian graces and the saving power of God, as Shakespeare still remembers at the end of the sixteenth century, when he has King Henry VI pray for the dying Bishop of Winchester:

> O thou eternal mover of the heavens,
> Look with a gentle eye upon this wretch!
> O, beat away the busy meddling fiend
> That lays strong siege unto this wretch's soul,
> And from his bosom purge this black despair![29]

The presence of the devil at the deathbed is depicted in illustrations that accompanied the *ars moriendi* throughout the fifteenth century and that reached even those who could not read in the form of block prints produced by the early printers. As Eamon Duffy points out, these prints "portrayed the deathbed as the centre of an epic struggle for the soul of the Christian, in which the Devil bent all his strength to turn the soul from Christ and His cross to self-loathing or self-reliance."[30] In dramatic opposition to the devil, the ministering priest held aloft a crucifix, displaying the power of the passion as the site of Christ's defeat of Satan on behalf of humankind and encouraging the dying to appropriate that power on their own behalf.

The material impact of the oppositional preoccupation with choosing God and resisting the devil at the end of life went beyond the production of manuscripts, books, and block prints. It is no exaggeration to say that much of what we think of as characteristically late medieval was shaped by this concern. A large proportion of new wealth was expended in gifts to parish churches and private chapels, with the intent of demonstrating the piety of those who had earned it and thereby preparing the donor's case for being loosely attached to earthly goods at the time of deathbed reckoning and the Day of Judgment. Every visitor to Westminster Abbey is aware of Henry VII's gifts to create a magnificent new chapel with fantailed vaulting, but Henry's prudent generosity did not end so close to the royal domain. His gifts to Great St. Mary's in Cambridge are no less important as pious contributions to the university church, though Christopher Brooke has recently discovered evidence that the munificence attributed to Henry may actually have been bestowed by Richard III.[31] The point is not which king deserves credit but that both were so determined to establish it. Henry's story could be told many times over for thousands of other lay Christians in the late Middle Ages. No doubt conspicuous consumption played a part in such gifts as well, but to assert that nothing more impelled them is to miss the religious dimension of the social context that gave rise to them.

Displays of personal generosity were impossible for the poor, of course, but as a vernacular preacher made clear, the poor were at less obvious peril on their deathbeds and the Day of Doom, because they had fewer earthly goods to tempt them into worldly complacency: "Tho[gh] god sende the litill, thou art never the lesse beholden unto hym for too skilles. On ys, thou haste the lesse to yeve hym accountes of at the daye of dome; and anothur, the lesse ioye that thou haste in this worlde, the more thou shalte have in heven."[32] A common theme of medieval preaching was Jesus' parable of the sheep and the goats, distinguished from one another on the Day of Judgment by their consideration for the poor and dispossesed, and dramatic renderings of the same parable are also a prominent part of all the Judgment plays in the extant mystery cycles, where the devil claims those who did not repent their willful commitment to luxurious consumption at the expense of others.

An efficacious deathbed struggle against the devil was not, then, the prerogative of the rich. It was a spiritual struggle that confronted everyone, and material donations were expressions of charity that prepared one to face the devil on the deathbed. Though the poor (who were, of course, the majority of the population) were unable to display their charity to the community in the manner of their wealthy neighbors, they were allotted a place in every parish's memory of those who had contributed against the day of reckoning. For the names of all donors were entered on the parish bede roll, no matter how small the donation, and prayers were offered every Sunday for the souls of those named there. Moreover, during the annual requiem for benefactors of the parish, the name of each contributor was read aloud by the priest, from those who had built or remodeled the church to those who had given two-pence (Duffy, pp. 334–35). No one, in short, was denied an opportunity to prepare for resisting the devil at death by expressing charity through material generosity.

Birth and death were not the only times when pre-Reformation Christians were aware of the devil's malignant opposition. Between the beginning and the end of the Christian life, marked by the ordeals of baptism and dying, everyone ritually encountered the devil repeatedly as a frightening opponent in the course of an agrarian cycle that derived its ultimate meaning from the liturgy. Despite the rapid growth of towns in the late Middle Ages, the vast bulk of the population still made its living from the land, and the rhythms of agricultural life dominated European consciousness. What the liturgy provided, then, cannot be accurately described as merely spiritual comfort. In a way that is characteristic of sacred culture, the liturgy also profoundly shaped consciousness about material life on a daily basis, where the power of ritual experience was involved with life, death, and wellbeing:

What that power procured was the salvation of man; or, to recapture the larger overtones of the word *salus*, the deliverance of the Christian from the whole concatenation of dooms, dangers, anxieties and tribulations which loomed over him in his corporal as in his spiritual existence: overtones more exactly rendered by the German *Heil* than by any English equivalent.[33]

The most important half of the liturgical year was the period between Advent and Easter, which had come to include, by the late Middle Ages, Ascension, Whitsunday, and Corpus Christi.[34] During this time a sequence of feast days commemorated the life, passion, resurrection, and ascension of Christ, which were definitively efficacious in the cosmic defeat of Satan. The correspondence of this period with the time between the winter and summer solstices meant that the communal remembering of Christ's cosmic suffering and victory occurred at a time of year when suffering from cold and a meager food supply was also endured and came to an end. Still, that coincidence does not mean that the "real" significance of the liturgical celebrations was a residual pagan fertility rite, as Chambers inferred. It is more accurate to say that the real meaning of assimilated fertility rites and the community's survival of the passing seasons' hardships had long since become Christian.[35]

In any case, the Christocentric feasts openly re-enact the cosmic victory of Christ over Satan in innumerable ways. The concluding Christmas feast, for example, was Candlemas, celebrated on February 2, commemorating the purification of Mary and the presentation of the infant Jesus in the temple. The name of the feast derives from the candles carried in a procession of the worshipers and presented for blessing to the priest, along with a penny donation. The prayer accompanying the blessing explicitly identifies its apotropaic function, asking that wherever the candle "shall be lit or set up, the devil may flee away in fear and trembling with all his ministers, out of those dwellings, and never presume again to disquiet your servants" (Duffy, p. 16). On Palm Sunday, the yew, box, or willow branches carried in elaborate procession were similarly blessed and were similarly efficacious in banishing the devil (Duffy, p. 23).

One of the most elaborate annual feasts was Rogation, the only liturgical procession retained by the sixteenth-century Reformers, celebrated for three successive days before Ascension, the sixth Thursday after Easter. The Rogation procession was the most extensive of all, for it followed the entire parish perimeter, or "bounds," with church banners, bells, singing, readings from the gospels by the priest, and pauses at wayside crosses, all designed to cleanse the parish of evil influences and bless the fields. On the first two days the procession was preceded by a dragon, whose tail was shorn away for the third day's procession, symbolizing the overthrow of the great dragon, Satan (Duffy, p. 279). The gospel reading for Ascension Day, immediately following Rogation, helped to link the two feasts, for it was Mark 5, the story of Jesus' exorcism of the man possessed by a demon (Duffy, p. 217). Like some other Christian feasts, this springtime celebration originated as a counterpart to a pagan festivity (the Roman Robigalia), specifically designed to promote fertility, and the fertility implications of Rogation itself are obvious.[36] The point, again, is neither that Rogation was really a "heathen festival," in Chambers' phrase, nor that the liturgical calendar was spiritual and irrelevant to the material lives of agricultural communities. On the contrary, the meaning of material life was derived from Christian ritual. Alasdair MacIntyre makes a similar point when he discusses moral thinking in traditional societies, or what Sommerville calls "sacred" societies, where "religion was characteristically not a separate segregable aspect of life . . . but was rather the mode in which every aspect of life was related to the divine."[37] Certainly the motivations that accompanied a three-day procession and feast on the part of the entire parish must have been remarkably various – at least as various as the motivations that prompt Chaucer's springtime pilgrims. Still, the assimilation of a wide variety of motives to Rogation's drama of the cosmic Christian struggle is unmistakable.

Many non-Christocentric feasts in the liturgical year were equally charged with power to oppose evil, though less clearly linked to a symbolic sequence of the seasonal cycle. Michaelmas (September 29) celebrated the eschatological binding of Satan and all his forces, a future victory that was anticipated daily by St. Michael's presence at the deathbed, where faith was most severely tested by demonic power. On All Souls' eve (November 1), the parish bells rang till midnight, and consecrated candles were burned in windows to ward off demonic power. The stories of particular saints, usually honored locally, invariably recalled God's power over demons, either in a saint's life or by means of a saint in the life of someone else: St. Mary Magdalen had seven devils exorcized from her by Jesus himself; St. Agnes successfully interceded for the life of a prefect's son who had been strangled by demons; St. Margaret was swallowed by the devil in the form of a dragon, which she exploded by making the sign of the cross (Duffy, pp. 172–73). The folktale attributes of hagiography are obvious; the point is that all the saints' legends, no matter how naive, are consistently oppositional in their thinking, identifying Satan as the cosmic enemy, the source of all harm and the ultimate threat to all good things.

In short, recent social historical descriptions of traditional pre-Reformation Christianity yield a very different view of the devil from the one that Chambers entertained, and the impact of that view on early drama will be a primary theme in the pages that follow. Chambers' distinction between liturgical and vernacular drama is certainly untenable where devils are concerned, because devils are also active in Latin liturgical drama, which should not be surprising, given the function of the liturgy and the sacraments in opposing the devil. As early as the ninth century, in the *Ordo Dedicationis Ecclesiae* used by the bishop of Metz, the devil was exorcised in the process of consecrating the building, much as devils were exorcised from unbaptized children. In the surviving text of this service, the bishop stops three times in procession before the north portal of the church and makes the demand that the Gospel of Nicodemus had associated with the harrowing of hell: "Tollite portas . . . et introibit rex gloriae," to which one inside the church responds, "Quis est iste rex gloriae?" After the third exchange, the one in the church leaves "quasi fugiens."[38] Diabolus also asks the same impertinent question twice in the early thirteenth-century *Ordo Paschalis* from Klosterneuberg (Young 1:425, 428). In a more explicit rendering of the harrowing, a Bamberg service book from 1587 again requires that one "qui Diaboli personam simulans" recite the antiphon, "Quis est iste Rex gloriae?" (Young, 1:174). To be sure, this is a late example and may reflect the influence of vernacular plays on the same theme. But the example still makes the point that devils were admissible in liturgical plays, where they performed the same function that they performed in other early drama. In a fourteenth-century *ordinarium* on the ascension of Christ from Moosburg, an "image of the devil" is cast down "with abominable fires of sulphur and pitch, or with the colors of waters mixed in and with other things" in contrast to the effigy of Christ, which is raised to the top of the church by a rope (Young, 1:487; my translation). Diaboli also appear in the late twelfth-century *Ludus de Nativitate* and *Ludus de Passione* from Benediktbeurn.[39] In every case these devils are additions to the biblical story, but in no case are they "secular" detractions from it; on the contrary, they illuminate the stories in which they appear by making explicit the devil's opposition to Christ, in whose name the devil is defeated by the Christian social body and banished from it.

The modified story of secularization that I am suggesting has not been anticipated by others who have responded to Chambers, though interpreters who are more sympathetic than Chambers to the plays' religious subjects have argued that stage devils are consistent with structural and thematic patterns of the plays' informing theology. This view of devils has taken various forms, as Chambers' view has, from V. A. Kolve's argument that laughter at devils in a modern production of the Towneley cycle provided a "comedy of victory" over evil, to Hans-Jürgen Diller's analysis of "speech forms" to demonstrate that the "harsh, bitter, and funny" realism of the *platea* "is part of the original make-up of the genre, not a late, popular and irrelevant addition."[40] While Diller acknowledges the social ambiguities of devils and their human accomplices, Kolve puts evil creatures firmly in their social place, arguing that comedy gives them their due only at the bottom of the cosmic hierarchy: "God is in control, the evil and the demonic behave stupidly because that is their nature, and the proper reaction to this example of the rightness of things is laughter."[41] Socially, this view is precisely the opposite of that described by Chambers and his socialist heirs, for in Kolve's view stage devils function to reinforce the existing power structure.

What this book argues is that devils need not be understood either as exuberant subverters of a hegemonic social order or as proto-Enlightenment examples of failed attempts to challenge cosmic order. For stage devils are closely related to the devil of traditional religion, who is consistent with but not reducible to the devil of theology. Operating supportively within the bounds of traditional religion, stage devils reveal communal values by default, illustrating (often satirically) what fifteenth-century English society saw as most destructive of its sacral cohesion. In drama, as we shall see, the demonic threat to society was not from "below," i.e., from the lower classes. The late fourteenth-century peasants' rebellion and its occasional successors in the fifteenth century did not deter playwrights from consistently identifying the demonic threat with the crown and the aristocracy, including members of the ecclesiastical elite.[42] The mystery plays do embody social ambivalence, as we shall see in the following chapter, but it is very different from the ambivalence described by Chambers and his critical heirs. Moreover, the social function of stage devils changes late in the tradition, when devils are indeed associated exclusively with commoners. This development, however, is a product of increasing competition between commercial acting companies and of changing patterns of dramatic authorship. Ironically, the association of stage devils with the lower class, attributed by Chambers and others to repressive Christianity, actually came about only after plays had become secularized and traditional oppositional thinking made less impact on their dramaturgy.

CHAPTER TWO

The devil and the sacred in the English mystery plays

STAGE DEVILS AND TRADITIONAL RELIGION

The devil's oppositional role in traditional religion is particularly important in understanding the social function of devils on the stage. In E. K.
Chambers' view, vernacular drama's recognition of secular problems
was impossible for liturgical drama, because it was preoccupied with
spiritual and otherworldly concerns. He therefore understood occasional moments of social satire in the mystery plays, often voiced
through devils, as evidence of secularity and evolutionary progress. He
was right about a sense of opposition in early drama, as we have seen in
chapter 1, but the opposition did not involve secular and sacred; rather,
it involved God and the devil. Where society was concerned, the devil's
opposition defined community by default, illustrating emblematically
what community was not by opposing what it was. Just as the devil
played this role in countless liturgical celebrations throughout the ritual
year, so he plays it in the mystery cycles. As we have them now, these
plays are not the earliest drama in English; in some cases, the texts are
early sixteenth-century, and a complex palimpsest of influences is discernible in them. Nonetheless, the mystery plays are the closest of early
vernacular dramatic forms to ritual, and they therefore represent a perpetuation of traditional religious views until well into Elizabeth's reign,
when they ceased playing.

The extant cycles begin with the archetypal anti-social act, which is
also demonic: Lucifer's departure from the undivided community of
heaven. The opening pageant of the creation and fall of the angels thus
defines community in sacred terms and defines its opposite as what disrupts or opposes it. The theology of this play has received careful and
thoughtful treatment, but Lucifer's fall as an oppositional paradigm for
community division – and thus for political and social conflict of all
kinds – has not been adequately appreciated.[1]

Though each cycle treats the fall of Lucifer differently, they all develop an opposition between "mirth," "joy," or "bliss" in the community of heaven before his revolt, and communal strife and division afterwards. A narrative development is thus a social, psychological, and moral development as well. Towneley establishes the first part of this contrast in a cherubin's celebration of Lucifer as an *innocent* part of the creation before his revolt, praising God as the maker of "Lucifer so bright" in celebratory wordplay on Lucifer's name:

> Bright ar we,
> Bot none of vs so bright as he:
> He may well hight Lucifere,
> Ffor lufly light that he doth bere;
> He is so lufly and so bright
> It is grete ioy to se that sight.
> We lofe the, Lord, with all oure thoght,
> That sich thyng can make of noght.[2]

In reaction, Lucifer declares his role as spoiler and destroyer as soon as he speaks, for he rejects the subordinate angel's charitable celebration of gratitude, humility, and praise of fellow creatures. In individualistic self-assertion, he identifies bliss and mirth only with himself and his mastery over others, rather than with the community as a whole and his solidarity with it:

> For I am lord of blis,
> Ouer all this warld, i-wis,
> My myrth is most of all;
> Therfor my will is this:
> Master ye shall me call.   (6/94–98)

The consequence of Lucifer's divisive declaration is the division of the heavenly community into opposed allegiances and states of mind. Hell is full of bickering and mutual recrimination. Primus Demon angrily but accurately articulates Lucifer's responsibility for their fall and the rejection of their own kind: "Thou art foull comyn from thi kyn" (7/143). The "mery place" of Eden (10/229) now partakes of the "ioye" and "blis" of heaven (10/231), and misery and woe now characterize Satan and his followers:

> Who wend euer this tyme haue seyn?
> We, that in sich myrth haue beyn
> That we shuld suffre so mych wo?   (11/250–52)

"Joy" is mentioned again by Lucifer at the end of the fragmentary play of the Creation, but only because he and his followers have lost it, to the benefit of humankind. Having destroyed heavenly mirth to his own loss, he now plans to destroy earthly mirth:

> Bot herkyns, felows, what I say:
> The ioy that we haue lost for ay,
> God has maide man with his hend,
> To haue that blis withoutten end,
> The ix ordre to fulfill   *nine orders [of angels]*
> That after vs left; sic is his will.
> And now ar thay in Paradise;
> Bot thens thay shall, if we be wise.   (11/260–67)

The plot of the plays that follow is thus set up: the lost joy of Lucifer and his fellows will be visited on humankind, but opposing it will be the creative and preserving power that made the cosmos in the first place and then rejected its primal enemy.

But more than a plot is set up by the fall of Lucifer. What *The Creation and Fall of the Angels* also re-enacts is the founding event of the communities for which it was played. Secundus Demon explicitly links the archetypal scene with its spectators, whom he addresses directly, asserting that they share the condition of what they witness:

> Alas, we may warrie wikkyd pride,   *curse*
> So may ye all that standys beside.
> We held with hym ther he saide leasse,   *told lies*
> And therefor haue we all vnpeasse.   (8/156–59)

In reminding the community of its story, the event also articulated the community's present values, defining oppositionally both what it was ("mirth") and what it was not ("unpeasse"). The scene thus establishes a parallel series of hierarchical oppositions: gratitude and self-congratulation, communal solidarity and individualism, humility and pride, love and hate, trust and mistrust. But in the *Creation and Fall of the Angels* these abstractions are embodied in a story about the founding of the cosmos, and that story was the story of its audience as well: the origin of their own history was also the origin of their moral affirmations, whether they understood the pageant individually, socially, or politically.

Chambers identified this kind of founding event with liturgical drama and thus distinguished it from the mystery plays. Distinctions between the two are real, but Chambers saw this particular difference as evidence of secularization, whereas the mystery plays accomplish the same purpose as liturgical drama but in a different manner. In the liturgy, as in ritual of all kinds, primal events are effectively re-enacted, not merely imitated. In the mystery plays, the events of salvation history were not literally repeated as they were in the liturgy, the sacraments, or sacred processions, yet the force of that history for the community was scarcely less than if the events had literally been re-enacted, because everything the story meant to the community was fully present in it to those who watched and to some extent participated – as when they were directly addressed, pushed aside, pursued, or merely invited to respond with approbation or disapprobation to what they witnessed.[3] In the pageant of Lucifer's fall, the devil is not a late extraneous element; he is an essential part of what ties the story most profoundly to its audience, not merely in terms of doctrine but in their moral lives and their social relationships.

Politically the fall of Lucifer was inevitably understood in feudal terms, and among the four cycles Chester is particularly attentive to nuances in the feudal relationship between God and the angels.[4] None of the cycles, however, makes Lucifer's fall analogous to a peasant revolt against a landholder, as one might expect in a strongly hierarchical society.[5] Rather, fidelity to the sacred narrative in the mystery plays makes Lucifer's rebellion a palace revolt. While the Towneley cherubin's loving deference to the unfallen Lucifer is unique, all the cycles emphasize Lucifer's extraordinary power and favor with God, and what they chiefly excoriate is pride, the besetting sin of those with heavy investments in the social and political hierarchy. Lucifer's adherents are almost always the socially privileged, not peasants, and the demonic destruction of community occurs in repeating the sin of Lucifer – that is, in abuses of power by the powerful. Recognizing, acknowledging, and condemning upper-class abuses, as these plays continually do, effectively reinforces the moral assumptions that underlie communal cohesion, because those assumptions are based on the narrative depicted in the plays and on the sacraments which relive that narrative.

The N-Town cycle goes so far in condemning class abuse as to depict approvingly a revolt against a hierarchical superior. As soon as Lucifer orders the angels to worship him, the Boni Angeli explicitly refuse to obey Lucifer's order, though he is their created superior:

> We worchipe God of myth most stronge,
> Whiche hath formyd bothe vs and the.
> We may nevyr wurchyp hym to longe,
> For he is most worthy of magesté.
> On knes to God we falle.
> Oure Lorde God wurchyp we,
> And in no wyse honowre we the![6]

Rejecting orders that countermand God's order is not only allowable but requisite in heaven, even when the orders come from a hierarchical superior – a position defended by Thomas Aquinas.[7]

The mystery plays' first pageant thus establishes a political pattern that runs throughout all four of the complete cycles, as well as partial ones, like those from Coventry and Norwich. This pattern identifies pride and rebellion against God with nearly everyone in the stories who possesses wealth, social prestige, and political power. Arnold Williams recognized this pattern long ago and pointed it out: "With the exception of the Three Kings, who are after all away from home and without authority, all kings and 'bishops' are villains."[8] Saving the appearances of Chambers' theory, Robert Weimann attributes this social bias to authorship of the plays by members of the lower clergy, who sponsored such ecclesiastically rebellious festivities as the Feast of Fools.[9] But Weimann's conclusion is problematic, for we know little about authorship of the cycles, but we have several instances of highly placed preachers condemning the misuse of power and social position.[10] Even if clerical authorship could be proved for the plays, then, it would not necessarily involve clerics of low rank. The social critique in these plays emerges from widely held religious assumptions about communal value, not simply from the social status of the critic.

In addition to depicting a palace revolt, the fall of Lucifer also involves little, if any, of the comedy that is often attributed to devils as if it were their inherent characteristic. The seriousness of mystery-play devils was recognized by Chambers' contemporary, L. W. Cushman, in a comment that has been almost entirely ignored.[11] More recently Hans Jürgen Diller has observed that the mystery-play devils characteristically invite *Schadenfreude*, rather than hilarity.[12] Only N-Town includes the merest suggestion of scatological humor in the first play: when Lucifer encounters hell, he exclaims, "For fere of fyre a fart I crake!" (*N-Town Play*, 24/81). Given the remarkable theological sophistication of N-Town's devils, this instance seems a characteristic interpretation of carnivalesque detail in keeping with the plays' ritual celebration of communal values.[13]

The pageant of Lucifer's fall models the relationship of mystery-play devils to the devil of traditional religion. In the plays, devils always appear in keeping with Lucifer's disruption of primordial community, and they appear relatively infrequently. Only three out of thirty pageants in the Towneley cycle contain devils, though Towneley is often thought of as the most devilish of the four, perhaps because of the rambunctious appearance of Tutivillus in the *Judgment*.[14] The cycle with the most pageants containing devils (eleven out of forty-one) is N-Town, whose solemn intellectual density confirms the seriousness of devils.[15] Still, devils are relatively scarce, even in N-Town, and when they do appear, it is seldom in the carnival attitudes that are often described as their essential character.

STAGE DEVILS, DEATH, AND JUDGMENT

A good example of stage devils' affinity with the devil of traditional religion is their association with death in the cycle plays. The part played by devils in dying is explained in chapter 1; what is important for the mystery plays is the part that individual dying played in the life of the social body. For the deathbed struggle was not merely a matter of personal piety and orthodox affirmation; it was a matter of affirming community or denying it, as Lucifer does in *The Creation and Fall of the Angels.* Resisting the devil in one's final moments depended to a large extent on how well one had prepared for it, and this involved more than an appropriate spiritual attitude; it involved a life's story of practicing the seven corporal acts of mercy. The story might even be short. John Mirk tells of a rich man who used a piece of bread as a weapon to throw at a poor man in order to drive him away; after the rich man died, the Virgin saved him from damnation by producing the bread as proof that he had fed the hungry.[16] The point is not that Mirk was naive or superstitious; he was making a rhetorical point about the efficacy of charitable deeds in defeating the devil.

The point seems to have been taken, for a large proportion of new wealth generated in the fifteenth century was spent on places of communal worship in order to demonstrate that the benefactors were mindful of others' needs and not intent simply on their own comfort and luxury. In these cases, more than a crust of bread was committed to the public good as a way of preparing for the deathbed temptation and the Day of Judgment. Gail Gibson details the generous bequests of three wealthy East Anglians in the fifteenth century: John Baret, John Clopton, and Anne Harling, who all disburdened themselves of significant portions of their wealth in gifts to local churches.[17] In doing so, they responded, as did hundreds of other lay Christians in the late Middle Ages, to the common homiletic theme of the parable of the sheep and the goats, separated on the Day of Judgment according to their practice of the seven corporal acts of mercy. As with the devil and ecclesiastical processions, so with the devil at the deathbed: personal

piety and acts of devotion were understood as social values, practiced
for the community on which they made an undoubted material impact.

That impact is evident in the mystery plays, as it is in art, churches,
literature, pilgrimages, and innumerable other details of fifteenth-
century life. Where the deathbed itself is concerned, the cycles provide
many examples of demonic power in life's extremity. Significantly, when
the devil succeeds, he does so in the lives of the rich and powerful, a
development of the pattern established in the *Creation and Fall of the Angels*
that identifies pride and the demonic violation of community with the
socially privileged. Yet the suffering of the deathbed is never remitted,
even for the faithful. When Mary asks Jesus if she can be relieved of
fiendish temptation in the York *Death of the Virgin,* Jesus replies that she
cannot, though he promises divine comfort because her life has been
virtuous:

Bot modir, the fende muste be nedis at thyne endyng
In figoure full foule for to fere the.
Myne aungelis schall than be aboute the,
And therfore dere dame thou thar noght doute the,   *you need suffer no self-doubt*
For douteles thi dede schall noght dere the.[18]   *deeds / harm*

What we actually see, however, is the overwhelming of "dede" by "dere"
in the deathbed suffering of the wicked. Two of the cycles (Chester and
N-Town) thus introduce non-canonical devils into the scene depicting
the death of Herod, and the inspiration in both cases is contemporary
belief about the devil and dying.

In the Chester play, Herod dies soon after slaughtering the innocents,
and Demon appears briefly to claim his soul and drag his corpse from
the stage. Demon's victory indicates that Herod's life record makes him
a citizen of the kingdom Lucifer established in his revolt. In fact, Herod's
killing of the children is modeled on Lucifer's self-punishing action in
The Creation and Fall of the Angels: boasting that he is godlike and attempting to destroy a rival god, Herod actually destroys his own son, unwittingly killed in the arms of a wet-nurse by one of the soldiers during the
slaughter in Bethlehem. Herod thus represents a parody of God and
God's power: fancying himself divine and attempting to kill his rival's
son, he in fact kills his own son and dies in despair. "Booteles is me to
make mone, / for dampned I must bee," he laments, seeing "of feindes
swarmes – / I have donne so many harmes – / from hell comminge after
mee."[19] Having no "dede" to cite, unlike the York Mary, but only "many
harmes," he has nothing to prove charity in his life as a resource in the
struggle against despair:

> I have donne so much woo
> and never good syth I might goo;
> therfore I se nowe comminge my foe
> to fetch me to hell. (201/426–29)

As Rosemary Woolf points out, his next two lines are a bold parody of late medieval testamentary wills: "I bequeath here in this place / my soule to be with Sathanas" (430–31).[20]

The N-Town play makes clearer than its Chester counterpart that the suffering associated with death is not occasioned by death itself but by the fiends, who are, as it were, the servants of death. As in *Everyman*, death is personified, representing the claims of God against Herod. If anything, Herod is even more boastful in the N-Town play than in Chester. Feasting his courtiers after the slaughter of the innocents, Herod intemperately lists the luxury of his dinner table (192/144–49), caring nothing about the seven acts of mercy nor about his obligation to remember others' needs against the day of death and reckoning. Mors enters in the midst of this banquet, drawn by Herod's bragging: "Ow! I herde a page make preysyng of pride!" (193/168). The socially slighting "page" contrasts strongly with Herod's claims to be "wurthely servyd at my degré" (193/156), and Mors' accusation of "pride" recalls Lucifer's archetypal revolt. Indeed, Mors' assertion of God's lordship over Herod parallels the N-Town Boni Angeli's assertion of God's lordship over Lucifer in *The Creation and Fall of the Angels*:

> But of his wykkyd wyl, lurdeyn, yitt he lyede!   *lout*
> Goddys sone doth lyve! Ther is no lord but he.
> Ouyr all lordys he is kynge. (193/173–76)

Ironically echoing Herod's boasts about the children, Mors declares his intention to claim Herod:

> Bothe hym and his knyghtys all,
> I xal hem make to me but thrall.
> With my spere sle hem I xall
> And so cast down his pride! (194/203–6)

The part played by a devil in this scene is small but significant. As in the Chester play, when Mors strikes Herod and his two knights, Diabolus drags them away, promising "pleys," "mirthe," and "sport" to his victims (235, 236, 243).[21] Diabolus justly claims Herod by the way Herod dies, and the promise Diabolus makes to his victims demonically parodies the communal "mirth" that God established in heaven by creating the angels – the same mirth that Lucifer lost in his rebellious pride.

Closely related to death is the Last Judgment, the reckoning of human deeds at the eschatalogical death of the human race, and all four of the complete cycle plays bring devils on stage in this pageant, ready to claim those who belong to them. The criteria for belonging to the devil invariably involve failure to practice the seven corporal acts of mercy, and all four cycles stage the parable of the sheep and the goats, with the devil avidly claiming those who did not repent their willful commitment to luxurious living at the expense of others.[22] Thus, at the end of each of the cycles, we are reminded that the kingdom Lucifer established in his rebellion against God was a kingdom that defines community oppositionally by default, for here, as elsewhere, the social function of devils is to clarify the failure of community, which is the failure of charity.

In the Chester *Judgment*, this purpose is achieved by animating a conventional iconographical motif, the Dance of Death, whose origins lie in homiletic reflection on the transience of wealth and worldly success.[23] A sequence of social types appears in hierarchical order, from pope to merchant, one each for the saved and the damned, all briefly repenting a life record of deeds that violated charity, the essential principle of social cohesion. These confessions are remarkably candid about moral and social failure. Even the most prominent among the saved (i.e., the pope) laments a life that "was wood [*obsessed*] / worshipps for to wynne" and wits spent "to come to great degree" (440/51–53). On his own behalf, the pope, like his other saved counterparts, pleads only the passion of Christ and his own patient suffering in purgatory. Later rejecting Papa Damnatus, Jesus specifically cites his failure to help "the leaste of myne / that on yearth suffered pyne" (461/637–38). Eamon Duffy's comment is apt: "the thought of mortality was endlessly harnessed by preachers and dramatists, not to call people away from social involvement but to promote virtue and sociability in this world" (p. 303).

In this context, the devils function as prosecuting attorneys, ensuring that their claim to the damned is honored. Their victory is pyrrhic, however, for while they eagerly assert their right, they do so according to terms God established long before, and they thus implicitly concede the justice of God not only against the human damned but against themselves. When Demon Primus (later addressed as "Sathan"), claims his right to Papa Damnatus, he appeals to the principles of God's kingdom (its justice, mercy, and establishment in Christ's passion) in order to assert his right to one who violated those principles (457/525–32), yet the prime violator, ironically, is Satan himself, without whom there would be no kingdom of the damned. Here, as in his fall at the beginning of the cycles, Satan is the implacable enemy of humankind, the origin of "all our woe." Without him there would be no severance from God, no violation of the perfect community briefly celebrated by the Towneley cherubin. Counteracting his malicious influence (including exploitation of the poor by the rich) was one of the primary functions of liturgical celebration and one of the primary purposes of the mystery plays.

Critical assessment of the N-Town *Judgment* is difficult, because it is unfinished, but the devils in the York and Towneley plays function as they do in Chester, albeit with a great deal more elaboration and social directness in Towneley's case. In York, the devils' role is abbreviated: just twelve lines out of 380 in the whole pageant. Nevertheless, their essential function, as in Chester, is that of prosecutors who demand their right to those who have violated community. When I Diabolus urges his fellows to "arraye us for to fight" (411/217), he is not repeating the mistake the devils made in the *Harrowing of Hell*, when they attempted to battle Jesus physically; rather, he is referring to a legal fight: "go we faste oure fee to fange [*to get our reward*]" (218). The Towneley author, working closely from the York play, expanded this thought, clarified its reference, and reinforced its contemporary application:

It sittys you to tente	*befits / pay attention*
In this mater to mell	*get involved in this matter*
As a pere in a parlamente	
What case so befell.	
It is nedefull	
That ye tente to youre awne,	*pay attention to your own [interest]*
What draght so be drawne. (406/174–80)	*whatever legal action*

Here and elsewhere, the Towneley author enlarged the role of the devils, until twelve lines in his source eventually grew to almost 400, but the expansion is not gratuitous, it does not subvert the play's solemn theology, and it is certainly not secular; rather, it relates the biblical narrative concretely to the social reality of the play's auditors, clarifying how the story they witness is their own story, both individually and collectively.

Towneley's lively social satire is always attentive to the imagined context of the devils' claim to the damned before the judgment seat of Christ. Recounting the evil deeds that the accused have committed, Primus and Secundus Demon thus refer explicitly to three of the seven deadly sins: pride (407/208, 220), lust (208), and anger (407/224). These are individual moral failings, of course, but they are also social failings, the inevitable pattern of violated relationships in the kingdom of Satan, which is defined by oppositional contrariety and inversion. Charity is thus absent, and the seven corporal acts of mercy are not practiced. Hypocrisy is cited by Secundus Demon as a contemporary social failure, as well as an individual fault:

Bot before hym he prase hym,	*to his face*
Behynde he myssase hym.	*speaks derogatorily about*
Thus dowbill he mase hym.	*doubly confuses (double crosses)*
Thus do thai to-day.	(407/231–34)

Discovering paid detractors and false witnesses in his list, he makes clear who their primary victims are:

Faithe and trowth, maffay,	*by my faith*
Has no fete to stande.	
The poore pepyll must pay,	
If oght be in hande.	(409/274–77)

Tutivillus, a Towneley devil often noted for his engaging garrulousness and verbal facility, serves to direct the same social satire to specific contemporary vices, always with the dramatic and theological context in mind. His lavish enumeration of luxurious fashion, for example (413/417–20), is a specific and exuberant gloss not only on pride but on the failure to observe the merciful act of clothing the poor, which Jesus refers to later in commending the saved: "When I was clothles ye me cled" (418/618). Tutivillus refers to the "synnes vii" and names five of them (413/443, 414–15/482–84, 495), and his interpretation of them is invariably social, involving such violations of community as aggressive upward mobility, adultery, luxuriously self-indulgent clothing, social scorn, neglecting church-going, and the like. All are conceived, in effect, as varying ways of removing oneself from the sacred social body that was originally established by divine love, opposed from the beginning by the malevolent power of the devil, and continually renewed by the sacramental celebration of Christ's passion. Tutivillus' verbal extravagance is indeed impressive and funny, and it retains powerful elements of social inversion that may derive from carnival devils. These characteristics, however, serve a social vision that was informed by the broader context of traditional religion. Like the seasonal liturgical festivals, Tutivillus and his fellows retain the energy of age-old folk tradition in a distinctively Christian setting.

STAGE DEVILS AND THE PASSION

The most striking evidence of the mystery plays' attention to the demonic suffering that accompanies dying is their extended focus on the betrayal, rigged trial, beating, torture, and execution of their principal character, who is a landless peasant. Satan's responsibility for Jesus' death is a complex matter in all the cycles, but his responsibility for Jesus' suffering is never questioned, and it amounts to an extended demonic temptation of the kind that traditional Christians prayed to be delivered from. All the cycles devote several pageants to these events, which belong generically to the woe that Satan successfully introduced to the human race, including the suffering that peasants endured at the hands of their social superiors. In fact, the brutality of the passion plays seems to represent a victory of Satanic sorrow over the incarnate God himself. On the other hand, the plays celebrate the paradox of Satan's defeat in his apparent victory and thus vindicate the ultimate effectiveness of sacred redemptive power, for the events depicted in the passion were uniquely efficacious in warding off the devil. The eucharist, ubiquitous symbols of the cross, commemoration of the five wounds, the crossing of oneself, veneration of the nails, crown of thorns, and spear, all are familiar cultural manifestations of the power of Christ's passion to overcome the power of evil.

Two of the cycles (N-Town and York) treat Satan's paradoxical self-defeat in the story of Pilate's wife, and though each handles the story differently, both introduce devils to help them do it, and both use the episode to suggest Satan's essential weakness, even at the height of his most determined duplicity and cunning. As in the York *Judgment*, the demonic role in the York *Dream of Pilate's Wife* is slight: Diabolus makes only one appearance in a speech of eighteen lines out of 548 in the play (259/157a–75). His function is to motivate Pilate's ambivalence about the prisoner brought before him. Suddenly recognizing that Jesus is God's son, Diabolus decides to abort the divine plan of salvation by convincing Pilate's wife that Jesus is innocent, so she will persuade her husband to acquit him. This plan works to the extent that Percula successfully persuades her husband of Jesus' innocence, but it fails because of Pilate's need to deal with the political reality of Anna's and Cayphas' uncompromising determination that Jesus be sentenced to death. In other words, Satan's cunning is defeated by the fruits of the cunning that he has himself produced in the human community: political striving, implacable hatred, lying, slander, duplicity, envy, treachery.

The feudal dynamics of the scene are unmistakable: as in *The Fall of Lucifer*, the properties of government are inevitably understood in contemporary terms.[24] Pilate is a king, and Cayphas and Anna are his "prelates" (262/271, 266/403). Diabolus archly refers to Jesus as a "gentilman" (259/160, 168), but the social scorn of Jesus' human enemies is blatant: they repeatedly call him a "warlock" and dismiss his father as "but a write" (269/504). Cayphas' and Anna's slander creates particularly rich irony, because they counter Percula's report of Jesus's innocence with an assertion that Jesus used "wicchecrafte" to raise a fiend and deceive a gullible woman (263/293–300). In their attempt at vicious slander, they unwittingly state the truth about the demonic source of Percula's dream and thus ironically defeat the devil's attempt to defeat the divine plan of salvation.[25] The result does not reduce the demonic suffering endured by Jesus, but it clarifies the irrepressibly redemptive power of his passion and the self-defeating power of what opposes it.

The ironies of the York play are heightened in the N-Town *Satan and Pilate's Wife*, when Satan himself, rather than Pilate, becomes the focus of Satan's struggle to defeat Jesus, so that Satan has a more prominent role as the personal adversary of God. Satan's abuse of power has theological roots in a patristic account of the atonement, as Timothy Fry has argued, but the N-Town play casts Satan's action in the form of a contemporary political abuse of power as well, so that politics, doctrine, and story are inseparable, as in the cycle's first play.[26] Satan's hatred of Jesus mirrors contemporary courtly strife. Satan is out to avenge the dishonor he suffered when Jesus dared to "defy" him in the temptation: "That rebuke that he gaf me xal not be vnqwyt!" (315/21). Moreover, he despises Jesus socially: "For all his barfot goyng, fro me xal he not skyp" (315/23). He confidently reminds himself of the formidable array of weapons he has prepared to destroy Jesus and bring him to his "derk dongeon" (315/24): the cross, the nails, the spear – ironically, of course, all potent symbols of redemption to a contemporary audience. After a warning from Demon about what Jesus might do to hell, Satan changes his strategy. Abandoning the idea of the direct assault, he determines to be cunning: "But som wyle help, I have a shrewde torne [*Unless some trick help, I will suffer a bad turn*]" (316/43). His recourse to wiliness is not successful either, but whatever its outcome, Satan's procedure is modeled on courtly competition. As the premier spiritual adversary, Satan's enmity takes recognizable social and political form, and his class identity is unmistakably aristocratic.

What we find in the N-Town *Satan and Pilate's Wife*, then – and indeed, everywhere in the mystery plays – is that the devil is identified with social oppression, not with social resistance. Critics seeking topical meaning in the mystery plays have shown that the devil's kingdom, led by himself but including human characters who inflict various kinds of demonic suffering on themselves or others, is invariably identified with powerful and socially privileged individuals: landowners, courtiers, bishops, lawyers, merchants, wealthy yeoman.[27] Even the Towneley Cain, while obviously a farmer, is a prosperous landowner, hard-working, thrifty, industriously acquisitive on his own behalf, and the Chester alewife, though no more than a small businesswoman, is committed to seeking her own advantage at the expense of others, exemplifying a wilful violation of the liturgical social body and its charitable sinews.[28] The satire in both cases is directed not at commoners themselves but at their failure of responsibility to their neighbors – a trait they share with many others, particularly their social superiors. This satire is neither extraneous nor secular; it is a direct expression of a story about the creative and redemptive power of God, opposed by willful self-seeking and the rejection of sociable expectation.

That rejection is developed most richly through stage devils in the N-Town *Passion Play I*. Except for a brief appearance in the York *Dream of Pilate's Wife*, devils are not present in the passion play of any other cycle, yet the long prologue of Demon in the N-Town play is not a comic excrescence: it ties this play explicitly to *The Creation and Fall of the Angels*, it establishes the principles of the story that follows, and it dramatically emphasizes the relevance of the story to the audience watching it.[29]

The prologue is in two equal parts: lines 1 to 60, a dramatic monologue revealing Satan's frame of mind, his motives, and his plan for defeating his archenemy, and lines 61 to 124, where Satan suddenly adopts the persona of a courtier, dressed lavishly in the very latest style and advocating every kind of social arrogance associated with the "newe faccyon" (248/80).[30] While this division is evident in reading the prologue, an audience perceives it differently. For Lucifer calls attention to his costume for the first time in the second half, but the costume is the same from the beginning, and the message is therefore visually implicit from the outset: the same Lucifer who rebelled against God, who tempted Christ unsuccessfully, and who inflicted horrible suffering on him is embodied in contemporary luxury and social oppression. The courtly satire is not tacked onto the doctrinal background; the two are inseparably fused in the story the audience watched, and it was made their story not only by Lucifer's use of direct audience address but by the way he was costumed.

The opening arrogance of Lucifer's lines therefore has a theatrical doubleness that is difficult to appreciate fully in reading them. When he claims to rule as "youre lord, Lucifer," "Prince of this Wer[l]d and gret Duke of Helle" (245/1–2), his three self-bestowed honorific titles are hyperbolic, recalling the boasting associated with arrogant tyrants who invariably embody the deadly sin of pride. This is another such character, not only in his boasts but in his luxurious contemporary costume. At the same time, however, he explicitly identifies himself as the one who tried to defeat God but was himself defeated in heaven and in the temptation, and who now determines, as in the N-Town *Satan and Pilate's Wife*, to avenge himself cleverly: "Thus xal I venge by sotylté al my malycyous grevauns, / For nothyng may excede my prudens and dyscrecyon" (248/59–60). His determined "sotylté," akin to his "craft" in *Passion Play II*, relates to N-Town's pervasive contrast between "wyt" and "wysdam," and points again to the specific nature of courtly power – its indirection, dissimulation, and treachery.[31] This is the same character who will inspire the "treson" of Judas in the scenes that follow (272/209), addressing him as "derlyng myn" (281/951), and motivating the kiss that Judas proposes in response to Leyon's complaint about the charitable community of Jesus' disciples: "o dyscypil is lyche thi maystyr in al parayl, / And ye go lyche in all clothyng" (275/807–8). Judas' action not only disrupts the community of the disciples in the same way that Lucifer disrupted the community of heaven but also emphasizes the inappropriateness of Satan's gaudy clothing in the prologue, designed only to display oppressive wealth and power.

Satan's comments about the quality of his rule thus anticipate what happens later in *Passion Play I*, from the "ryth sotyl ordenawns" proposed by Rewfyn (269/619) to the extravagant costumes of Annas and Cayphas (252/164 SD; 253/208 SD). Satan both describes and enacts the principles of his regime, which are also the principles of abusive contemporary regimes he alludes to in his self-selected titles, in his costume, and in the diabolical advice he gives in succeeding lines. By the same token, the principles of Jesus' kingship are enacted as well, in a consistent contrast to Satan's. Jesus' exorcism of seven devils from Mary Magdalen contrasts with Satan's successful influence over Judas, and Mary's terms of gratitude ("Now I am brought from the fendys brace, / In thi grett mercy closyd and shytt" [271/669–70]) contrast with Satan's vengeance and cunning, which motivate the false justice that betrays, overwhelms, and destroys Jesus. When Jesus makes his triumphal entry into Jerusalem, four citizens enter "barfot and barelegged and in here shyrtys" (263/449 SD) because they cast their gowns on the road for him to ride on – a striking contrast with the sumptuary display of Satan and his followers. Satan despises Jesus for what he calls "hese werkys ful grettly merveyllys" (247/36) that are enacted in the scenes that follow: his humility, his power to heal and give life, and his preservation of human beings from the fiend with his death – all principles of ritually defined community that Satan violates, both in his fall and in everything he does in opposition to Christ.

Passion Play I ends before the crucifixion, the greatest of Jesus' works on behalf of humankind ("For mannys love I may do no mo / than for love of man to be ded" [283/979–80]), but the crucifixion is included proleptically. For the play stages the last supper in what is, in effect, a simultaneous pre-enactment (in the imagined time of the play) and re-enactment (in the time of the audience) of the crucifixion, bringing this play very close to liturgical drama. As historians have noted, commemorating the broken body of Christ was, paradoxically, the foundation of liturgical community, the establishment of the social body by whom and for whom the mystery plays were performed, sometimes and in some places actually on the Feast of Corpus Christi.[32] The social anachronism of Satan's prologue, as well as of the preaching of John Baptist, Peter, and Jesus himself, is a result of fifteenth-century oppositional thinking projected "historically" onto the primal event that established the play's audience as part of a socially cohesive community – that is, onto the crucifixion, which is the model of the eucharist, celebrated for the "first" time in this play but according to a procedure that was distinctively fifteenth-century. The devil is dressed and behaves like an arrogant courtier because envy and hatred are characteristic ways for courtiers to violate community, because the devil fell through pride, and because the devil envies and hates Jesus, the establisher and preserver of sacramental community, just as the devil envied and hated God, who established the blessed community of heaven. These are theological insights, to be sure, but they are inescapably moral and social insights as well, and their ubiquitous presence in various forms in all the cycles indicates their wide acceptance and recognition in the communities for which and by which the plays were performed.

STAGE DEVILS AND SOCIAL AMBIVALENCE

Attention to the social function of devils in the mystery plays requires some comment on the actual social context in which devils were staged. In other words, how does the social vision implied by these plays' presentation of the devil compare to what we know about fifteenth- and early sixteenth-century society? The answer to this question, I think, reveals the actual ambivalence of the mystery plays. They have long been thought to be divided against themselves in a way that Chambers imagined almost a century ago, when he envisioned an upper-class veneer of Christian orthodoxy overlying a solid peasant core of residual paganism and social resistance. What the plays tried to do officially and theologically was thus constantly subverted by the energetic eruption of folk elements, devils being prime among them. "The medieval mind," as A. P. Rossiter put it, contained "uncombinable antinomies" whose evidence is in the comic elements of drama.[33] For reasons described in chapter 1, this view of social ambivalence in medieval drama would seem to reveal more about the mind of those who maintain it than about the so-called medieval mind. Nonetheless, the perception of ambivalence of some kind is accurate, and identifying what that ambivalence consists of is worthwhile.

The plays are truly ambivalent about what opposes community when they identify the devil as adversary. A merely spiritual enemy is one thing, but insofar as community was social, its opposite was social too, and the identification of community with one's own parish, the center of one's social and ritual experience, meant that community and its opposite were often defined in literally parochial terms. In fifteenth-century Norwich, tension between the city and the local Benedictine cathedral priory was produced by the perception of the monks as foreigners, because they had no local family ties, unlike the secular clergy.[34] In at least one instance, Rogation processions produced fights between neighboring parishes, because people from both neighborhoods thought the other parish was ridding itself of demons at its neighbor's expense (Duffy, p. 136).

The principle of social cohesion was thus, paradoxically, the source of social conflict as well, since both derived from a strong sense of identity with one's local parish. Other factors than religious belief encouraged this sense of identity, of course: slow and limited communication and transportation and the labor-intensive requirements that kept most people close to home in providing for daily living. Combined with the ubiquitous influence of the liturgy, these patterns of social life help to account for suspicion of strangers. Thinking of social evil as the opposite of community meant that foreigners were automatically suspect, and the unbaptized were difficult to accept because they literally belonged to the devil. Anti-Jewishness was therefore an inevitable structural feature of late medieval society: not only did Jews reject Christian belief, but they had called for the death of Christ, as the gospels made clear. Jews were therefore thought of as very close to the great enemy Satan himself, a prejudice that explains the way they are presented in the mystery plays and the Croxton *Play of the Sacrament*, as well as in later plays like Marlowe's *Jew of Malta* and Shakespeare's *Merchant of Venice*, where Shylock is explicitly identified with the devil and his house with hell.[35]

This parochialism generates ambivalence in the plays because it is at odds with their ostensible depiction of the story of humankind, not merely of the European Christian community, let alone of one city or parish. After seeing the infant Jesus, the York Simeon declares that he has seen "The helth for all men that be levand / Here for ay [*all people living on earth forever*]" (159/417–18), and the Towneley Sibilla is equally emphatic in the universality of her vision:

> All men was slayn thrugh Adam syn,
> And put to pyne that neuer shall blyn,   *punishment / cease*
> Thrugh falsnes of the feynd.
> A new kyng comes from heuen to fyght
> Agans the feynd to wyn his right;
> So is his mercy heynd.   *gracious*

> All the warld shall he deme,   *judge*
> And that haue seruyd hym to wheme,   *please*
> Myrth thaym mon betyde.
> All shall se hym with thare ee,   *eyes*
> Ryche and poore, low and hye;
> No man may hym hyde.   (69–70/169–80)

Just before his ascension, the Chester Jesus commissions his disciples "To teach all men" (373/101), and at the same point in his ministry, the N-Town Jesus orders the apostles, "to the worldys ende vttyrly / My wyttnes only be" (383/42–43). To be sure, the symbolic placement of Jews and Saracens beyond "the worldys ende" is done on the basis of their disbelief, as Stephen Spector and Gail Gibson have pointed out,[36] but distinctions are never made in these plays on strictly doctrinal grounds: one mark of a sacred culture is that oppositional distinctions embrace social life, as well as religious experience.

Another kind of social conflict associated with ritual community has been pointed out by Mervyn James, in this case arising not from encounters with outlanders but from differences within the community itself.[37] Communal celebrations not only expressed the solidarity and order of the parish or town but also stressed the fault lines of social organization, engendering disputes over privilege and precedence. "Conflict," as James puts it, "was the dark side of the moon of unity" (p. 8), and conflict erupted frequently. While James details conflict in the Corpus Christi procession, others have documented competitive strife between guilds over production and presentation of the plays, and even in the liturgy, where in some cases a ritual of reconciliation, such as the kissing of the paxbred or the distribution of holy bread, became an occasion for division and actual violence over social place and appropriate deference.[38]

In such cases, the hierarchical organization of society and the observation of deference and rank were in conflict with the Christian virtue of humility, for the jealous guarding of honor and social place was difficult to distinguish from pride, the besetting sin of social privilege. Chaucer notices this inherent conflict with remarkable acuity in *The Canterbury Tales*, and the cycle playwrights treat it by assigning contemporary aristocratic excesses to Lucifer and his human followers. In doing so, they took their inspiration in part from the social leveling celebrated by Mary in the Magnificat, which is recited or sung in some form in all the cycles.

As in their affirmation of universality, however, the mystery plays are often ambivalent about class differences, for they also fail to resolve the conflict between hierarchy and humility. In the N-Town *Passion Play I*, the blessed community of Jesus and his disciples is distinguished from the demonic worldlings who harass Jesus: whereas the worldlings are dressed luxuriously as befits their high social status, Jesus and the disciples are dressed all alike, as Leyon complains to Judas, and they consistently address each other simply as "friend" or "brother," in contrast to honorific feudal titles used by Jesus' opponents. Nonetheless, the disciples' seeming egalitarianism coexists with a stage direction for the last supper, when Christ is seated at the table together with "hese dyscypulis ech in ere degré" (276/348 SD). Hierarchy, then, somehow obtains among the disciples, though the author is silent about its social markers in this case.

Another instance of class ambivalence appears in the Chester cycle, in the Dance of Death that takes place during the last judgment. Even in this setting, where all that matters is presenting one's record of charity before God, people appear in order of social prominence, with the highest first. Moreover, no one below the rank of merchant appears at all. Martin Stevens may well be right that "while only a few 'estates' have speaking roles in the Chester Judgment, the stage would have been occupied by every social type, from pope to beggar,"[39] but even if that were the case (and no stage direction indicates that it would have been), only the most socially prominent literally have a voice; others are consigned to silence, as befits their social obscurity, even though Jesus himself is a peasant in the plays, and even though the plays of the last judgment explicitly cite one's attitude toward the poor as the basis for how one is judged.

This kind of social ambivalence in the mystery plays seems undeniable, and other instances could be cited, but in the present context, the most important point to make about it is that *it is not linked with the devil.* In other words, social attitudes in the mystery plays are not divided between an "official" upper-class ideology, theologically correct and socially oppressive, on one hand, and an "unofficial," peasant, residual resistance on the other hand, that appears subversively in the form of irreverent devils. Insofar as Jews are treated as if they were devils in the mystery plays, what we see is not an oppressed conflation of the marginal and the powerless, which would be socially consistent, but an oppressive conflation of the marginal (Jews) with the powerful (bishops) that reflects moral categories (prideful oppression) and provincialism (ignorance about real Jews), not social reality. Morally repugnant as it is, the identification of an alienated minority with the devil is culturally comprehensible, but that identification is also compelling evidence that the majority of baptized Christians – namely, the peasants – would not have been able to identify with the devil as their champion against social oppression. If we look for that kind of champion, we find it not in the devil but in Jesus, himself a peasant, embodying certain aspects of the trickster (beguiling the guiler, for example), and the one who speaks the parable of the sheep and the goats in the last judgment, just as his mother recites the Magnificat before his birth as a prophecy of what he represents. The social function of the devil in the mystery plays is to be the oppositional Enemy; in that capacity, it is incomprehensible that he could ever be on the side of the poor and the oppressed, for the plays insist time and again that without the devil, poverty and social oppression would not exist in the first place.

CHAPTER THREE

Stage devils and sacramental community in non-cycle plays

The devil's opposition to sacramental community makes sense in the mystery plays, which have increasingly been understood in light of the sacred social body. Other kinds of early drama, however, seem less indebted to a ritual conception of community. The fifteenth-century *Play of the Sacrament*, from Croxton, Norfolk, is an obvious exception, but neither morality plays nor saints' plays were associated with the eucharist or with Corpus Christi.[1] Saints' plays were performed on saints' days; morality plays, at any time of the year; and neither seems to have involved the community in the same way the mystery plays did, since the life of a particular saint or of a representative abstraction did not offer, as dramatic subjects, the same scope for social cooperation and competition that was offered by the communal staging of salvation history, and neither seems to have involved anything like the Corpus Christi procession.

Yet the non-cycle plays were also oriented to the sacraments, as we shall see, and their distinction from the mystery plays is an accident of critical history rather than a feature of the plays themselves. This is particularly true where stage devils are concerned, for the evolutionary argument about devils as a comic dessert added to a serious doctrinal entrée is closely related to the way we have come to distinguish the mystery plays from other kinds of early drama. A. W. Pollard wrote one of the most influential early textbooks in this field, responding in each of eight editions (1890 to 1927) to ongoing work by E. K. Chambers, W. W. Skeat, and W. W. Greg. Like his contemporaries, Pollard is teleological in his account of early drama: everything before the late sixteenth century "prepared the ground from which the Shakespearian harvest was to spring in all its glorious abundance," though some fields were more fruitful than others.[2] Thus the moralities were comparatively poor, because personification tends "to didacticism and unreality," and is therefore "wholly undramatic," with the result that "the popularity of the later Morality significantly coincides with the dullest and most barren period in the history of English literature" (p. xliii). Pollard's generalized dismissal of personification as an inferior dramatic device necessarily includes the Vice, who is thereby judged inferior to the predominant devils in the mystery plays. Yet Pollard makes this assertion in the face of the fact that personified abstractions also appear in the mystery plays, and that devils and vices were consistently staged together in pre-Reformation morality plays.

Pollard's severe judgment against the late morality plays was first challenged some seventy years after his first edition, in the work of Bernard Spivack and David Bevington, who decisively vindicated dramatic personification and the Vice in particular. Yet even in their important revision of the critical tradition, they retained a strong sense of historical teleology. Spivack's interest in distinguishing personifications from flesh-and-blood characters was determined by his thesis about the influence of the Vice on late Elizabethan dramatic characterization, and he therefore exaggerates the place of devils in the mystery plays, while understating it in moralities: "The Devil, who in the Christian mythos is the father of evil, has only a negligible place in the morality drama. In the cyclical mysteries and in the miracles he is a familiar personage."[3] Yet Spivack's generalization concerning saints' plays is based on a small, and possibly unrepresentative, sample: only two saints' plays are extant in English, and devils are a late addition to one of them, the Digby *Conversion of St. Paul* (c. 1480–1520). According to Spivack, devils appear in "only nine of the almost sixty surviving" morality plays (p. 130), but it should be added that this proportion is in line with the proportion of pageants that stage devils in each of the extant mystery cycles.[4] Moreover, while Spivack is right that Tudor playwrights preferred to stage the Vice rather than the devil in extant morality plays, devils actually appear more frequently in the later tradition than they do early on, so they do not somehow give way to vices as the morality play "progressed," "developed," or "matured."[5] Mystery-play devils were also staged continuously until shortly after the advent of commercial theatres in London in the 1570s, so a fair assessment of the existing record suggests a continuous interest in devils and personified vices throughout the sixteenth century. Indeed, in view of the sudden increase in the incidence of devils in London commercial plays after Marlowe's *Faustus* and Greene's *Friar Bacon and Friar Bungay*, it would be more accurate to say that in the course of the sixteenth century vices eventually gave way to devils.

David Bevington demonstrates that playwrights increasingly paid attention to the exigencies of commercial acting companies in the sixteenth century, but he takes this kind of progress as evidence of broader progress toward "secularity," so that "the growth of structure" also becomes a story about cultural development that is ultimately indebted to the story told by Pollard and Chambers. "The cycles perished with the Middle Ages while moralities bridged two worlds," Bevington writes, though both kinds were staged throughout the sixteenth century, and both ceased production shortly after the establishment of the commercial theatres in London. By this reckoning "the Middle Ages" ended in the 1570s and 1580s, though elsewhere in Bevington's account "the Renaissance" already makes its appearance in Medwall and Skelton.[6]

One difficulty with evolutionary schemes in literary history is that particular improvements too often exist in the eye of the beholder, especially when secularity is the criterion for progress. Spivack and Bevington thus follow E. N. S. Thompson in discovering significant secular progress away from the "merely spiritual" and "other worldly" in Medwall and Skelton at the beginning of the sixteenth century, while Louis B. Wright finds that dramatists in the 1560s and 1570s "still cling to an other worldliness."[7] If Wright is correct, then it is not clear what sort of "progress" Medwall and Skelton made more than a half century earlier.

The use of "hybrid" as a metaphor for growth and progress in early drama is a problematic manifestation of evolutionary assumptions. Spivack and Bevington both reserve the term for later Tudor plays like *Cambises* (1558–69) that combine personifications with quasi-historical characters. Wager's *Mary Magdalen* (1550–66) is thus part of this particular secularizing development, because it stages the Vice Infidelity along with Mary and other biblical characters. Yet neither critic mentions "hybridization" in the mystery plays and the Digby *Mary Magdalen* (1480–1520), presumably because these examples are too early or because they are not morality plays.[8] In either case, the argument is circular: taking hybridization as evidence of secularization, this line of reasoning defines "hybrid" according to a particular period and genre, explaining away or ignoring examples elsewhere. Rosemary Woolf, on the other hand, is consistent in applying the term "hybrid" to the much earlier Digby *Mary Magdalen*, but she does so in order to compare the gallant called Curiosity in the Digby play with Lucifer in the N-Town *Passion Play I*, whom she regards as a falling-off from rich biblical history in the direction of the morality play, and this judgment brings us back to Pollard's prejudice against morality plays.[9]

The difficulties that attend generic and evolutionary arguments (particularly where perceived esthetic quality or secularity are concerned) can be avoided by acknowledging cultural continuities throughout early drama. The earliest morality play that we know of, *The Pride of Life*, is late fourteenth-century, roughly contemporaneous with the earliest of the mystery plays; both kinds were staged throughout the ensuing two centuries; and both were abandoned after the establishment of commercial theatres near London. Another point of continuity in pre-Reformation drama, as this chapter argues, is that non-cycle plays evince the same sacramental sense of community as the mystery plays. In other words, they belong to the same "sacred" culture, in which devils and vices perform the same oppositional social function: to disrupt the sacred social body. The Protestant Reformation issued the first real challenge to this continuity, as we shall in chapter 5, but it is important first to recognize the continuity itself.

Robert Potter pointed out several years ago that the morality play belongs to a "tradition of sermons and penitential literature advocating repentance and preaching the forgiveness of sins."[10] He argued that the dramatic purpose of the morality play is therefore the same as that of the mystery plays: "the morality play performs the same ceremony in the microcosm of the individual human life as that of the Corpus Christi cycle in the macrocosm of historical time" (p. 8). This is an important insight for pre-Reformation plays: it sees beyond modern generic distinctions, and it recognizes the association of all early drama with traditional ritual. Moreover, the rituals in question, penance and the eucharist, were closely identified with each other and with renewal of the social body, as well as with renewal of the individual moral and spiritual life. Lay communion was taken only once a year, on Easter Sunday, and the period that preceded it, Lent, was designed not simply for personal abstinence but for the mending of relationships and making confession in the interest of restoring communal harmony. In a sermon on the Easter communion, *Mirk's Festial* thus charges that parishioners preparing for the annual rite be in charity with their neighbors and that they be shriven: "Wherfor, good men and woymen, I charch you heyly in Godys byhalue that non of you to-day com to Godys bord, but he be in full charyte to all Godis pepull; and also that ye be clene schryuen and yn full wyll to leue your synne."[11] In the exemplum that follows, the preacher relates how a bishop was granted a vision of parishioners coming to communion as if their moral and spiritual condition were revealed in their physical condition. What he saw were vivid personifications of envy, wrath, and lechery – all sources of communal division. This "vision" thus makes concrete the preacher's oppositional warning that "as wele as hym schall be that comythe to thys fest wele arayde in Godys lyuere, clothyd in loue and scharyte, also euell schall hym be that comythe yn fendys lyuere, clothyd in envy and dedly wrathe."[12] Envy and wrath are "fiends' livery," and they oppose "God's livery," which is love and charity, the basis of social wholeness.

A close collocation appears here that also appears thoughout early non-cycle drama. It consists of personified deadly sins (alternately called "vices") accompanying the fiend as sources of communal division and acting in opposition to the sacraments as means of restoring and maintaining social wholeness. *The Castle of Perseverance* (1380–1425) includes three of the seven sacraments – baptism, penance, and the eucharist – and the healing and unifying power of these rituals opposes the divisive power of fiends and vices. Humanum Genus is thus introduced as "nakyd of lym and lende [*loin*]," clothed only in "A sely crysme min hed hath cawth, / That I tok at min crysteninge."[13] His nakedness symbolizes his innocence, which is protected from the fiend only by his baptism ("A crysyme I haue and no moo" [324]), which in turn is his means of joining the Christian community. The protection and identity afforded by baptism is symbolically threatened when the "crysme" is covered by the rich garments bestowed on Humanum Genus by Mundus, who thus teaches "the wey / To the dedly synnys seuene" (693–94). The threat to Humanum Genus is both individual and social – both to his salvation as a representative member of the sacramental social body and to the integrity of the social body as a whole.

The assault of devils and vices on the protection offered by salvation is, of course, the substance of the action in *Perseverance*, and this assault finally fails because of the salvific rituals whose meaning the play makes concrete (visible and audible) through personified abstraction. "Thou art rewlyd aftyr the fende that is thi foo" (1262), laments Bonus Angelus to Humanum Genus, and Confessio demands rhetorically, "What dost thou wyth these deuelys seuene?" (1338). After Humanum Genus confesses his willful failure, Confessio formally absolves him in the manner that priests used in the sacrament of penance:

> He [God] forgeve the thi foly
> That thou hast synnyd with hert and mynde.
> And I, up my powere, the asoly. (1498–1500)   *by my power, thee absolve*

A few lines later, Confessio paraphrases the formula of absolution from the mass, translating the Latin into English:

> I the asoyle wyth goode entent   *absolve*
> Of alle the synnys that thou hast wrowth
> In brekynge of Goddys commaundement
> In worde, werke, wyl, and thowth.   (1507–10)

The eucharist and baptism are central in defending the Castle of Perseverance from the subsequent assault by the seven deadly sins. Abstinence thus repulses the attack of Gluttony:

> Certys I schal thy wele aslake   *weal reduce*
> Wyth bred that browth us out of hell
> And on the croys sufferyd wrake:
> I mene the sacrament.
> That iche blysful bred,   *same*
> That hounge on hyl tyl he was ded,
> Schal tempere so myn maydynhed
> That thy purpos schal be spent.   (2266–73)

What is imagined on stage at this point parallels contemporary meditation on the Seven Last Words of Christ on the cross. A prayer from the popular books of hours identifies the power of the Seven Last Words with deliverance from the seven deadly sins:

Lord Jesus Christ, who spoke the Seven Words hanging on the Cross on the last day of your life, and wished us always to have those words in remembrance: I beseech you, by the power of those Seven Words forgive me all that I have done or sinned concerning the Seven Deadly Sins, namely, Pride, Envy, Wrath, Sloth, Luxury, Avarice and Gluttony.[14]

The prayer was apotropaic, assuring the one who said it that "the dule [*devil*] no noon ule man shall not have no power to nye hym" (Duffy, p. 248). In other words, the prayer had the same effect that the virtues have in *Perseverance*: to drive away the devil and the vices.

A dramatic parallel to the appeal of *Perseverance* to the apotropaic power of Christ's passion probably existed also in York, where Alexandra Johnston has shown that the Pater Noster Play likely paired each of the seven requests of the Lord's Prayer with one of the seven deadly sins. For the Pater Noster play staged pageants that were also used in the York mystery cycle: the clause honoring God thus repulsed pride and was depicted by the fall of Lucifer, and the clause requesting daily bread repulsed sloth and was depicted by the institution of the last supper, because, as Mirk puts it, the slothful "woll nother travayll to help his body, ny his soule, but lyketh (?) as a swyne, etyth and drynkyth and slepyth."[15] The point is that personifications like the seven deadly sins were not mere abstractions and therefore somehow reductions of scriptural history. Rather, they helped to clarify the moral implications of scriptural narrative (and to that extent were concrete), at the same time that they embodied the power of evil in the daily lives of Christians no less than the devil himself did.

Christ's passion is invoked again in *Castle of Perseverance* after the death of Humanum Genus, when the four daughters of God debate the destiny of Anima. Humanum Genus' dying evocation of God's mercy has a heavenly counterpart in the four sisters' reconciliation in the death of Christ, as Peace makes clear:

> For hys loue that deyed on tre,
> Late saue Mankynd fro al peryle
> And schelde hym fro mischaunsse.   (3209–11; see also 3548–51)

Central to the play's resolution in Mankind's favor is the event commemorated in every mass and partaken of by lay Christians once a year in the Easter service. In short, dramatic action in *The Castle of Perseverance* is no less focused on the passion and its liturgical significance than are the mystery plays.

That focus, moreover, involves more than individual salvation, for it is closely tied to the play's social vision. Just as Humanum Genus' baptism, his "christening," is a sign of his induction into the community of Christians, so his lapse into the devils' camp is not merely an individual moral failure; it is the failure of a society, whose wholeness derived from the mass. This is why the play puts such emphasis on social failure, as the preacher does in *Mirk's Festial*. The central image is one of conflict, but the battle involves more than a psychomachia; it both delineates the principles of social disintegration and offers specific examples.[16] Thus Avarice urges Humanum Genus to exploit his neighbors in seeking gain only for himself: he should practice simony, extortion, "false asise," help no one unless it is to his own advantage, fail to pay his servants' wages, destroy his neighbors, refuse to tithe or help beggars, "And thanne schalt thou ful sone ryse" (841–48). Humanum Genus is a quick study, relishing the thought of doing what Avarice bids him:

> I schal nevere begger bede   *offer*
> Mete nyn drinke, be heuene blys;   *by*
> Rather or I schulde him clothe or fede,   *ere, before*
> He schulde sterve and stynke, iwys.   (871–74)

What he describes are unambiguous rendings of the social body, as an anonymous fifteenth-century confessor makes clear in noting questions to himself for his parishoners to answer as they prepared for confession:

Haue ye hadde enie envie to your neighbores or to youre euen čsten and be gladde of here harmes & of here euel fare and loð of here good, or of ðe adversite or desese ðt haõ falle to hē and be sorie or hevie of here prosprite or welfare . . . and of here good name and good fame. Haue ye bacbitid and dispreised yô evē čten or tolde evell talis of hē to a pew [impugn] here good name or wolde not heere noo good spoke of hē bi yô wille but lette it or stopped it as moche as ye might.[17]

What the priest warns his parishioners against – and what Humanum Genus delights in – are violations of charity, as Charity herself makes clear in *Perseverance*, when she responds in character (i.e., without rancor) to the vilification of Envy:

> Oure louely Lord wythowtyn lak
> Gaf example to charyte,
> Whanne he was betyn blo and blak
> For trespas that nevere dyd he.   (2173–76)

The reconciliation of the Four Daughters of God at the end of the play is another model of charitable community, in contrast to the divisive violence that devils and vices have engendered. Though the daughters disagree with each other, they are not querulous, vicious, colloquial, or overbearing, like their demonic counterparts, and they eventually reconcile their differences with a holy kiss (3519).

The same social vision, again focused in the sacraments, is evident in *Wisdom* (1400–50), though this play's dramaturgy is much more formal than that of *Perseverance*, possibly reflecting courtly or monastic auspices, rather than popular urban performance.[18] A sacramental context is present from the beginning, when Wisdom instructs Anima as if he were a catechist, emphasizing that the death of Wisdom (Christ) redeemed Anima from death and gave rise to "the sacramentys sevyn," of which the first is baptism, because it "clensythe synne orygynall."[19] Wisdom does not enumerate the other sacraments at this point, but he later enjoins Anima to penance and sincere contrition. Having performed this rite, she is released from the dominance of the seven deadly sins (961–79), and exits, singing a hymn based on the Book of Lamentations, "as yt ys songyn in the passyon wyke."[20] Wisdom again instructs her, pointing out that the "asythe" or atonement (1096) made by the crucifixion is provided for her through the sacraments:

> Fyrst ye were reformyde by baptyme of ygnorans
> And clensyde from the synnys orygynall,
> Ande now ye be reformyde by the sakyrment of penance
> And clensyde from the synnys actuall.   (1109–12)

Anima, in chorus with her restored faculties, Mind, Will, and Understanding, sings a hymn based on Psalm 125:2 and 3, verses "spoken by the celebrant of the mass since the ninth century" (Eccles's note to 1064 SD).

Complementing the liturgical and sacramental emphasis in *Wisdom* is an evocation of social disruption that closely parallels the military image of divisive violence in *Perseverance*. The source of communal disorder is the violation of communal norms, which are established by the liturgy and threatened by the power of Lucifer, who actually appears in this play along with the seven deadly sins, as in *Perseverance*.[21] Specific elements of communal disorder are often the same as those mentioned in *Perseverance*, because they are violations of the sacramental social body.

Possible topical allusions may be present in this play, as well as in *Perseverance*, but Wisdom's sense of normative community is identical to that in *Perseverance* and has been largely overlooked in the search for allusions to particular social problems as evidence of progress toward the promise of secular drama in the future.[22] To be sure, *Wisdom* may be concerned with contributions to social disorder that the monasteries in particular were likely to make, especially when powerful churchmen became involved in the maintenance of standing armies, either in gathering them themselves or in assisting a secular nobleman in organizing and maintaining them. But maintenance may well be an example of generic evil, rather than a specific social target, for maintenance was practiced exclusively by the aristocracy, who easily fell prey to the besetting sin of pride, the sin of Lucifer, highest of all creation. A similar treatment of maintenance appears in the convincing and detailed portrait of rural oppression in *The Second Shepherds' Play*, which is blamed by Primus Pastor on "mantenance / Of men that ar gretter," and the social vision of that play also derives from the eucharist, whose origin the play celebrates and to which it alludes in its remarkable comments about eating a sheep.[23] The point is that the basis of social order and disruption is the same in *Wisdom* as it is elsewhere in traditional religion – not only in other plays but in sermons, primers, and commonplace books; maintenance is merely a particular example of Lucifer's power to destroy the social body.[24]

The solemn catechism that opens *Wisdom* thus points to more than individual moral instruction; it evokes social wholeness, with Anima closely attending to Wisdom who is Christ. The rending of this social body is evident in the frenetic dances and dumb shows that accompany the corruption of Anima's mights, Mind, Will, and Understanding, who learn how to destroy their neighbors, just as Humanum Genus does, though they do so with satirical litigious viciousness that sometimes anticipates the seventeenth-century city comedy of Jonson, Middleton, and Marston. Will thus complains that the jealous husband of his "cosyn Jenet N." spoils Will's sport (833–40). Mind offers to chide Janet's husband "Tyll he leve that jelousy" (847), but Understanding has an even better idea: "Arest hym fyrst to pes for fyght" (i.e., for disturbing the peace), indict him in another shire, and have him thrown in Marshalsea prison (849–56).

This urban realism is precisely detailed, with specific references to the contemporary legal scene in London. Nonetheless, the solution to it is the ritual of penance, which restores charitable community, as Wisdom makes clear in his sermon on the nine points of pleasing God:

> Lett not thy tonge thy evyn-Crysten dyspyse,
> Ande than pleyst thou more myn excellens   *performest*
> Than yff thou leberyde wyth grett dylygens
> Wpon thy nakyde feet and bare
> Tyll the blode folwude for peyn and vyolens
> Ande aftyr eche stepe yt sene were.   (1039–44)

This advice is arguably topical – in rejecting asceticism in favor of measured monastic involvement in secular life – but topical readings do not obviate the moral observation that good deeds achieve nothing without charity, a point that Charity makes in *Perseverance* ("Al thi doynge as dros is drye, / But in Charyte thou dyth thi dede" [1604–5]), and that Wisdom makes in different words a few lines later: "Lo, Gode ys plesyde more wyth the dedys of charyte / Than all the peynys man may suffer iwys" (1062–63).[25]

Though baptism is mentioned as one of the seven sacraments in *Perseverance* and *Wisdom*, as we have seen, the ritual of baptism is actually staged in two non-cycle plays in which stage devils also oppose the sacramental body: *The Conversion of Saint Paul* and *Mary Magdalen*, both from 1480–1520. Baptism in these plays is the rite of adult conversion, for both Saulus and the King of Marseilles begin their lives as non-Christians. In fact, Saulus is so determinedly pagan that he persecutes Christians, loyally serving the priests, Cayphas and Anna, who are imported into this play because they are the oppressors of Jesus in the passion cycles of the mystery plays.[26] Like the devil, Saulus thus opposes sacral community: he is the essence of what is alien, frightening, and destructive, because he is not only outside the sacramental social body but threatens its very existence. Ananias' baptism of Saulus makes this point clearly, identifying Saulus' "dedly wound / That was infecte with venom nocent" with "fendys powres so fraudelent," both ritually banished with "thys crystenyng": "where thys doth attayne, / In euery stede, he [the fiend] may not obtayne!" (319–24). In distinctively fifteenth-century terms, Paul is thus transformed from God's enemy into God's champion by the apotropaic power of a sacrament.

That power, moreover, has a decided social function; it is not merely individual. For destructive opposition to community is evident not only in Saulus' persecution of Christians (from which baptism symbolically purges him) but also in a comic scene, added much later, between two devils, Belial and Mercury. The fact that the scene is added makes it a test case for the early critical thesis that all devils were late accretions in response to an increasing appetite for secular subjects, with the result that the plays degenerated into farce and clowning. The thesis does not pass the test of this play, for the devil scene, though interpolated possibly as late as the mid-sixteenth century, nonetheless complements a comic scene in the original and clarifies the significance of baptism as an apotropaic sacrament.[27]

The devils are introduced to lament the loss of their human servant, Saulus, after his conversion has been reported to Cayphas and Annas. Beliall enters "wyth thunder and fyre" (411 SD) boastfully declaring his power and majesty, trusting his "busshopys" and "prelatys" (418, 419) to conspire the death of "All soch as do worship the hye God supernall" (422). Beliall's boastful threats against Christians are proof, in effect, of what Ananias said about "fendys powres" when he baptized Saulus. Another devil called Mercury enters "with a fiering" (432 SD) and concurs with Beliall's incredulity at Saulus' conversion, because most people enjoy only sin, "Pryde and voluptuosyte ther hartys doth so fyre" (446). Inspired by Mercury's comment, Belial boasts about his power over people who follow him. "Ther was neuer among Crystyans lesse charyte / Than ys at this howre," he brags, naming Pride, Envy, Concupisence (who "rayneth as a lord thorow my violence"), Gluttony, Wrath, and Covetousness as the means of his domination over humankind (489–95). Though the seven deadly sins are not actually staged in this play, as in *Perseverance* and *Wisdom*, they are verbally personified as the enemies of human beings, both individually and socially, and in this they are like the devils themselves, with whom they are closely allied, for the sins are direct expressions of demonic power, not mere abstractions or theological constructions. In other words, even when sins are identified as moral abstractions, they still have a concrete potency that is indistinguishable from their influence in biblical stories, like this one, where devils appear without being accompanied by personified vices.

The baptism of a biblical saint in the Digby *St. Paul* has a counterpart in the Digby *Mary Magdalen*, when St. Peter baptizes a legendary pagan king: in both plays, the sacrament functions in the same way, in that it opposes demonic power by establishing a model of charitable community, as well as sanctifying an individual adult conversion. In this case, charity even crosses social lines, bringing a monarch and common sailors into generous harmony with each other.[28]

The banishment of devils in two Digby saints' plays thus derives from the apotropaic power of saints, whose special favor with God is evident not only in their own remarkable conversion but also in the sacramental social body they are able to create in the face of demonic resistance. This kind of apotropaism at the heart of the two recognized saints' plays surviving in English also helps to explain the presence of devils in the N-Town *Assumption of Mary* (fifteenth century), which has not been considered as a saint's play, though perhaps it should be.[29] It resembles the Digby *Mary Magdalen* in several ways: both celebrate a female saint, both include powerful preaching by the saint, both stage the saint's power over demons and her assumption into heaven.[30] Two devils enter the N-Town *Assumption* to abet the disbelief and sacrilegious intentions of the Christian community's powerful enemies, Episcopus and three Princeps, who intend to abuse the body of Mary after her death. As soon as their hands touch the bier, they freeze to it, just as Jonathas' hand freezes to the host in the Croxton *Play of the Sacrament*. In response to this miracle, Primus and Secundus Princeps quickly repent (436 and 468–69), in an abbreviated sacrament of confession (like St. Paul's and Mary Magdalen's in the Digby plays) that immediately inducts them into the sacramental community, in contrast to Episcopus and Tertius Princeps, who continue to scoff and curse. For this, the disbelievers are seized by two demons and carried off to hell, just as the disbelieving Herod is carried to hell by a demon in the N-Town *Death of Herod*. In a symmetrical but opposite action, Mary is received into heaven by Dominus, her son, from whom she derives her power over disbelief, over enmity within the social body, and over the power of hell itself.

The effect of the sacraments in overcoming devilish power and establishing charitable community also helps to explain *Mankind* (1465–70), last of the pre-Reformation plays to be considered here that stage devils or devils together with vices. The importance of the sacrament of penance in *Mankind* has been studied in detail by Sister Mary Philippa Coogan and Kathleen Ashley.[31] Coogan points out that *Mankind* echoes the liturgy for Ash Wednesday and the first Sunday in Lent and twice suggests the sacrament of penance: once implicitly in English and a second time more formally in Latin, when Mercy absolves Mankind, a liturgical representation that Coogan sees paralleled in *Perseverance*, *Wisdom*, *Play of the Sacrament*, and *Everyman*.[32] Building on Coogan's argument, Ashley identifies several common homiletic themes from Shrovetide that reappear in *Mankind*, such as "working in the field or sowing seed" as "figures for proper use of the Word" (p. 144), a contrast between "the lies of the Devil" and the truth of Jesus (p. 145), an emphasis on the "binding snares of Satan," and "the need to arm oneself for battle against the forces of evil" (p. 146). "To its original audience," Ashley argues, "the play therefore exhibited a theological and thematic coherence that escapes a modern reader divorced from the medieval and liturgical tradition" (p. 148). Ashley's reading is particularly helpful in explaining the oppositional presence of the devil Titivillus.

What needs to be added to this account of penance and the Shrovetide liturgy in *Mankind* is the social effect of the sacraments in resisting the power of vices and the devil. For *Mankind* is like other pre-Reformation plays in its concern with the community, as well as the salvation of the individual, and this concern is not secular; it is an expression of faith in the sacramental social body. Mercy himself is comparable to Wisdom in *Wisdom*, despite the plays' remarkable dissimilarities in other respects, for both Mercy and Wisdom embody essential characteristics of the second person of the trinity, and they exhibit their traits not only in name but in behavior. Mercy refers repeatedly to the passion of Christ in his opening homily, actually identifying himself theologically as Christ at one point: "I haue be the very mene for yowr restytucyon."[33] This is another instance of a personified abstraction – in this case a virtue, rather than a vice as in the York Pater Noster Play – merging with an event from salvation history in such a way as to explicate its moral significance. When he is mocked and abused by the vices, he is patient and forbearing, exactly like "Owr Sauyowr, that was lykynnyde to a lambe," in Mercy's own description of Christ (34). As an exemplary friar, Mercy models sacramental community in his solicitous attention to Mankind, just as Wisdom models it in his attention to Anima.[34]

The vices oppose community, despite their social habits, because they oppose charity, in name as well as behavior – in their determination to interrupt and abuse Mercy, in their obscenity, and in their persuasive modeling of riotous company and fast living for Mankind, both the character and the audience. The vices appear to be less powerful than Titivillus, since he is effective in breaching Mankind's moral defenses, whereas they are not, but the devil and the vices work toward the same end in this play, and that end involves more than personal moral and spiritual corruption; it also involves threats to sociability in the form of the charitable relationship that Mankind and Mercy initially represent in their dealings with each other. The restoration of charitable community comes about in the same way it does in *The Castle of Perseverance* – by the intervention of Mercy, depicted in the earlier play as one of the four daughters of God and in *Mankind* as an attribute of God's self. A mimed ritual absolution thus performs the same function in both plays, visibly restoring sacramental community, as well as redeeming a representative individual from the oppression of the fiend.

Vices are just as effective as devils in corroding sacramental order in the plays we have seen thus far, because vices serve the devil's purpose in destroying the spiritual health of individuals and the wellbeing of community. Importantly, the same function is performed by personified vices alone (i.e., unaccompanied by devils) in other pre-Reformation plays. The virtual identity of devils and vices when they appear together should make this no surprise, yet it needs to be pointed out in detail, because it has not been noticed in previous studies of how evil was staged in early English plays. Moreover, attention to plays that stage vices alone helps to account for the essential dramaturgical continuity between devils and the Vice, as he emerged in the early sixteenth century, as we shall see in chapter 4.

Three representative plays that span the range of pre-Reformation English drama can be cited to make this point – one from the early fifteenth century and the other two from the late fifteenth and early sixteenth centuries.[35] The early play is the N-Town *Trial of Mary and Joseph* (fifteenth century), which functions effectively as a saint's play, like the N-Town *Assumption of Mary*, though neither play has been considered independently of its context in a putative mystery cycle. The vices in the *Trial* are identified as personified abstractions in the dialogue: Raise Slander and Backbiter, a vice who appears in a similar role in several morality plays. The playwright imagines the vices as witnesses in an ecclesiastical court, thus combining trenchant satire of contemporary social abuses with the apocryphal story (from Pseudo-Matthew) of the trial of Mary and Joseph for fornication.[36] The vices exhibit a perverse sense of fellowship in their mutual commitment to the destruction of others, boasting that they can raise more slander in an hour "Than evyr ther was this thowsand yere" and sealing their friendship in a kiss that parodies the kiss of the Four Daughters of God in the N-Town *Parliament of Heaven*.[37]

Despite their obscene and blasphemous detraction of Mary and Joseph, the vices' power is overwhelmed in the end by the power of God as exhibited in the virgin, a plot structure that also appears in the N-Town *Assumption of Mary* and is typical of surviving continental miracles of Our Lady. Episcopus orders Mary to drink from "the botel of Goddys vengeauns" (234), because it is designed to reveal unchastity in the imbiber, but it leaves her untouched. Not so Raise Slander: forced by the court to imbibe in his own turn, he falls into an agony of pain that induces him to repent and beg mercy of Mary, which she charitably grants without hesitation: "Now god Lord in hevyn omnypotent, / Of his grett mercy youre seknes aswage" (368–69). Episcopus is so moved that he too falls on his knees and asks Mary's forgiveness. In contrast to the destructive influence of the vices, the play's concluding tableau of restored relationships is suffused with charity, mercy, forbearance, and forgiveness – a tableau identical to that in many of the morality plays, as well as the N-Town *Assumption of Mary*. In *The Trial of Mary and Joseph*, this tableau is brought about by the saint's power to oppose evil and by the abbreviated sacrament of penance that appears in both Raise Slander's and Episcopus' cries of repentance.

The influence of vices in the sacramental pattern of pre-Reformation drama is particularly noteworthy in the final two plays to be considered here, Medwall's *Nature* (c. 1496) and Skelton's *Magnificence* (1515–26), because their courtly auspices differentiate them in many respects from popular plays. Both associate their hero's initial period of innocence with reason, rather than with baptism; indeed, the emphasis on reason is so pronounced that these plays seem to look forward to the Enlightenment, two hundred years after them, rather than to their own time, in the early sixteenth century. This is one reason that these sophisticated plays have been cited as decisive evidence of incremental secularization in drama before the Reformation.

Thus in *Nature* Man describes himself as being at the pinnacle of creation because of his ability to choose for himself:

> Yet for all that have I fre eleccyon
> [To] do what I wyll, be yt evyll or well,
> And am put in the hande of myne own counsell.[38]

This apparent assertion of autonomous completeness in "myne own counsell" contrasts strikingly with the traditional assumption of original sin and the need for baptism, as they are expressed, for example, in *Wisdom*. Man's advisor, Nature, confirms his view, urging him to "Let Reason the governe in every condycyon," if he wishes to avoid "great myschef and ruyne" (1159–61), because "Thou hast now lybertye and nedest no maynmyssyon" (1166). The liberty asserted by Reason seems a step beyond the portrayal of Mankind as a dependent infant in *Perseverance*, where he requires baptism to preserve him from the fiend, whom Medwall's Nature never mentions. When Reason himself appears as Man's counsellor, he seems to assert that the potential fall of Man is from reason, not from grace (1269–73), and Innocency echoes Nature in his insistence on Man's unfallen state:

> Wherfore I dare the surelyar testyfye
> For innocencye that he ys yet vyrgyn
> Both for dede and eke consent of syn.   (1355–57)

A similar emphasis on reason is evident in Skelton's *Magnificence*. Felicity's opening statement defines Magnificence's situation as a conflict of human faculties:

> will hath reason so under subjection,
> And so disordereth this world over all,
> That wealth and felicity is passing small.[39]

Magnificence stands to lose Felicity, according to this description, not by the threat of the devil in opposition to the sacraments, but by the individual surrender of reason to will. In discussion with Liberty, Felicity again emphasizes the importance of reason: "Howbeit liberty may sometime be too large / But if reason be regent and ruler of your barge" (37–38), and Measure praises the "linked chain of love" that binds Liberty, Felicity, and Measure (200–1). This "chain of love" is not charity, however, as in *Perseverance* and *Hick Scorner*; it is worldly virtue per se, visibly unattended by divine power.

Insistence on the primacy of reason in *Nature* and *Magnificence* seems a departure from the heavily sacramental emphasis in *Perseverance* and *Wisdom* earlier in the fifteenth century. For with reason comes autonomy, and with autonomy comes a secular sense of human identity as self-determined and independent. Reflecting this sense of change, Bernard Spivack calls *Nature* "a transitional play and a milestone in the new dispensation. . . . its eschatalogy is a faded echo and its moral emphasis mainly humanistic" (*Allegory*, p. 214). Bevington similarly sees "a degree

of secular transformation" in *Magnificence*. "Secularization," he continues, "is one of the unmistakable developments in the chronology of the
English moral play, and *Magnificence*, like *King John*, represents a
significant step forward" (*"Mankind" to Marlowe*, p. 136).

The assumption of secularity in Skelton and Medwall, however, is due
to the influential Enlightenment oppositions introduced by Chambers to
the study of early drama, for these two plays do not, in fact, represent a
departure from the traditional dramaturgy that involves an oppositional
scheme of vices and the sacraments. To be sure, *Nature* and *Magnificence*
reflect the influence of the "new learning" that was increasingly in vogue
in academic and courtly circles in late fifteenth- and early sixteenth-
century England; the emphasis on reason is characteristic of the humanist movement, which captured the imagination of the social elite during
the reigns of Henry VII and his son.[40] But humanists were not opposed
to traditional religion per se, at least in the years before the Reformation,
no matter how scathing their rejection of clerical abuses. A well-known
example of skeptical reason coexisting with traditional religion is
Thomas More, who was a protégé, like Henry Medwall, of Cardinal
Morton. Medwall's imagined conflict between reason (championed by
Nature) and Sensuality (a vice) is deeply traditional, indebted to Lydgate
and Hilton and appearing also in *Wisdom* (133–60) and in the Digby *Mary
Magdalen*.[41]

In keeping with this tradition, qualifications of human reason are
clear from the beginning of *Nature*, and the difference from *Wisdom* or
Perseverance is one of emphasis, not of substance. Addressing the audience
in a 105-line monologue, Nature acknowledges the "dower of [God's]
grace" (1.65) and urges humble acceptance of God's will: "Enforce you
therfore, hys creaturs eche on, / To honour your maker wyth humble
obeysance" (1.70–71). The emphasis on humility is characteristic of plays
written under the influence of traditional religion, for humility is the
companion of charity (as asserted in *Youth*, published several years later)
in establishing sociable community, because humility is the antidote to
pride, the archetypal sin of Satan. The threat to community, as Nature
points out, is "Thappetyte of vyce" (1.105).

Though the traditional context is less emphatic in *Magnificence*, it is
acknowledged several times in the play. When Measure asserts that "For
default of measure all thing doth exceed," Felicity agrees: "All that ye say
is as true as the creed" (217–18). This seems a bold assertion, since
Measure has been offering purely this-worldly wisdom, but one wonders
how real the difference would have been to Skelton and his audience,

who lacked the advantage of hindsight. For them, virtue so obviously derived from traditional Christian belief and practice that they presumably could not affirm the first without affirming the second. When Magnificence also affirms the importance of measure and asks Measure's opinion of what he has said, Measure replies: "God forbid that it otherwise should be" (246). The assumption, again, is that the order of virtue is divinely sanctioned.

By the end of both plays, the traditional context is unmistakable, as the restored fortunes of both Man and Magnificence follow the sacramental pattern of confession and penance. In *Nature*, when Man grows old he also grows remorseful, but while he thus seeks virtue by the compulsion of nature, the virtue he finds is more than natural. Mekenes now warns him against an enemy that is not "passyons sensuall," as Nature had said earlier; rather, the enemy is the one depicted at the beginning of all the mystery plays:

> Who so woteth hystoryes of scrypture well
> Shall fynde that for pryde and presumpcyon
> Lucyfer, whyche somtyme was a gloryouse angell,
> For that hys offence had suche correccyon
> That both he and eke meny a legyon
> Of hys order was cast down to hell
> By ryghtfull justyce perpetually there to dwell.   (2.1097–1103)

Mekenes continues the story with Adam, who followed the same pattern, thereby visiting the punishment for pride on the whole human race (2.1111–14). This gives rise to a familiar oppositional abstraction that explicates Mekenes' narrative: "The rote of all syn ys Pryde, ye know well, / Whyche ys myne adversary in all that he may" (2.1125–26). What enables Mekenes to oppose the personified Pride effectively is the death of Christ which "us redemed fro paynes endles" (2.1114).

In response to this allusion to the Passion (and implicitly to the eucharist), Man asks for Mekenes' help and counsel in making confession and offering satisfaction (2.1136–38), just as Anima turns to Wisdom and Mankind to Mercy. Man's relationship to Reason is not an autonomous agent's relationship to his own best faculty; it is the traditional Christian's relationship to the sacraments. Reason approves when Man tells him that Repentaunce has brought him to Confessyon, "And anon I was acquaynted with Hartys Contrycyon" (2.1398). "Have good perseveraunce, and be not in fere," Reason advises, "Thy gostly enemy can put the in no daunger" (1402–3). The "gostly enemy" of Man is not his own will, as seemed to be the case at the beginning of the play; the enemy is Satan, as always in traditional religion. Reason concludes the play by addressing the audience, drawing them into a renewed sense of sacramental community:

> Let us by one accord togeder syng and pray
> Wyth as humble devocyon as we can or may
> That we may have grace from syn thus to ryse
> As often as we fall, and let us pray thys wyse.   (1409–12)

The play thus ends with an expression of social harmony, as everyone sings a hymn or religious carol ("some goodly ballet"), in a strong confirmation of the play's ritual focus.

Skelton's *Magnificence* ends with less overt acknowledgment of the liturgy, but it is no less emphatic about the proper orientation of reason to the sacraments. In abandoning reason (allegorically identified with Measure at the beginning of the play), Magnificence eventually abandons his hope for life itself, wishing for his own destruction. The remedy for this dilemma, however, is not restored reason but the sudden and unexpected arrival of Good Hope, who is not a faculty of Magnificence but a sign of grace, like Mercy in *Mankind*, who arrives at the same moment in Mankind's despair. Like Mekenes in *Nature*, Good Hope (not Measure) is the solution to problems caused immediately by Magnificence himself but ultimately by "your ghostly foe" (2330), who also causes the problems in Medwall's play. There can be no doubt that Good Hope comes by divine agency, because he says so, identifying himself as the "potecary" to "your physician," who is "the grace of God" (2350–52). Moreover, Good Hope comes by the efficacy of the Passion, and the restoration of Magnificence is therefore implicitly through the eucharist:

> love that lord that for your love was dead,
> Wounded from the foot to the crown of the head;
> For who loveth God can ail nothing but good.
> He may help you, he may mend your mood.   (2364–67)

The repentance of Magnificence also suggests the sacrament of confession and penance no less clearly than Man's repentance does in *Nature*. Now "armed with good hope," Magnificence repents of his willfulness, asks God's mercy, and humbly commits himself to God's will, "Under Good Hope enduring ever still" (2379–83). Redress reassures him that he is "now in the state of grace" (2404) and gives him a new habiliment – a costuming detail that appears earlier in *Wisdom* and later in *Youth* and *Hick Scorner*. Perseverance urges Magnificence: "ever let the dread of God be in your sight; / And know yourself mortal, for all your dignity" (2495–96). As in many other non-cycle plays, the ministering of the virtues to a representative and responsive human figure involves more than individual salvation; it is also an emblem of renewed community.

In the context of the sacramental social body, the vices of both *Nature* and *Magnificence* are unmistakable agents of the "ghostly enemy," and the vices serve the same function by themselves that they serve in the company of devils in other plays. That function, moreover, involves more than individual moral and spiritual corruption; it involves the destruction of social harmony, which is restored in the end only by the defeat of the vices through the power of the sacraments. Both Medwall and Skelton are brilliant satirists, evoking in fuller and more compelling detail the social fractures of their courtly context than do any of the popular playwrights. Yet the motive for social satire is the same in their plays as in other pre-Reformation drama.

Thus in *Nature*, when Man confesses to Charyte (2.1168), Charyte explains how Envy destroys community. Envy enjoys only the sorrow of others; though he speaks fair, "yet wythin hys hart he ys full of doublenes"; and he is the source of slander and backbiting (2.1178–87). Those who are possessed by Envy are destroyers of community, and the social chaos engendered by Envy in *Nature* is therefore identical to the violence and abuse produced by Backbiter, both in *Perseverance* and the N-Town *Trial of Mary and Joseph*. The remedy for Envy, moreover, is charity, the double love of God and neighbor: "byfore all thyngys love God entyrly. / Next that, thy neyghbour love as thyne own body" (2.1191–92). Lyberalyte points out that Man cannot excuse his avarice with alms, if the goods he gives away were ill got (2.1280). "Thou must have compassyon and also be lyberall / Unto thy neyghbour at hys necessyte" (2.1286–87). As in *Perseverance* and *Wisdom*, virtuous deeds are only efficacious when they are motivated by charity, because charity is the foundation of sacramental community.

Though all the vices in both *Nature* and *Magnificence* perform socially disruptive functions, Envy's closest correlative in Skelton's play is Cloaked Collusion, who is associated with pride from the moment of his entry: "Here let Cloaked Collusion come in with a haughty expression, strolling up and down" (572 SD). He may also be associated with clerical hypocrisy, if his "cope" (601) is ecclestical. If so, then his threat is all the more serious, since he corrupts the very heart of sacramental relationships. In any case, he does indeed corrode trust: "Double-dealing and I be all one; / Crafting and hafting contrived is by me" (696–97). In fact, he has mastered the manipulation of emotional displays to trick others in histrionic fashion, and he boasts of his ability to dissemble in laughter and groaning (698), to study other men's laughter so he can hurt them (707–9), "And craftily can I grope how every man is minded" (724–25). The result is trouble on a national scale, as Cloaked Collusion gleefully acknowledges: "By cloaked collusion, I say, and none other / Cumberance and trouble in England first I began" (714–15). His delight in causing trouble to others is so refined that he professes no joy but others' sorrow (731–34), as Envy does in *Nature*. Cloaked Collusion is a convincing progenitor of the later Vice and of innumerable human characters inspired by the Vice.

While the wit and originality of personified vices in Skelton and Medwall is important and deserves emphasis, it also needs to be understood against a background of sacramental community, whose literal and archetypal opponent was the devil. Playwrights at court had more opportunity to witness the nuances of social pride and arrogance and more motive to enact them in plays for an elite audience. Still, the court playwrights' conception of the social body was identical to that of popular playwrights, like the authors of *The Castle of Perseverance* and *Mankind*, because of a shared assumption that ritual was the source of social cohesion, which was opposed by the devil and the seven deadly sins. By the same token, the social body in courtly moralities is identical to the social body in the mystery plays. Communal division originates in plays about the creation and fall of the angels, and it is perpetuated by the one who started it and by those whom he corrupts. The simplicity of this story is deceptive, for it gave rise to effects that are strikingly complex and profound, and it accounts better than anything else for the characteristic shape of the dramaturgy of evil in all forms of pre-Reformation drama.

CHAPTER FOUR

Stage devils and early social satire

In the mystery plays, social satire is invariably associated with devils and with those who side with devils, as we noticed in chapter 2, because the sacramental social body is normative for community, which devils oppose. Social coherence derives from the sacraments and particularly from the eucharist, which is established in the passion of Christ, an episode more fully developed than any other in the biblical cycles. Its centrality is evident in its anticipation by plays before it, its shaping of plays after it, and its symbolic presence in all relationships, as they exemplify charity or its absence. In this view, though satire encompasses and expresses social resistance, satire does not arise from social resistance in the first place but from moral affirmation, which recognizes the gap between affirmation and practice.

Non-cycle plays maintain the same standard of sociability as the mystery plays, as we have just seen, and even though they tell a different story, they therefore generate the same kind of social satire. In these plays too, the sacraments are central to the individual moral life and to the life of the community, even when their subject appears to be secular, as in Skelton's *Magnificence*. No matter what the genre, as perceived by modern criticism, playwrights thus seem to have learned from each other and from common sources in using devils and personified vices as a means of establishing the expectation for sacramental community by default. In other words, the social function of stage devils is oppositional, not in subverting moral expectation but in manifesting and exemplifying the defeat of virtue in the life of the community.

This fundamentally moral and narrative sense of normative sociability is expressed in several features of dramatic satire that are consistent across the lines drawn by modern criticism between one early dramatic genre and another. The principle of consistency is the shaping influence of sacramental social assumptions in the formation of fifteenth-century dramaturgy. This influence was so strong that it established the essential elements for the Vice, which became the most popular and widely imitated instance of social satire associated with stage devils, even though the Vice first arose and flourished during the Henrician Reformation. The sacramental motivation for devilish social satire has not been recognized, because early critical assumptions and arguments remain influential – the assumption of organic secular progress in early drama, for example, which produced the argument that stage devils were socially subversive and were eventually replaced by vices as part of the secularizing process.

The normative sense of social cohesion gave rise to one of the most striking features of satire associated with pre-Reformation stage devils: its focus on social abuses that were perpetrated almost exclusively by those at the upper end of the social hierarchy. We have seen this feature in the mystery plays, but it appears no less pervasively in non-cycle drama as well. The satire is directed at many aspects of court life, but three in particular stand out because of the frequency and ingenuity with which playwrights attack them, and because of the influence of these attacks on later drama. These three are sartorial excess, destructive infighting, and dissimulation in seeking advantage over others. The explicit standard for determining these social abuses was the sacramental social body, which provided the context for satirizing them as the oppositional failure of community.

"CLOTHYNGE FYNE"

"Conspicuous consumption" seems to be an inevitable outcome of concentrated wealth, as Thorsten Veblen pointed out when he coined the phrase in his *Theory of the Leisure Class* a century ago, and if wealth was concentrated anywhere in the fifteenth century, it was at court, whether in Westminster or in regional centers of power, both secular and ecclesiastical. Without the benefit of Veblen's incisive structural analysis, contemporary observers of the social scene resorted to moral explanation, identifying luxurious living with pride, first of the seven deadly sins and the cause of Lucifer's downfall from the highest point in the order of creation. Sumptuary excess thus had a place both in an abstract moral scheme and in the narrative of salvation that originated in the Bible and continued in the life of every Christian and every Christian community, providing the means by which traditional believers made sense of their existence.

Similarities among five satirically clad "gallants" in various pre-Reformation plays therefore arise from the same narrative and moral motive for satire in each case. We have seen one of these already in chapter 2: Lucifer in the N-Town *Passion Play I* (fifteenth century), who advocates social injustice in fifteenth-century terms at the same time that he plots to destroy Jesus, because both actions are attacks on the sacramental body. But the dubious honor of being the earliest satirical gallant in extant English drama likely belongs to Superbia, in *The Castle of Perseverance* (1380–1425). Personified vices also appear as ostentatiously dressed gallants in the Digby *Mary Magdalen* (c. 1480–1520) and Medwall's *Nature* (c. 1496), but when Lucifer himself appears again as a gallant in the morality play called *Wisdom* (1400–50), he does so in defiance of a longstanding critical inclination to assign devils to "medieval" mystery plays, and vices to the putatively more secular morality plays.

The historical interchangeability of devil and vice fits no narrative about preference for one or the other but points to identification of evil with the one who originated it, an identification that is also made in a non-dramatic fifteenth-century source, "A Treatise of a Galaunt":

> For in thys name Galaunt ye may see expresse
> Seueyn lettres for some cause in especiall,
> Aftyr the seuyn dedly synnes full of cursydnesse,
> That maketh mankynde vnto the deuyll thrall.
> Was nat pryde cause of Lucyferes fall?
> Pryde ys now in hell, and Galaunt nygheth nere.
> All England shall wayle that eure came he here.

> G for glotony that began in paradyse.
> A for Auaryce that regneth the world thorough.
> L for luxury that noryssheth euery vyce.
> A for Accydy that dwelleth in towne and borough.　　　　*sloth*
> V for VVrathe that seketh both land and forough.
> N for noying Enuy that dwelleth euery-where.
> T for toylous pryde: these myscheuen oure land here.[1]

This acrostic gallant conflates the seven deadly sins with the story of Lucifer's fall and his enmity against humankind, and the same conflation also appears repeatedly in fifteenth-century drama.

Superbia presents himself as a gallant in *The Castle of Perseverance* among a group of three deadly sins occupying the acting station ruled by the devil, who is very much a feudal overlord accompanied by retainers. He thus introduces Pride as "my prince in perlys ipyth [*decorated in pearls*]," and Pride later advocates the "new jettys [*fashions*]."[2] In fact, Pride scorns those who are merely fashionable, advocating instead that one always be *ahead* of fashion, at the cutting edge of sumptuary innovation, for if one merely maintains fashionable attire, others will think "the but a goos":

> Therfore do as no Man dos,
> And euery man sette at a thost   *turd*
> And of thi self make gret ros. (1063–65)   *boasting*

Superbia's pride is so specific to the early fifteenth century that his costume description helps in dating the play.[3] Precise social observation did not await "the renaissance," as is too often claimed; rather it characterizes the earliest of "other-worldly" morality plays.

Superbia represents sartorial satire most forcefully in *The Castle of Perseverance*, but it is not confined to him. Mundus is also "prekyd [*attired*] in pride," as he addresses the audience directly and abusively from high on an acting scaffold (159). His boasting is followed by that of his companions in the monarchical trinity of hell: Belial (also called "Satanas") and Caro. Each one introduces more of the seven deadly sins as his retainers, in formal feudal fashion, and Caro boasts of vast wealth: "With tapitys [*tapestries*] of tafata I timbyr my towrys" (239).[4]

This emphasis on demonic luxury is relevant to Humanum Genus' covetousness, the fifteenth-century way of thinking about concentrated wealth. Humanum Genus' first expression of wistful longing is to "be ryche in gret aray" (337), in contrast to Bonus Angelus' warning not to "coueyt werldys goode" because Christ and his followers lived "all in pouert" (350–52). Mundus' promise of "rycchest robys" (477) and Voluptas' of "sendel [*silk*] softe" (554) are closely linked to fantasies of power: "To thy cors schal knele kaiser and knyth" (588–90).

The temptation is too much for Humanum Genus. "What schulde I recknen of domysday," he exclaims, "So that I be riche and of gret aray?" (607–8), as he follows Folly and Lust-and-Liking off stage. They dress him in a luxurious costume that contrasts with his first appearance, when he was "nakyd of lim and lende" (279), clothed only with the sacrament: "A sely crisme min hed hath cawth, / That I tok at min christeninge" (294–95). His new clothing not only expresses his individual surrender to covetousness and pride but signals a breach of communal trust. Rejecting the admonition to clothe the naked (one of the seven acts of mercy), Humanum Genus arrogantly abuses the poor, refusing to offer beggars anything and wishing they would "sterve and stinke" before he would clothe or feed them (871–74).

This refusal is a reminder of the moral motive for satire in pre-Reformation drama, for the Towneley and Chester plays of the Last

Judgment also link sumptuary excess with Jesus' rejection of the damned for their failure to clothe the naked.[5] To categorize these plays as "otherworldly" or "merely spiritual" is to ignore how deeply rooted their satire is in contemporary standards for social justice, which expected the rich to care for the poor. This standard was obviously not conceived in light of structural social or economic analysis, but the plays' emphasis on the upper classes as the source of social violation indicates that the standard functioned as more than a compliment to the personal piety of the rich or as protection for the feudal hierarchy in church and monarchy.

In the Digby *Mary Magdalen*, the gallant Curiosity is indisputably aristocratic, like the N-Town Lucifer and Superbia in *Castle*. When Bad Angel introduces Curiosity as "Pryde, called Corioste,"[6] World has already described the seven deadly sins as "The seuyn prynsys of hell, of gret bowntosnesse" (324), and Satan himself has called them "my knythtys so stowth" (373). These are more than honorific or military designations appropriate to the coming battle for Mary's soul; they are unmistakable designations of social class. World, Flesh, and Devil are all introduced as kings, as they are in *The Castle of Perseverance*, with Satan echoing Mundus in boasts about his fine clothing: "I, prynse pyrles prykkyd in pryde, / Satan, yower sovereyn" (358–59). Satan and his cohorts thus present a consistent picture of power and luxurious display based closely on the contemporary courtly scene.

Moreover, *Mary Magdalen* places Curiosity in a familiar moral and narrative context. Lucifer aims to besiege the soul of humankind (364) and bring it to destruction in revenge for the "joye / That Lycyfer, with many legyown, lost for ther pryde" (366–67). The same vengeance also motivates Satan throughout the mystery plays, as we have seen, because he failed to impose his will on the blessed community of the angels. Satan's attack on Mary thus represents his attack on all Christians, both individually and in society, where the most serious lapses are evident among the upper classes, because they are subject to the greatest temptations, as Lucifer himself was among the unfallen angels.

Mary in the Digby play is an aristocrat, the daughter of Cyrus, lord of Jerusalem, and Satan's enmity against her is explicit, as he determines "To werkyn hur sum wrake" (380) and laughs maliciously when news comes of the tempter's success (555). As in *Castle*, World, Flesh, and Devil boast abusively in direct address to the audience from scaffolds, not from the *platea*, signalling their enmity to the whole human community, as well as Mary in particular.[7] The "castell of Mavdleyn" (59) is both an aristocratic possession, inherited by Mary after her father's death, and a

symbol of Mary's spiritual condition, providing a visible object for
demonic attack, like its counterpart in *Castle of Perseverance*. While
Lechery and the Bad Angel enter the castle to tempt Mary, the other
Deadly Sins *"besege the castell tyll [Mary] agre to go to Jherusalem"* (439 SD).
Dramaturgically the devilish assault is thus manifest, though it is presented to Mary only in the guise of a flattering visit from a noble and
sophisticated lady.

After Lechery succeeds in drawing Mary out of the castle, Curiosity
enters the play to seduce her. His appearance is brief and episodic, but
it expresses the sartorial and class satire associated with him. He calls
attention to himself as "A frysch new galavnt" (491), boasting "a shert of
reynnys [*Raines*] with slevys peneawnt" (496), a "stomachyr," "dobelet,"
and "hossys" (501–2), and his social attitude is predictably arrogant: "I
wol awye [*be in awe of*] sovereyns, and soiettys [*subjects*] I dysdeyne!" (500).
Curiosity is part of the demonic assault on Mary, and the delineation of
fifteenth-century extravagance is due to the timeless nature of pride, for
Mary is not only a biblical character but also a personified representative
of humankind in general and of the high-born in particular, with their
special vulnerability to moral failing through pride and great wealth.
The author of *The Arte or Crafte to Live Well and Die Well* thus imagines the
eschatalogical torment of the proud as a revolving wheel upon which
they are bound, as Lear imagines himself bound, because in their lives
they would "evermore be lyft up above these other, and lyve in dyscorde
without peas . . . and for thys cause theyr herte is in contynuall moevynge
the whiche is never fedde with honoure."[8]

Despite the oft-repeated claim that Henry Medwall's plays mark a
departure from the ascetic morality of earlier plays, in the late fifteenth-
century *Nature* Medwall adheres closely to established traditions, and his
social satire derives from sacramental affirmation, as we saw in chapter
3. In fact, two overdressed gallants appear in *Nature*, and the first of them
is Pride, as in *Castle* and *Mary Magdalen*. The only differences are that
Medwall's Pride boasts about himself at much greater length than his
predecessors (for almost 100 lines), and that the fashions have changed:
Pride brags that his short gown with wide hanging sleeves would be
enough to make some men a doublet and coat.[9]

The second gallant in *Nature* is the generic hero, Man, whose surrender to the vices is marked by a sumptuary metamorphosis from simplicity to luxury, as in *The Castle of Perseverance*. Indeed, Man's descent into
vicious gallantry parallels Humanum Genus' point for point: he is
seduced by World, advised by Pride to keep ahead of the latest fashion,

mocked by the vices for his gullibility, compared to Lucifer in his fall (2.1097–1103), and urged to share his goods with the poor as a sign of his genuine repentance (2.1293–96). Man accepts this advice when he willingly follows Repentance "to Confessyon / And anon I was acquaynted with Hartys Contrycyon" (2.1397–98). In *Nature*, the cure for prideful self-indulgence is the sacrament of confession and penance, which is also the healing of social fractures, as in earlier morality plays.

The most atypical of the five gallants is not in *Nature*, though *Nature* comes late in the pre-Reformation tradition and by evolutionary logic should therefore depart furthest from the tradition; rather, it is in *Wisdom*, an earlier play, where sartorial satire belongs to a motif of clothing that runs throughout the entire play and is the most complex in early English drama.[10] Here the opposition is not between moderate simplicity and luxury, as in other plays (including *Nature*), for both Wisdom and the unfallen Anima are royally costumed, according to unusually specific and complete stage directions. Wisdom is Christ in this play, but he is *Christus victor*, the king of heaven, not the peasant of the mystery plays, whose model of poverty is also appealed to in *Castle*. The playwright thus departs from a pattern that appears consistently in other early plays, where the peasant Christ is paradoxically a king by virtue of the spiritual power that accompanies his social humility.[11]

But this departure marks no change in *Wisdom's* social and moral vision, for it assumes sacramental community as much as other pre-Reformation plays, and from this vision the play's sartorial satire also arises. Anima is costumed royally, like Wisdom, to symbolize her creation in God's image: "Yt ys the ymage of Gode that all began; / And not only ymage, but hys lyknes ye are."[12] Her royal garments are overlaid with a black mantel, because she is "dysvyguryde" by the sin of Adam (118), which can be reversed only by the sacraments (124–25). "Yowr dysgysynge and yowr aray," Wisdom tells her, indicate the two parts of the soul, with royal white signifying reason and the black mantle signifying sensuality (149–56).

Since Wisdom warns Anima that she has three enemies, "The Worlde, the Flesche, and the Fende" (294), it is no surprise that Lucifer appears "in a dewyllys aray wythowt and wythin as a prowde galonte" (324 SD), as soon as Wisdom has finished instructing Anima. Entering alone, he addresses the audience directly and abusively, as devils and vices usually do in other plays, then departs briefly, sheds his outer devilish costume, and re-enters "as a goodly galont" (380 SD). In contrast to other gallants, he does not boast about his costume, nor does he delineate its features; instead, he proceeds as Milton's Comus does, debating cleverly with Anima's three mights, Mind, Will, and Understanding, quoting the Bible in Latin, and arguing sophistically against ideals of moderation and restraint:

> What synne ys in met, in ale, in wyn?
> Wat synne ys in ryches, in clothynge fyne?
> All thynge Gode ordeynde to man to inclyne. (475–77)

The three mights' submission to Lucifer's temptation emphasizes the human effects of luxurious gallantry, in keeping with the play's satiric focus on sin's effects in the human community, as well as in the individual soul. Lucifer advises the mights to "change that syde aray" (510), and they are quick to comply, donning a "new aray" (551) that they deem to be "freshest" (556). The link between conspicuous consumption and concentrated wealth is noted by the playwright, but he construes it in moral terms, as when Understanding gleefully meditates on avarice:

> And my joy ys especyall
> To hurde uppe ryches, for fer to fall,   *hoard*
> To se yt, to handyll yt, to tell yt all,
> And streightly to spare! (581–84)   *reluctantly / spend*

The effects of the seven deadly sins are interpreted socially in the names of the personifications that accompany Mind, Will, and Understanding (six each). The original seven sins thus proliferate themselves in a feudal aristocratic ritual involving lords and their retainers, like the seven deadly sins and their overlords, World, Flesh, and Devil in *Castle*. These satirical manifestations become local and specific in the retainers' boasts about what they do in London and Westminster, the seats of wealth and royal power (789–872). While *Wisdom* is the most theologically complex of the early moralities, the play is not otherworldly, ascetic, merely spiritual, or unconcerned with the material lives of its auditors. On the contrary, its concern with material life is the thrust of its moral message, which in turn is the motivation of its social satire.

While no other self-advertising gallants appear in other pre-Reformation plays, the use of sartorial satire is pervasive and invariably serves the purpose of illuminating the sacramental ideal of the social body by default, as devils and vices do. *Mankind* (1465–70) is unique in requiring its actors to have on hand identical coats of varying lengths, so that Mankind's coat can appear to be cut ever shorter by the exploitative vices. But the motive for their doing so is familiar. It is identical, for example, to Pride's motive in *Nature*, when he boasts about his short coat and urges Man to adopt the fashion that goes "now a day" because it is the "new guyse" (1.1024–25), phrases that the author of *Mankind* takes as the names of two of his vices. Lucifer's advice to the mights in *Wisdom* to "change that syde aray" (510) is echoed in New Guise's allusion to Mankind's "side gown" and his advice to make a fashionable "jakett therof."[13] *Mankind's* rascally vices behave in much the same way as the depraved mights of *Wisdom* do, singing and dancing bawdily, thieving, womanizing, exploiting honest folk – all violations of the social body. Their urban sophistication and determined upward mobility are social markers that distinguish them from the peasant Mankind, a generic figure akin to Langland's plowman, so that the social vice we see in action is aggressive self-elevation, as in other plays, while the victim of smart social abuses is a peasant who earns his living by manual labor.[14]

Bombastic boasts of worldly wealth and power are the most recognizable (and performable) characteristics of tyrants in early drama, often accompanied by specific reference to sumptuous costumes, the easiest props of wealth for actors to acquire, transport, and display. Luxurious costumes or sartorial satire thus appear in every dramatic genre before the Reformation: in the social satire that the Wakefield Master gives to the devil Tutivillus in the Towneley *Judgment* (339–51), in the Digby *Conversion of St. Paul* (1480–1520), and Skelton's *Magnificence* (1515–26). Costume changes were an obvious way to signal the opposition of devilish pride to Christian humility, and the props of elegance provided grist for the mill of social satire in a sacramental context.

"EUERY MAN TO KYLLYN OTHER"

The baronial wars of the fifteenth century provided stark and ubiquitous evidence of aristocratic rivalry, inspiring Shakespeare's choice to feature ruinous upper-class competition as the centerpiece of his first history plays more than a century later. But whereas Shakespeare brought a considerable grasp of the political process to the fifteenth-century situation, his predecessors thought in almost exclusively moral terms when they wrote for the stage, attributing civil dissension to the influence of the devil in his unceasing assault on the sacramental social body. Their way of thinking has parallels in other pre-Reformation writing. In a sermon for Rogation, John Mirk writes that devils "rerythe warres; thay makyth tempestys in the see, and drownythe schyppes and men, thay makythe debate bytwyx neghburs and manslaght therwyth."[15] The writer of *Dives and Pauper* similarly sees devils at work in "dissencioun and werre be [*war by*] destruccioun of charite, be myspryde, couetyse, lecherye, wratthe, envye."[16]

The assumption that dissension and war are the oppositional work of the devil is as influential in plays as in sermons and prose commentaries. Rancor and recrimination are characteristic of devilish community from the moment of hell's creation in the mystery plays, as we saw in chapter 2, and resentment quickly turns violent in the York *Creation and Fall of the Angels*, as 2 Diabolus rounds angrily on Lucifer for bringing them to such a sorry pass: "We, lurdane, haue at yowe, lat loke!"[17] Violence flows in a more predictable direction – from leader to followers – in the York *Harrowing of Hell*, when Satan's scorn of Jesus' challenge to his kingdom turns to rage, and he twice shrieks at his own subordinates to "dynge that dastard doune" (180, 203). Satan's spiritual myopia is manifest in his belief that the battle is literal and physical, and it contrasts with the vision of the Old Testament faithful whom Christ has come to redeem, for they recognize him for who he is. At the same time, the demonic battle enables the playwright to make a satirical point, by borrowing familiar taunts, threats, and an abusive command style from contemporary warfare.

This kind of demonic infighting in the York and Towneley *Harrowing* has an exact counterpart in *The Castle of Perseverance*, when the devil attacks his henchmen irascibly, like a frustrated field officer, after learning of Humanum Genus' defection to the virtues. Ironically he describes their spiritual condition, hoping that they find no grace and die an evil death (1769–70), and his verbal abuse quickly turns physical: "Et verberabit eos super terram [*he shall beat them on the earth*]" (1822 SD). When Satan's outrageous attack on his own subordinates is repeated in turn by Flesh and World, the effect is undoubtedly comic. Indeed, the conflict between devil and vices in *Castle* is the earliest extant instance of the slapstick vice conflict that became a standard feature in virtually every morality play. The risible effect of knockabout stage action is self-evident; what needs emphasis is that it functions in these plays as morally inspired satire of upper-class emulation from its first appearance. The comedy of vice conflict is one instance among many of traditional playwrights borrowing the energy of folk custom to make a serious moral point. Detractio thus glosses Satan's attack on his own vices in *The Castle of Perseverance*: "Ya, for God, this was wel goo, / Thus to werke wyth bakbytynge" (1778–79). Directly addressing other backbiters, Detractio urges them to follow his example, down to the last one, "Of Goddys grace he schal be rafte / And euery man to kyllyn other" (1789–90).[18]

A similar example of demonic infighting occurs in the Digby *Mary Magdalen*, at a similar moment in the play. After Jesus casts the seven devils/deadly sins out of Mary, Satan bursts out in loud and comical lament for her loss and then sits in judgment on Bad Angel (who is also Pride). The playwright ironically laces social satire and mockery of the chaotic demons with allusions to redemptive grace, as writers of the passion plays often do: "Wy hast thou don all this trespas, / To lett yen woman thi bondys breke?" (731–32). Satan implicitly acknowledges his destructive opposition to humankind and the superior power of redeeming mercy. Bad Angel makes the point precisely in attempting to excuse his defeat: "The speryt of grace sore ded hyr smyth / And temptyd so sore that ipocryte" (733–34). The inversion of terms is both funny and morally serious: smiting, temptation, hypocrisy, all attributed to God in the devil's view.

Since the seven deadly sins are depicted as devils, the stage shows devils torturing devils, or hell divided against itself, as in *Castle*, so that in both plays the principles of cohesion in hell are derivative and constantly break down. Its power is effective only against unrepentant sinners, whose attempts to create community invariably decline into imitations of hell. Moreover, the "frest" of the seven deadly sins is Pride, who "suffers" first in Mary's conversion but is also the Bad Angel, a devil, as well as the chief of the personified abstractions, so that in the conflict with grace, hell defeats itself. Hence Satan's order that the devils set fire to "this howsse" (741) in order to punish the devils that let Mary go. Though firing the scaffold of hell is spectacular and theatrically unforgettable, its point is morally serious. The playwright borrows the oppression and vindictiveness of Satan from what he knew of oppression and vindictiveness in human affairs, but for him they were modeled on their counterpart in hell, just as the corrective model for human community was the kingdom of Jesus.

In contrast to the rowdy devils of *Castle* and *Mary Magdalen*, the devil in *Wisdom* is always suave and smooth, because we see him not as the manager of tempters working elsewhere but almost entirely in the company of his intended human victims; this is why he is more like Curiosity in *Mary Magdalen* than the devil who beats his subordinates. But the effect he has on the human "community" of Anima's mights, Mind, Will, and Understanding, reproduces the courtly dynamics of devilish community itself in other plays, an effect that is repeated in *Hick Scorner*, written several years later, when competitive acrimony breaks out between Freewill and Imagination, who are human attributes rather than vices.

Wisdom's courtly audience is the kind that Medwall also wrote for in *Nature*, and his mimicking of competitive emulation among the vices produced some of the most subtle and biting satire of courtly viciousness in early drama. Though the vices are presumably united in their effort to corrupt Man, Sensuality gratuitously informs Pride that Man went to a tavern and slept with Margery – the very Margery who stole Pride's shirt the other night (1.1113–43). The point of this story is simply to gull Pride, who is enraged at the thought that the ingenu Man, whom they all despise for his naivety and innocence, should have seduced Pride's mistress. When Sensuality excuses himself for pausing to wipe his nose during this tale (1.1122), he is really laughing into his handkerchief at Pride's expense. Moments like these anticipate the satire of Jacobean city comedy a century later, yet they derive from the failure of sacramental sociability, the standard for community in pre-Reformation religious drama of all kinds.

Medwall reproduces a more complex kind of vicious infighting later in *Nature*, this time involving courtly auditors in a manner that implicates them directly in the vices they are watching at work to corrupt Man in a play. In effect, courtiers are thus compelled to recognize that they are "Man" as well. Listening to Bodily Lust describe a visit to the stews, Pride determines to go there himself and asks the audience the way, "For I cam never there" (2.401–3). Apparently receiving no help, he seizes on one person in particular: "Ye know the way, parde, of old! / I pray the tell me, whyche way shall I hold?" (2.404–5). Pride's victim failing to reply, presumably surprised and flustered by the unexpected question, Pride turns again to the audience as a whole: "Wyll ye se thys horson cocold? / I trow he can not here!" (2.406–7). The humiliation of a noble auditor by a common actor involves more than social humbling. For one person, at least, the spectacle of vice comedy ceased to be a joke he was watching and became a moment of intense discomfort that related directly to pride and its effects on humankind.[19]

Vice conflict in Skelton's *Magnificence* is equally sophisticated, though Skelton does not involve the audience as Medwall does. A crescendo of courtly gestures and put-downs begins with Courtly Abusion's entry singing "Huffa, huffa" (745), the traditional stage exclamation of gallants and pretentious worldlings. Collusion no sooner mocks the newcomer's pretentious attire (764–65) than Collusion finds himself quarreling with Crafty Conveyance, who claims to "rule much of the roast" (803). Collusion taking umbrage at this, Abusion observes that Conveyance wishes to "make a fray" (807) and threatens him with legal action, but

Conveyance coolly appeals to fashion – "it is but the guise" (808) – and Abusion is compelled to admit that he is not up on "the guise nowadays" (812), which involves words alone, not weapons.

Here too, vice quarreling is transformed into a satire of courtly posturing. The "guise nowadays" consists of gratuitous verbal abuse rather than physical blows, as in other vice conflicts, but the intention is still to promote oneself at the expense of one's neighbor, and the result is therefore a lapse into the social chaos that simultaneously results from the triumph of devils and constitutes more of the same. Skelton suggests that contemporary "courtly abusion" is a prime example of what destroys community, because it destroys charitable social relationships.

"CLOAKED COLLUSION"

Deception in itself is a human trait with no particular social barriers, but dissimulation in the interest of self-promotion was regularly understood by pre-Reformation commentators as a besetting sin of the upper classes, because indirection was an effective way to acquire and maintain wealth, status, and power, as Machiavelli eventually pointed out. Lacking Machiavelli's dispassionate appraisal, traditional social critics thought of dissimulation in exclusively moral terms: they saw what Machiavelli saw, often in precise detail, but rather than respond dispassionately, they rejected dissimulation as a product of the deadly sin of envy, one of the prime sources of disruption in the sacramental social order. Lucifer had fallen through envy and dissimulation, as well as pride, so dissimulation had a place both in moral thinking and in the story that accounted for the way things had come to be the way they were – the story that unfolds in the mystery plays.

Satan's envy of God motivates his rebellion in all the cycles, and it is quickly directed to humankind after Satan falls, when he understands that the human race has been created to replace the fallen angels. In Timothy Fry's view, Satan's envy turns to guile and motivates his cunning struggle with God throughout the N-Town cycle, and Satan is defeated in the end only by the greater "trick" of the Incarnation, Passion, and Resurrection.[20] Envy manifestly gives rise to dissimulation in the plays of Adam and Eve, as Satan dons the disguise of a serpent in order to tempt Eve. The cycle playwrights all make a connection between dissimulation and the court by having Satan approach Eve as if he were a gallant seducing an ingenue. In the York play he claims to be a "frende" who has come "for thy gude" (25–26).[21] When Eve asks, "Is this soth that thou says?" (74), Diabolus reaches the height of his dissimulation, lying in the very act of denying that he is doing so:

> Yhe! why trowes thou nogt me?　　*do you not trust*
> I wolde by no-kynnes wayes
> Telle nogt but trouthe to the.　　　　　　(75–77)

This and other examples of demonic and human dissimulation throughout the mystery plays are consistently associated with the court, with the seven deadly sins, and with assaults on the sacramental social body, as represented either by Jesus himself or by the baptized Christians who were the true community in pre-Reformation ecclesiology. As we have seen in the case of sumptuary excess and competitive infighting, when playwrights focus on the moral life, they bring the same assumptions to their task that they bring to the staging of biblical history, and this is also true when it comes to their use of dissimulation as a means of social satire. The moral life is rooted in the story told by the mystery plays, and dissimulating devils and vices therefore have the same effect in non-cycle plays that we have seen in biblical drama.

In *The Castle of Perseverance* dissimulation is associated principally with Detractio (Backbiter), who is carefully placed in the demonic hierarchy. Though not himself one of the seven deadly sins, Detractio is a retainer of Mundus, the king who first wins Humanum Genus' allegiance away from the kingdom of God, and Detractio introduces himself while Humanum Genus is off-stage being richly dressed by Folly and Lust-and-Liking at Mundus' command. In more familiar terms, self-protective and preemptive rationalization accompanies the concentration of power and wealth, conspicuous consumption, and upward mobility.

Detractio's tools are the same that *York*'s Satan uses in seducing Eve. Detractio boasts that he is "feller thanne a fox," in his use of "flaterynge," "lesyngys [*lies*]," and "letterys of defamacyoun / I bere here in my box" (668–72). His delight in the quarreling of his fellow devils is so keen that he deliberately foments it. Flatteringly addressing King Flesh, Detractio informs him that his retainers, Gluttony, Sloth, and Lechery, have let Mankind return to the Castle of Perseverance, whereupon Flesh rages at them and beats them, while Detractio gloatingly addresses the audience about his ability to use "fals fame" to "brekyn and brestyn hodys of stele" (1829–30). Detractio explicitly relates the spectacle of hell turning on itself to contempoary civil strife – the breaking of steel helmets throughout "this country" because of treachery and slander. As in the mystery plays, destruction of the social body is identified in *Castle* with the wealthy and the powerful, not with restive peasants. Backbiter's abetting of both envy and pride enacts the socially disruptive role that envy, slander, and dissimulation play in a hierarchical society, especially one that was marked by new wealth and increased competition for social position.

Dissimulation in *Wisdom* is closely related to the ubiquitous motif of "disfiguring" in that play. In his "dewyllys aray" Lucifer roars like a familiar stage devil (325), but when he disguises himself as a gallant, he becomes quiet and cunning. As in the mystery plays, Lucifer in *Wisdom* is motivated by envy (327), and his envy also turns to dissimulation: he will appear bright to beguile humankind, showing sin as perfection and virtue as wickedness, "Thus undyr colors all thynge perverse" (375–79). The material effects of Lucifer's spiritual guile quickly reveal themselves in Anima's "disfigured" wits. Understanding observes that wealth promotes upward mobility (587–88) and encourages dissimulation: no one blames the rich for covetousness, usury, or simony; instead "Yt ys clepyde wysdom" (601–4). Abandoning themselves to social predation, Understanding and Mind share confidences about how to behave if they are caught – offer bribes to prevent anyone injuring them and resort to every "craft" imaginable (857–61). Crafty expoitation of one's neighbor disfigures the soul, as Wisdom points out (901), and makes one easy prey for the devil, who originated the moral mechanisms of social chaos in the first place.

Some of the most influential innovations in satirical dissimulation were introduced by Henry Medwall, who wrote shortly before the Reformation but nonetheless established a repertory of techniques that playwrights after him repeatedly used – including Protestant playwrights. Medwall became familiar with diplomatic protocol as a protégé of Cardinal Morton, an ecclesiastical statesman of unusual ability and influence.[22] Not surprisingly, therefore, Medwall is the first English playwright to use the word "policy," and he does so in a way that would become familiar by the end of the sixteenth century, when "policy" was simply a polite term for "dissimulation" and was used to describe the techniques advocated by Machiavelli.[23] In *Nature*, World offers to introduce the naive Man to "dyvers persones that be ryght honorable . . . So wyse, so polytyke" (1.588, 592), who turn out to be the seven deadly sins. Learning quickly, Man invites Worldly Affection to join him, for "ye are polytyke" (1.674). When Pride urges Man to adopt a new "aray" and follow the "new guyse," he also recommends that Man learn "worldly wyt and polycy" (1.957). As a courtly playwright, Medwall follows popular dramatists in making Mundus ("the world") a prime route to spiritual failure, and he is not the first to render Mundus compellingly in contemporary courtly terms; his innovations are in satirical detail and degree, not in kind.

An example of Medwall surpassing his predecessors is in vice euphemism – a stage device that would become an identifying feature of the Tudor morality play. Dissimulating euphemism is hinted at in *Wisdom*, as we have just seen, when Lucifer dons the costume of a gallant, determining to exchange darkness for brightness and to present sin as "perfectness" in order to beguile Anima (375–77). Closer to Medwall is Lucifer in the N-Town *Passion Play I*, who brings "newe namys" for sin: "Ye xal kalle pride 'oneste', and 'naterall kend' lechory" (109), among several others (110–15).[24] Medwall similarly gives each of the seven deadly sins a new name, which they then use in the presence of Man, in order to deceive him. Pride, "The swete darlynge of the devyll of hell" (1.1209), is to be called "Worship" (1.1212). Covetousness "doth hys name dysgyse" as Worldly Policy; Wrath, as Manhood; Envy, as Disdain; Gluttony, as Fellowship; Sloth, as Ease; and Lechery, as Lust (1.1214–27). Medwall's allusion to the "no good" that Sloth loves to do (1.1225) is another detail that places *Nature* in a sacramental context, for one of the most commonly cited effects of sloth was to prevent people from attending mass and confession.[25]

Medwall's innovation of euphemistic name changes for the vices was first imitated by Skelton, who was, if anything, more brilliant than his predecessor when it came to satirizing dissimulation. For one thing, Skelton's vices are not the seven deadly sins but more precise renderings of courtly viciousness: Counterfeit Countenance, Cloaked Collusion, Courtly Abusion, Crafty Conveyance. Even this innovation, however, has a precedent in *Wisdom*, where each of Anima's corrupted mights has personified retainers whose names reflect some aspect of courtly and legal corruption.

The most lethal of Skelton's courtly vices is Cloaked Collusion, who enters Magnificence's retinue by means of a trick played by Counterfeit Countenance. Collusion is distinguished by his commitment to gratuitous trouble-making, like Detractio in *Castle*: "Double dealing and I be all one; / Crafting and hafting contrived is by me" (696–97; cf. 724–25 and 731–34). The fact that Cloaked Collusion is a priest (he wears a "cope" [601]) offers an important insight into anti-clerical satire in a play that affirms sacramental community. Collusion is so dangerous because corrupt priests are most like the devil himself, for their position at the top of the spiritual hierarchy puts them in a position analogous to that of Lucifer among the angels.

Courtly vice becomes a substantial element of Skelton's plot, when Magnificence dismisses Measure, hitherto his most trusted counsellor, thus depriving himself of all support except that of the vices, who are determined to ruin him. Magnificence is brought to this pass by Cloaked Collusion, who agrees to intervene with Magnificence in Measure's behalf, when Measure begins to realize that he is falling from favor. Begging Magnificence to remember Measure's good service (1638), Collusion whispers his real intent in Magnificence's ear, encouraging the suspicion that Measure bribed Collusion to plead for him. Collusion thus attributes treachery to the very man he is himself betraying, just as Lucifer lies to Eve when he protests that he is being most truthful in the York *Fall of Man*. Magnificence calls Collusion an "honest person" (1691), and Measure is completely fooled, believing that Collusion did all he could for him: "Nay indeed, but I saw how ye prayed, / And made instance for me be likelihood" (1697–98). Collusion's self-presentation and actions strikingly anticipate Iago, as Ann Wierum has pointed out.[26] But for both Skelton and Shakespeare, cloaked collusion derived from more than careful observation of the court. Both playwrights were also indebted to common assumptions that cunning and ill-will were inspired by Satan, the great Enemy, whose only joy was humankind's unhappiness, both individually and communally – a debt Shakespeare acknowledges and emphasizes in Iago's frequent allusions to hell and devils.

DEVILS, VICES, AND THE VICE

The best-known satirical by-product of a long tradition of stage devils is the figure who eventually became known as "the Vice." Yet his fame is due in part to the same teleological thinking that has predominated in treatments of stage devils and vices, for the afterlife of the Vice in plays written for the London commercial stage (especially those written by Shakespeare) has been the principal motivation for investigating the Vice himself, and evolutionary narratives have seemed the most obvious way to organize what critics found. Such narratives have tended to obscure another problem, however: the Vice appears late in the tradition and endures for only about fifty years, from midway through the reign of Henry VIII until shortly after the establishment of permanent commercial theatres near London. This is a brief period in the nearly 300-year history of devils in English drama, from the early fifteenth century to the late seventeenth. Though it is true that morality play authors preferred the Vice to devils during the period of the Vice's ascendancy in the mid-sixteenth century, it is also true that the mystery plays, with their preference for devils, continued to be staged throughout the same period, and that devils continued to be staged for another hundred years after the establishment of London commercial theatres – long after the Vice had become unfashionable.

It therefore makes sense to regard the Vice as a phase in the history of stage devils, rather than an evolutionary stage in a story of growth and development. It is also more accurate to say that playwrights like Shakespeare, Jonson, Fletcher, and Middleton belong to a continuous tradition of staging devils in English drama than that they looked back to the Vice in particular. Pre-Reformation devils and vices already exhibit the features for which the Vice is most famous, and we have seen that specific social satire appears in relation to devils and vices as early as *The Castle of Perseverance.*[27]

One of the principal objections to identifying the Vice with a continuous history of stage devils and personified vices has come from those who have construed the Vice as mirthful rather than vicious – a fool rather than a knave – and who have therefore sought his ancestry in French farce and popular folk drama, rather than religious drama. Evidence cited for this view is that the first use of the term "the Vice" is by John Heywood, in *The Play of the Weather* (1519–28) and *The Play of Love* (1533–34), where the Vice bears little resemblance to the devil of traditional religion. E. K. Chambers argued that Heywood derived his Vice from the domestic fool or jester, as an appropriate native addition to the continental traditions that he was adapting. Chambers thus gave rise to a strain of criticism that has identified the Vice with various folk traditions in Robin Hood and St. George plays, in addition to the Roman *mimus*, the fabliau, and the French *sottie.*[28]

Chambers no doubt illuminated the history of the Vice, but he sowed confusion about the social function of pre-Reformation devils and vices. Reading the folk and continental elements of the Vice back into earlier personified vices has resulted in ideas about subversion and "alterity" that take too little account of the culture that produced early drama. When fools and folk elements appear in religious drama, they support traditional religion, as we have seen. At the same time, they remain critical of social oppression, as has been readily recognized in the Towneley

First and *Second Shepherds' Plays*, though the same critique is virtually ubiquitous in pre-Reformation drama of all kinds.[29] In non-cycle plays, Folly is an exploitative vice who commonly serves the seven deadly sins as a promoter of social injustice. Stultitia appears in *The Castle of Perseverance*, where he advocates greed and aggressive upward mobility (504–17), and a hundred years later Folly does the same in *Mundus et Infans*. He is taught "with the courtiers," haunts Westminster, knows the law well, is a fellow of Covetise, and takes cases for "poor men that come from upland," "Be right or be it wrong."[30] It is difficult to see how peasants watching this play would be inclined to identify with a character whose explicit purpose is to exploit peasants. In the process of corrupting Infans, Folly takes the audience into his confidence in a dissimulating aside that mocks his intended victim as a gullible fool (p. 183). The aside does not invite audience complicity with Folly in subversive opposition to social oppression; on the contrary, the play satirizes social injustice on moral grounds in the person of Folly, who seeks to induct Manhood into vicious habits that he has mastered himself, including treachery and dissimulation. As Robert Jones argues, if asides like Folly's invite complicity with anything, it is with the vice of social injustice that Folly represents,[31] and the aside would therefore appear to be aimed at surprising the upwardly mobile with a satirical image of themselves.

Fascination with the folk origins of the Vice has led to neglect of precedents in the mystery plays, on the assumption that devils and the Vice have distinct origins. It makes more sense to see both as indebted to traditional religion and to folk customs.[32] The York Satan's dissimulation with Eve is a credible precedent for Folly's cunning way with Manhood, though Satan does not address the audience directly. In another pageant, however, and in pursuit of another innocent, he acts even more like Folly in *Mundus et Infans*. Entering "into the place" in the N-Town *Passion Play II*, Satan rages in alliterative verse, addressing the audience directly as he describes the assault he plans on Jesus, just as Titivillus describes his plan of attack in *Mankind*. Satan's tirade is interrupted by a fearful subordinate, who warns him that if Jesus comes to hell, its power will be broken.[33] Hearing this, Satan reverses course, announcing a change of plans to the audience, in the manner of the Vice who first appeared many years later. Satan says he will be crafty and go to Pilate's wife, bidding her send for her husband. Slyly concealing the purpose of this plan, Satan leaves the stage with a theatrically engaging promise: "Withinne a whyle ye shal se / How my craft I wole go pref" (55–56).

Indeed "craft" is the hallmark of this character, as it is of Folly in *Mundus* and of the Vice after him. In the manner of Cloaked Collusion, Satan boasts at having double crossed those he incited to mock Jesus: "Be he nevyr so crafty nor conyng clerke, / I harry them to helle as tretour bolde!" (9–12). This is a subtle combination of demonic dissimulation with hellish infighting, for Satan delights in betraying and destroying those who attempt to serve him as they deceive and betray others. Eventually, the apotropaic power of the passion prevails in the N-Town pageant, as it becomes clear that Satan has over-reached himself in his cleverness, again in a manner reminiscent of the Vice. He not only tricks himself into declaring the truth about Jesus' innocence to Pilate's wife but also fails to prevent Jesus' death, thus bringing about the harrowing of his own kingdom and the salvation of humankind.

Though the dichotomy between folly and knavery is too sharply drawn for pre-Reformation drama, it nonetheless has some usefulness as a possible explanation for Heywood's anomalous Vice. Observing that folly was a principal element of vice in traditional drama, a courtly humanist playwright, familiar with French farce, might well have abstracted mere mirth from Folly while adapting a generic name and some of the mannerisms (such as fireworks and stage patter) that derived from an acting tradition of demonic knavery informed by popular drama.[34] In any case, Heywood's *merely* mirthful use of "Vice" was not influential. The next play that names "the Vice" is *Respublica*, some twenty years after Heywood's plays, where the name is attached to Avarice, first of a succession of Vices who are equal parts knave and fool, like pre-Reformation devils and vices before them.[35] In *The Conflict of Conscience*, the Vice Hypocrisy mocks Tyranny for playing "too partes the foole and the K[nave]," yet the remark is in character, for no one plays the fool and the knave better than Hypocrisy.[36] Significantly, the remark occurs in a play written between 1571 and 1580, near the end of the Vice's stage career, and therefore points to continuity with earlier devils and personified vices who enact both folly and knavery.

The best explanation for how the vices became the Vice has been offered by Bernard Spivack and David Bevington with regard to the exigencies of small acting companies and the necessity of doubling.[37] Since the Vice was a large role, the one who played the part was required to do the least doubling, and he was also likely to be the senior actor in the troupe, who would have been most gifted and experienced in virtuoso acting. This helps to account for the doubling of the Vice and the principal virtue in many Tudor morality plays (anticipated by the doubling of Mercy and Titivillus in *Mankind*).[38] It also helps to account for the self-conscious theatricality of the Vice, who often calls attention to his acting ability when the play requires that he pretend to be someone other than himself.

Yet even this feature of the Vice is not necessarily a result of mere cleverness or a precocious interest in metadrama, for it was part of the moral and narrative context from which devils and vices arose. "Be [*by*] sygnes of the body outward," asserts the author of *Dives and Pauper*, the devils "knowen disposicioun of man and womman ynward, ben is to helthe or syknesse, to vyce or to uertu, and often be tokenes outward they knowen mannys thought ynward" (p. 152). This is a prescription for dramatic mimesis that comes from the heart of moral reflection. It explains one of Mak's devilish qualities in the Wakefield *Second Shepherds' Play* that is also strikingly theatrical: his ability to play on the emotions of the good-hearted shepherds from whom he steals. The dream he claims to have had about his wife giving birth provides a narrative account of his actions that effectively misdirects attention away from him as a sheep stealer, thereby enabling him to steal more securely. Knowing the inward quality of his audience from their outward actions, he is able to manipulate them emotionally to his advantage.

This particular species of dissimulation is not only inherently theatrical but is also associated by playwrights with the court. Mak affects courtly airs when he first approaches the shepherds, though it turns out to be an ineffectual act that earns only their disgust. Lucifer is dressed as a court gallant in *Wisdom* when he boasts that he knows "all compleccyons of a man / Werto he ys most dysposyde" (343–44) and can therefore "marre hys myndys to their wan [*weakening*]" (346), even "a holy man" (347). The noble and sophisticated lady who presents herself to the Digby *Mary Magdalen* after her father's death is really the deadly sin of Lechery, and she too knows how to read inward thoughts from outward tokens. Grief should be assuaged in pleasure, she urges, for grief is an abuse that breeds much disease, and Mary should make an effort to dismiss it in favor of "sportys whych best doth yow plese" (456–59).

In Medwall's *Nature* the suave Sensuality beguiles Man by weeping for the courtly friends that Man has deserted, though the "friends" are really the seven deadly sins, as in *Mary Magdalen*. Sensuality is the first of a series of weeping vices who vent their dissembling sorrow in Tudor morality plays as a trick to divert the moral attention of humankind.[39] "I can dissemble, I can both laugh and groan," boasts Cloaked Collusion in *Magnificence* (698), as if he were adapting his lines from *Dives and Pauper*.

When other men laugh then study I and muse,
Devising the means and ways that I can
How I may hurt and hinder every man. (707–9)

. . . .

Paint to a purpose good countenance I can,
And craftily can I grope how every man is minded. (724–25)

Behind a boast like this lay decades of dramatic storytelling that educated the community and entertained it at the same time by celebrating
what constituted it. The fall of Lucifer began with his duplicitous
participation in the blessed community of the angels, a primal act of dissimulation that every other such act inevitably looked back to, including
acts in the theatre. Yet objections to pre-Reformation drama per se as
dissimulation are extremely rare, finding voice almost exclusively in the
fourteenth-century Lollard sermon called *A Tretise of Miraclis Pleying*.[40]
The singularity of this document suggests that it represents a point of
view that failed to attract a wide following because of its strictness, sever-
ity, and lack of sympathy with prevailing notions of moral sociability,
which were not distinctly upper class.[41] Defining community by
participation in the sacraments permitted a breadth of moral response
that was not receptive to a reconception of sacral community in nar-
rower terms, as the early Reformers discovered to their intense frustration. Satan as the enemy of the sacramental social body was the enemy
of all baptized Christians, not merely of those who believed particular
doctrines or who practiced particular piety. Dissimulation and hypocrisy
were certainly well known, as we have seen, but they were identified with
those who violated communal expectations, not with those who celebrated the sacramental community in drama. In the sixteenth century,
the Reformers were compelled to redefine community, as we shall see.
The devil consequently became a different kind of enemy, and drama
itself eventually fell under the same moral suspicion as dissimulation in
public life and the church. But that turn of events requires attention in
another chapter.

CHAPTER FIVE

Protestant devils and the new community

THE MORE THINGS CHANGE . . .

The first change in the history of English stage devils is attributable not to incremental secularization, as in the evolutionary story of early drama, but to the Protestant Reformation, which introduced what can best be described as *religious* secularization.[1] For devils that appear in Protestant plays are no less morally and spiritually serious than devils in pre-Reformation drama, but the assumptions that motivate them are different, and the community they oppose is not that of all baptized Christians but that of the reformed party under the crown – a relatively secular entity when compared to the earlier target of devilish opposition on the English stage. The first Protestant dramatists, John Bale and John Foxe, were themselves formed by traditional religion; Bale spent more than twenty-five years as a Carmelite friar until his conversion to the reformed view in 1533. They therefore understood the devil's role in cosmic history, in the life of the community, and in the individual Christian's life, and they also understood how that role was embodied in drama.

Their deliberate attempt to redefine the devil's role was no mean task, but in the long run it succeeded, even if it did so by compromise, in the manner of the English Reformation as a whole. Demolishing prevailing views through satire and iconoclasm was the first step. Putting something new in place required the ability to assign new meaning and impose a new shape on ecclesiastical, liturgical, and dramatic tradition, to master assiduous historical scholarship on the new humanist model, to put scholarship to work in winning hearts and minds, to reinvent dramatic convention, and to persevere in all this against overwhelming resistance, both official and popular.[2] The task paid off when political events eventually took a decisive turn in the Reformers' favor, enabling them to establish a new tradition. Their opponents' effort to preserve and renew traditional faith, including its devils, was no less determined, and throughout most of the sixteenth century it was not clear which view was going to prevail. When the Reformers finally won out, their effort effectively determined the future, and subsequent history has been written mostly by the victors, including Whig historians and at long last E. K. Chambers.

Rather than standing in the way of new belief and practice, then, the coherence of traditional religion enabled Reformers to construct an equally coherent view of their own, which in many respects was a mirror image of what they rejected. Out of a system of oppositional differences, the Reformers invented a new system that defined aspects of the traditional truth as heresy and elements of former heresy as truth. They did not abandon excommunication, for example, though it was a solemn ceremony designed to define true community by rejecting those who did not belong. Rather, they responded by excommunicating those who would excommunicate them. When Henry VIII forbade the regular reading of the Greater Excommunication or General Sentence, his motive was not disbelief in it but profound belief, for the General Sentence banned those who appropriated the property of the church, and Henry had just ordered the dissolution of the monasteries, the first major secularizing move of his regime.[3] The Reformers' debt to traditional religion is evident in the extent to which they reproduced a variation of it.

To be sure, reformed rejection of the sacraments, the mass, and a whole range of traditional orthopraxis inevitably looked like skepticism about religious belief per se to traditional Christians, who regarded such skepticism as heresy and feared and loathed the Reformers as atheists. But the charge of atheism needs to be considered carefully in the sixteenth century, for in spite of its sometimes scurrilous rejection of traditional religion, reformed skepticism is not equatable with later philosophical skepticism. The two may be related; as a secularization of traditional religion, reformed skepticism may even in some sense be a forerunner of later philosophical skepticism, but they are not identical.[4]

The process of adapting and redefining is evident in the earliest Protestant plays, written by John Bale in the late 1530s, at about the same time as the passage of the Henrician Ten Articles, the first official formulation of reformed doctrine in England. This legislation was a reformed triumph of sorts, because the Articles endorsed only three sacraments (baptism, eucharist, and penance), rather than seven, but it was a compromise, since the three sacraments were still officially

commended as means of salvation. The Reformers' emphasis on salvation by grace through faith, rather than participation in the sacraments,
is a prime example of religious secularization, since it rejected the traditional affirmation that there was no salvation outside the church,
reduced the function of the church in society, and put the burden on
what individual Christians believed. Bale's new mystery plays, dealing
with the life of Christ, helped to propagate the Ten Articles by reinter-
preting the sacrament of baptism and the role of the devil in opposing
it. In *Johan Baptystes Preachynge* (1538) Bale came as close as he dared to
denying the salvific efficacy of baptism (aided by the fact that Christ's
baptism was a special case), but his interpretation for the first time
openly identified the devil with traditional religion itself – a model that
countless dramatists, including Shakespeare, would imitate after him.

Though the play is about Christ's baptism, Bale's title subordinates
the sacrament to the Protestant emphasis on biblical interpretation and
preaching. He assigns himself a part in the play as "Baleus Prolocutor,"
expounder of the scriptures and John's spiritual successor, and in this
role he explains how to understand the baptism of Jesus and the devils
who were traditionally banished by the sacraments. "Devylysh practyse"
is an undoubted reality for Bale, still manifested by hypocrites who reject
Jesus.[5] What banishes the devil, however, is not the sacrament of baptism
but following Christ in humility, and the sacrament is not important for
itself but for what it represents, as John carefully explains: "Thys
baptyme of myne to yow doth represent / Remyssyon in Christ"
(171–72). "Represent" is the key word, since reformed doctrine interpreted the sacraments as signs of salvation, not the thing itself.

For the uninitiated viewer, *Johan Baptystes Preachynge* may not have
seemed very radical, because Bale clearly works within well-known
conventions. When Satan himself appears, however, in *The Temptation of
Our Lord* (1538), he is suggestively disguised as a hermit, rather than a
courtly gallant or dissimulating royal counselor, as in pre-Reformation
drama. He introduces himself, with fawning hypocrisy, as a "brother . . .
of thy desart wyldernesse," who only wants to talk about goodness in
"symple cumpanye" (83–85). Though Bale also had ample precedent for
ecclesiastical hypocrisy on the English stage, none of the extant English
plays on Christ's baptism put the devil in clerical disguise.[6] Bale makes
his innovation explicit when Satan himself announces that "Thy vycar
at Rome" is his ally (337).

The innovation here is not Bale's anachronism, for scriptural drama
had long conflated biblical events with their contemporary significance

on stage. What is new for drama is the identification of traditional religion itself with the devil, even though Bale was indebted to Christian
tradition for the idea of the devil as the enemy of Christ and Christ's
followers. The Pharisees and Sadducees of *Johan Baptystes Preachynge* are
thinly disguised Roman clerics, and when John denounces them as
"murtherers of the prophetes" and "Lucifers proude" (255–56), Bale is
denouncing the unreformed ecclesiastical hierarchy in the late 1530s.
What Protestant devils stand *for* is defined oppositionally by what they
stand *against*, as in traditional religion, but they stand against something
new, as Baleus Prolocutor makes clear at the end of the *Temptation*:
"enemyes are they" that take the scriptures from the people, "And
throwe them headlondes into the devyls domynyon. / If they be no
devyls I saye there are devyls non" (420–24).

Bale's Protestant rendering of the devil and the sacrament of baptism
in his scriptural plays reappears in his interpretation of the Vice and the
sacrament of confession in *King Johan* (1538). Since confession was not
recognized in the Ten Articles, Bale had no concern about attacking it,
and his tactic is to identify it as a means of demonic incursion against
the true (reformed) community.[7] Parodically staging the actual ritual of
confession, Bale presents it satirically as a method used by the Roman
hierarchy to intimidate traditional believers into submission and to
foment sedition against divinely appointed kings.[8] Bale's Vice is in fact
Sedition, making Bale the first playwright to identify a traditional ritual
as a political action and to name it as a moral abstraction: "Offend Holy
Churche and I warant ye shall yt fele," Sedition warns King John, "For
by confessyon the Holy Father knoweth / Throw owt all Christendom
what to his holynes growyth" (271–73). Bale's motive in identifying a
political action as the prime moral failure of his play was not a political
interest per se; his motive was to promulgate a new vision of human
destiny, both individually and communally, on the reformed model.
Nevertheless, it was an inevitably secularizing vision, because it pitted
the monarchy against the traditional church, given Henry's declaration
of himself as the supreme head of the church in England.

Following Bale, Protestant playwrights repeatedly identified the devil
with the ritual and beliefs of traditional religion. Such demonization is
so familiar that it is hard to imagine its audacity and boldness in early
sixteenth-century drama, yet its frequent repetition by subsequent playwrights is a tribute to Bale's successful innovation in redefining what the
devil stood for. His influence on other playwrights is apparent in the per-
sistent pattern of having infidels and vices betray themselves by their

pious allusions to the old faith and by their vigorous Catholic oaths. The reduction of piety and oath-making to a satirical caricature of a particular religious party is a signal example of religious secularization in early Protestant drama.

In his unreformed phase, the hero of *Lusty Juventus* (1547–53) thus swears "By the blessed mass," and Hypocrisy the Vice intones "Sancti amen" as he enters.[9] In *The Longer Thou Livest the More Fool Thou Art* (1559–68), the irredeemable Moros refuses to learn, asserting that he "can ring the Saunce [*sanctus*] Bell / And fetch fier when they go to Mattins."[10] The character called Confusion in *Longer* may or may not be a devil,[11] but Wager undoubtedly identifies traditional believers, personified by Moros, with the biblical fool who "saith in his hart there is no god" (1599), thus reversing the Catholic charge that Protestants were atheists. Even in *The Disobedient Child* (1559–70), which rejects morality-play abstractions in favor of Roman comedy's social types, degenerate characters swear "By goddes precious" and "By Coxe bones," and they drop such expletives from their speech when they come to their moral senses.[12]

Playwrights after Bale were influenced not only by his innovative notions of what the devil stood for but also by his reformed idea of what the devil opposed. Bale was indebted to traditional religion for his identification of true community with the church, but since the church no longer consisted of all baptized Christians who participated in the sacraments, the sense of community was much smaller for Bale than it was for pre-Reformation playwrights. Indeed, his plays tend to reduce true community to one reformer and his God. This diminished notion of communal identity has less to do with emergent individualism than with the real situation of English Reformers in the mid-sixteenth century. For such characters as John the Baptist, Jesus in the wilderness, and King John are all, in effect, beleaguered suffering saints on a Protestant model. "To persecucyon   lete us prepare us than," urges Baleus Prolocutor in the *Temptation*, "For that wyll folowe   in them that seke the truth" (19–20). Baleus makes the same point again at the end of the play: "He is unworthye   of hym to be a member, / That wyll not with hym   some persecucyon suffer" (404–5). For Bale, as for his opponents, it goes without saying that whoever is not a member of Christ belongs to the devil.

One reason the Protestant community eventually expanded beyond a company of martyrs was its close tie to the monarchy. Henry VIII led the way in forging the bond between reform and the king when he declared himself, rather than the pope, to be head of the English church. Though he personally disliked reformed views, Henry realized that the Reformers offered vital support in his attempt to annul his marriage to Katherine of Aragon and marry a Lutheran, Ann Boleyn. Mary Tudor's surrender of headship again to the pope was perhaps as severe a blow to the Protestant cause as her government's rigorous pursuit of traditional heretics, and Elizabeth's revival of Henry's claim was an important sign of better times for the Reformers.

Evidence of the secularizing impact made by the new reformed community's identification with the crown is the players' concluding prayer for the monarch, which appears as early as the reign of Edward VI. Having abandoned the sacraments of confession, penance, and absolution, playwrights invented the prayer for the monarch as an appropriate way to represent a new source of social cohesion at the end of a play. The shape of the reformed community is clear in the earliest of such prayers, at the end of *Lusty Juventus*, when Lusty Juventus, now reformed from his hankering after the old faith, urges prayer for "al the nobilitie of this realme," who have been authorized by "his grace" "To mayntayne the publike welth," for they need to hear the complaints of those "which are wrongfulli opprest" and "seke a reformation" (1163–69). Making the king and the nobility responsible for social cohesion is an inevitably secularizing move, in contrast to the focus on the sacraments in pre-Reformation plays, yet this move did not have a secular motive, as *Lusty Juventus* makes clear in its action, for the aim was not a reforming of the political system but of doctrine and liturgy, the essential expressions of belief about destiny in this life and the next.[13]

The part that dramatic prayers for the monarch played in promoting the new idea of true community was small in comparison to Bale's and Foxe's reinterpretation of the English past. The rewriting of English history was one of Bale's principal inspirations and one of his most important legacies to Foxe. Both *King Johan* and Foxe's Latin play, *Christus Triumphans* (1556), are based on the new sense of what history showed about the papacy and kings, if one read history as the Reformers did, and Foxe's influential *Acts and Monuments* is based on the same assumptions.

This reformed view of history is important for a history of the devil in drama, because Bale and Foxe made the devil's opposition to the true church central to their vision of the past and its bearing on their present. In keeping with his identification of traditional religion with the devil, Bale followed continental Reformers in understanding the papacy as

Antichrist, reading the Book of Revelation as a key to history since the time of Christ. Like the redefinition of heresy and truth, this insight also involved a reversal of assumptions in traditional religion and was thereby indebted to it. In the Chester mystery cycle, gullible kings believe Antichrist's assurance that they need have no fear if they believe in him: "I put you owt of heresye / to leeve me upon."[14] They discover their error only when those whom Antichrist resurrects are unable to take the eucharist. In effect, the play stages a miracle of the host, and the true source of Antichrist's power is revealed when a demon boasts that Antichrist performed miracles "through my might and my postee" (664) as he draws Antichrist's soul out of his body to carry it to hell.

Bale's Antichrist is identical to Chester's, except that Bale's is the pope, sponsor of belief in eucharistic miracles, which happen only by demonic power, according to Bale, if they happen at all. The confusion produced by this kind of conflict is registered by a traditional believer's complaint that a dissolved abbey was one day "the House of God, and the next day the House of the Devil: or else they would not have been so ready to have spoiled it."[15] For Reformers, however, Satan sat in Rome, not in the English church, at least so long as a reforming king was at its head, and Antichrist's alliance with hell was revealed through Protestant understanding of the Bible and its prophetic revelation of history – including English history. Increasingly, Bale came to believe "that S. Jhons Apocalips hath as well his fulfilling in the particular nacions, as in the universal church,"[16] a conviction that underlies his account of English martyrs in *The Acts of English Votaries* (1546).

Bale's strong sense of absolute binary opposition between true faith and heresy was therefore not his invention. It had its origin in traditional religion, where it is manifest in the contrast between sacramental community and the devil in prè-Reformation drama. The same contrast is developed in the iconography and characteristic shape of the narratives in Foxe's *Acts and Monuments* (1563). Bale's oppositional thinking is apparent in the title and substance of another of his works that influenced Foxe, *The Image of Both Churches*, and this kind of thinking inevitably invites deconstructive readings, as several critics have recently shown.[17] Deconstructing Bale, however, puts the emphasis on his intellectual limitations at the risk of ignoring what his way of thinking tells us about his situation – where his binary thinking came from, what original intellectual effort went into his reinvention of tradition, and what contribution he made to the formation of English national identity as distinctively Protestant.[18]

Bale's and Foxe's historical sense informs John Day's woodcuts for the *Acts and Monuments*, whose iconography complements the devils in Protestant plays. On the title page of sixteenth-century editions (Plate 1) are the same contrasts that we have seen in the innovative dramaturgy of Bale and those he influenced. The page is divided vertically into two columns, with "Come ye blessed &c." inscribed above the left column in the 1570 edition, and "Go ye cursed &c." above the right. The reference is to Jesus' parable of the sheep and goats in Matthew 25, the same text that governs the opposition of saved and damned in the mystery plays' pageants of the Judgment. On Foxe's title page, too, Christ sits in judgment, beckoning with his right hand, rejecting with his left. A column of images that represent the new reformed community is thus on God's right hand; the demonic opposition, on God's left.

The two columns are distinguished by their respective visions of liturgy, social body, and eschatology – categories that imply each other on both sides of the divide. The eschatalogical future is depicted at the top: on the left are seven crowned martyrs, clothed in white robes of righteousness and carrying palms of triumph (Rev. 7:9); on the right, five defrocked and tonsured clerics are dragged downward by devils who resemble in every detail the woodcut demons that were published in books of popular traditional devotion until the reign of Elizabeth. Below the eschatalogically triumphant martyrs on Foxe's title page are seven others, who literally and symbolically establish the wholeness of the new community in the breaking of their own bodies amid a fiery death at the stake, an image whose textual counterpart is Foxe's description of Laurence Saunders' preparation for burning at the stake in Coventry in 1555:

he was wonderfully comforted, in so much as not only in spirite, but also in body, he receaued a certayne taste of that holy communion of Saincts, whilest a most pleasant refreshing did issue from euery part and member of the body vnto the seat & place of the hart, and from thence did ebbe and flow to and fro, vnto all the partes againe.[19]

Opposed to this image of the new sacred social body on Foxe's title page is its demonic parody from the old faith: a priest elevates the host in a eucharist whose blasphemous idolatry is signaled by the approving gaze of an onlooking devil.

In the lower right-hand corner of the wood-cut, the same devil also intrudes into the liturgical space of the old faith, appearing to bless it preposterously with his left hand. A priest addresses his homily to a

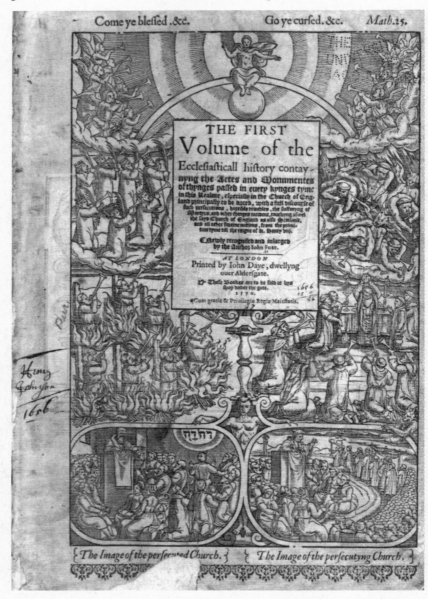

1. Title page from Foxe's *Acts and Monuments* (1570)

crowd preoccupied with the vain repetition of the rosary, while a Corpus Christi procession wends its way toward a shrine in the background. In contrast, the new community focuses on the Word of God, seeing it in the Bibles open in their laps and hearing it from a preacher who mediates it directly, as indicated by the shimmering Tetragrammaton. The influence of Bale's *Image of Both Churches* is evident in the subscriptions for each column in the 1570 edition: "The Image of the persecuted Church" on the left, "The Image of the persecutyng Church" on the right.

A more traditional source for Day's iconography is evident in the 1535 title page of Coverdale's Bible (Plate 2), which Hans Holbein also arranged according to a principle of binary opposition. In Holbein's woodcut, however, the opposition is typological, presenting a progression from old to new across the page from left to right, so that goodness and evil are in reversed positions from those they occupy on Foxe's title page: on the left, the sinful Adam and Eve with the serpent have their counterpart on the right in the redemptive Christ treading on a dragon and devils; Moses giving the law has his counterpart in Christ delivering the sermon on the mount, and so forth. This kind of opposition is traditional, updating similar iconographic contrasts in the *Biblia Pauperum*, for example. The only Protestant innovation in Holbein's iconography is the image of Henry at the foot of the page, delivering the Bible, as head of the church, to his bishops. The Tetragrammaton at the top of the page thus has its earthly manifestation below, in the godly king's reverence for the Bible.[20] Though a small innovation, Henry's image is nonetheless a revealing iconographic example of religious secularization, since it asserts the primacy of royal power in religious affairs.

Completing the oppositional iconography of the new community in Foxe are depictions of royal power that have been discussed by several critics. Invariably, as in Bale's *King Johan*, the power of monarchs is subdued by that of popes. A spectacular series of half-page woodcuts in the 1583 *Acts and Monuments* depicts popes and their representatives in the act of humiliating kings and emperors: Celestinus IV crowns Emperor Henry VI contemptuously with his foot; Emperor Henry IV stands waiting three days to see Pope Gregory VII; King John offers his crown to Pandulphus, and so on.[21] Often the depictions are accompanied by the phrase, "Image of Antichrist." But in three cases, monarchs dominate the papacy. The initial "C" that begins the whole book is elaborately decorated to depict Queen Elizabeth with the pope beneath her feet; the opening page of Book Seven has a woodcut of Henry VIII with

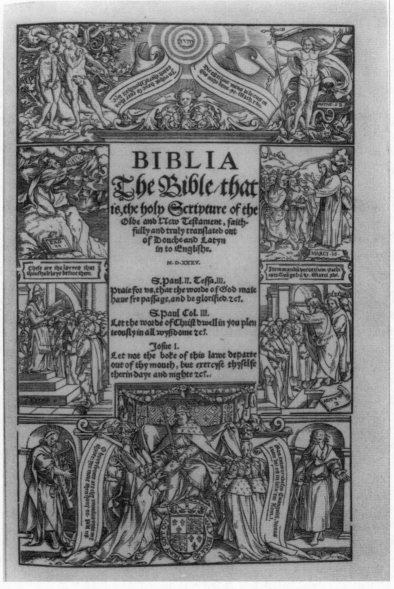

2. Title page from Coverdale's Bible (1535)

his feet resting on Pope Clement; and the opening page of Book Nine shows Edward VI delivering the Bible to his prelates, as his father does on the title page of Coverdale's Bible. Pictorially, only the three Tudor reforming monarchs thus reverse the historic trend, and the woodcuts powerfully suggest that England has a uniquely Protestant and providential destiny.[22]

A careful reader of Elizabeth's story in Foxe would discover more than a triumph over papacy, however. As William Haller points out, Foxe makes the young Elizabeth one of the martyrs, suffering at the hands of her sister along with others in the faithful remnant.[23] By presenting Elizabeth both as a subduer of the papacy and as a proto-martyr, Foxe made her spiritually and psychologically the head of the true church in England, thus reinforcing the idea of community as defined by suffering and increasing the queen's appeal to ordinary citizens who saw themselves in the innumerable commoners who are burned and tortured for their faith in Foxe's pages.[24]

Foxe's book is important to students of Tudor drama, because it helps to clarify what the dramatists aimed to achieve. Even in many plays that were "offered for acting" by small traveling acting companies in the 1560s and 1570s, the weight of humanist learning is still heavy, as it is in Bale and Foxe, and the assumed audience would seem to be well educated and staunchly Protestant.[25] It is hard to see how such plays could have had much popular appeal, as long as Protestantism itself was not popular. Still, the drama undoubtedly made some contribution to establishing a new and distinctively Protestant culture in England, and plays whose learning is less heavy are likely part of the same movement that adapted popular songs to a godly Protestant purpose.[26]

Protestant drama is also like the *Acts and Monuments* in making a contribution to religious secularity. The more sharply it defined itself over against its predecessor, the more clearly it represented a delimited sense of community, a new idea of "us" and "them." The new community was defined by the now familiar benchmarks of reformed faith: salvation by grace through faith, the priesthood of every believer, the necessity for individual belief. In themselves, of course, these are religious affirmations, and they pertain no less to the ultimate destiny of human life than does participation in the sacraments. Nonetheless, in their emphasis on individual salvation, on the absolute rejection of what they replaced (evident in Protestant demonizing of traditional faith), and above all in their link to monarchical power, these religious affirmations are comparatively secular – that is, they shift the religious focus from the institutional church and the sacraments over which it alone presides to the individual, the monarchy, and parliament, which passed the legislation approving the Reformers' changes. Here, if anywhere, is evidence of secularization in English life, and the devils of Protestant drama are part of it.

. . . THE MORE THEY REMAIN THE SAME

One consequence of adapting traditional drama to Protestant purpose was that dramatists obliterated the original social function of the conventions they borrowed. What anti-Catholic drama gained in a keen polemical edge it therefore lost in social observation and satire. In contrast to Chambers' assumption that increased secularization entailed increased social awareness, the secularizing tendency of Protestant drama actually resulted in less trenchant social satire than appears in the sacramentally inspired drama of traditional religion. Bale's Dissimulation in *King Johan* does not satirize self-seeking upward mobility, as Dissimulation had done repeatedly in traditional drama; rather, Bale's Dissimulation enacts yet another facet of Catholic hypocrisy and oppression, eventually incarnating himself as Simon of Swinset, the monk who poisons King John. Blatantly ignoring the unprecedented concentration of wealth that accrued to Henry VIII and those he favored following the dissolution of the monasteries, Bale identifies injustice exclusively with the Catholic church, which alone concentrates wealth: "False Dyssymulacyon doth bryng in Privat Welth," as Sedition remarks (771).

Foxe's iconography also reflects this early Protestant displacement of social injustice with demonization of the pope. The endleaf of Volume 1, in the 1583 *Acts and Monuments*, depicts Justice with a scale (Plate 3), in a woodcut that complements the title page. In the pan on the left (i.e., on Justice's right) is a Bible, sunk almost to the ground with its weight and surrounded by Jesus with his soberly costumed followers. Into the other pan a pope in full vestments pours a hoard of coins (or perhaps obles), decretals, decrees, rosaries, sensors, jeweled crosses, goblets, and other precious items. A tonsured priest attempts to pull down the right arm of the scale, and a devil hangs onto the bottom of the pan, which swings high in the air, despite the mound of treasure in it. The woodcut is an allegory of salvation, and what Justice weighs are competing Catholic and Protestant views, just as God judges the Catholic and Protestant communities in the title page woodcut (the same right/left

3. Allegory of Salvation from Foxe's *Acts and Monuments* (1583)

opposition is evident in both). Nonetheless, Justice holds the sword of state, and her traditional associations are with social issues, not soteriology. Day's woodcut is like Bale's plays in subsuming social justice into a preoccupation with competing ideas of doctrine and the church.

Other early Protestant plays follow the same pattern. When Hypocrisy approaches Lusty Juventus, the Vice pretends to be a friend and acts hurt when Juventus fails to recognize him (*Lusty Juventus*, 558–63). This involves dissimulation of the sort we have seen in Medwall and Skelton, as Hypocrisy pretends to honor Juventus ("your mastership"), and falsely expresses concern for changes in "man, maners, and fashion." Wever is not satirizing upward mobility in this passage, however, despite the suggestiveness of his language. As the scene develops, it becomes clear that he is borrowing satire of the pushy parvenu to create an allegory of the Reformation, with Lusty Juventus as the nascent Protestant movement itself and Hypocrisy as Catholic persuasion to return to the fold. "Yes I haue knowen you euer since you were bore," asserts Hypocrisy, "Your age is yet vnder a score," and he reminisces about the good times they had "When you wer yong and tender" (566–71). Professing to speak "Wythout any dissimulacion," Hypocrisy declares his name is Friendship, that he is closely related to Juventus, and that he loves him "so hartely, / That there is none so welcome to my cumpany" (574–85). The sly insinuation is courtly, as in Skelton and Medwall, but its satire is not aimed at the court; rather, it is used to support the allegory of the old faith's appeal, including false friendship, a common lineage, the lying declaration that one is being truthful, and the ominous desire ("love") for a "victim." Wever thus empties the convention of its social implications and substitutes anti-Catholic satire.

Not all reformed observers, however, turned a blind eye to new Protestant wealth and power, and when those who saw it pointed it out, they drew on pre-Reformation traditions that had been formed by centuries of social observation and satire. Robert Crowley was one of the most outspoken, publishing a satire called *Philargyrie* in Skeltonic rhyme as early as 1551. Crowley may be indebted to Skelton for more than his verse form, for Crowley's title character derives from a play by Skelton called *Nigramansir* – known to Warton but now lost – in which "Phylargyria, or Avarice" is put on trial before a devil, along with Simony.[27] In Crowley's satire, Hypocrisy is Catholic, as in most anti-Catholic invective, but he serves Philargyrie, who promises reform and destroys Hypocrisy, only to become worse than the thing he had destroyed. Since Crowley takes specific aim at the accumulation of wealth following the dissolution of the monasteries, he applies pre-Reformation social satire to problems of concentrated wealth and power in the reformed community. This is a more complex picture of that community than Bale's and Foxe's notion of suffering martyrs.

Increasingly, Protestant playwrights turned their attention to the same problems Crowley addressed, and the result is a resurgence of satire involving devils and vices that derives from pre-Reformation social satire on stage, even though that satire originated in a sacramental conception of social wholeness. "Resurgence" is crucial in describing this development, because the evolutionary view of early drama sees later Protestant playwrights' attention to social issues as a step in the inevitable progress toward secularization. Generalizations about the "other-worldly" focus in pre-Reformation drama are a rhetorical way to make the evolutionary argument work, but they have produced an inability to recognize or understand opposition to social injustice in pre-Reformation plays, and that inability has in turn resulted in a failure to recognize the debt of later Protestant playwrights to their pre-Reformation predecessors.

When Theology, Science, and Art converse sagely in *All for Money* (1559–77), Theology remarks that money corrupts even those who study theology and remarks ominously, "Without they amend, God will strike them with his sworde."[28] This is the prophetic denunciatory voice of Bale or Foxe, but it is directed at concentrated wealth per se, not at Catholics, and it therefore revives the social commentary of pre-Reformation drama. In *Like Will to Like* the Vice Nichol Newfangle informs the audience that Lucifer has taught him everything "that vnto the maintenance of pride might best agree," and he lists instances of literal sartorial abuses precisely like those that are satirized in earlier morality plays: "gowns with long sleeues and winges," "ruffs like Calues' chitterlings," and the like (sig. Aii^v–Aiii). Nichol's satirical target is not traditional faith but social affectation. His lines could as easily have been penned in 1467 as in 1567, and they indicate the establishment of a Protestant elite that invited satirical denunciation no less than the old social elite had done before the Reformation. The Vice in *Enough Is as Good as a Feast* (1559–70) is called Covetous, and when he proposes that he and his fellows change their names, the point is social satire, not anti-Catholic satire: Inconsideration becomes Reason; Temerity becomes Agility; Precipitation becomes Ready Wit; and Covetous himself becomes Policy. Wager almost certainly knew that Covetousness in Medwall's *Nature* also renames himself Worldly Policy.

Such "pure" examples of Protestant social commentary are relatively rare; often they are combined in complex ways with the new ideal of Protestant community, and the result has not been adequately understood or appreciated. The idea behind this effect is stated by Foxe himself, in his description of the reign of Edward VI as "a breathing time . . . graunted to the whole Church of England: So that . . . there was now no daūger to the godly, vnless it were onely by wealth and prosperity, which many times bringeth more dammage in corrupting mês minds, then any time of persecution or affliction" (1583 edn.; 2: 1297). Foxe's concern for the perceived dangers that peace and prosperity represent for the godly follows from his equating true godliness with suffering and martyrdom. Persecution sharpens one's spiritual edge, in this view, and prosperity just as surely takes it off. Foxe thus depolores just the kind of spiritual apathy, born of pragmatic commitment, that Shakespeare's Bastard espouses in *King John*: "Bell, book, and candle shall not drive me back / When gold and silver becks me to come on" (3.3.12–13).

The problem of Protestant greed and hypocrisy is treated centrally in several Protestant plays from the 1560s and 1570s, including some that stage devils as the enemies of community. A good example is Thomas Garter's *Virtuous and Godly Susanna* (1563–69), which is, in effect, a Protestant saint's play, since the heroine's fidelity is rewarded by the unexpected appearance of *"the spirite of Danyell"* (1061), who acts redemptively on behalf of a godly woman, just as saints had done in plays like the Digby *Mary Magdalen*. Though Daniel speaks like a Protestant preacher, he denounces the elders' abuse of power, not Catholic doctrine. The elders are two personified abstractions, Sensualitas and Voluptas, who are inspired by Satan, like all traditional vices, and Satan follows his dramatic predecessors by boasting that he wallows "now in worldly welth," creeping into each heart until "Of blood I haue my fill" (31–33).

Susanna's exemplary character is expressed in her chastity, but her chastity is not presented as an end in itself; rather it is the means by which she proves her faithfulness in the midst of prosperity, and it therefore makes her the moral opposite of the corrupt judges, who repeatedly gloat over their wealth and invincible power. Before the elders harass her, Susanna thanks God for her blessings, asking that they will not reduce the strength of her moral commitment, so that she "may if any storme doe fall, account it for the best" (680–83). Her internalized ideal of the suffering martyr is tested by the vicious judges, whose victim recognizes their harassment as the "storm" she had feared: "Oh Lord, oh God, oh King of blisse, what stormes does stop my breth" (767). Still, she reckons that to risk her reputation is better than "to attempt my Lord my God with this so vyle a sinne" (772). Since Susanna is happily married (she and Joachim are, in effect, the nexus of a godly community), sexual intercourse is not the issue for her, as it is for innumerable saintly virgins in *The Golden Legend* and, much later, for Dekker's and Massinger's Dorothea in *The Virgin Martyr*. What is at stake is Susanna's faithfulness to God when prosperity gives way to adversity. True Report in fact affirms Susanna's innocence before Daniel attests to it, because he remembers hearing Susanna pray for "a little peece of thrall" in the midst of plenty to prevent her taking her prosperity for granted (828–30). When the devil reappears, after Susanna's vindication, he admits that God has withstood his force, "And them that I doe seeke to get, he keepes them in his hande" (1387). This complaint could as well be voiced by the devil at the end of any pre-Reformation play, and Garter's devil has no hint of anti-Catholicism about him.

Nathaniel Woodes' *The Conflict of Conscience* (1570–81) is the latest and most striking example of playwrights turning their attention to social problems in the new Protestant establishment.[29] To be sure, Woodes' play is also virulently anti-Catholic and seemingly preoccupied with questions about free will and divine determinism, a point in which it anticipates Marlowe's *Dr. Faustus*. Still, its continuity with other Protestant plays that address problems of social justice is an important feature that it also shares with pre-Reformation morality plays.

Woodes' Protestant protagonist, Philologus, is patterned closely on the concept that Lupton laments at the beginning of *All for Money*: "Howe is the Scripture with many abused / With mouth it is talked, but with liuing denyed" (3–4). Woodes explains his character's name with reference to the breach between moral affirmation and practice:

But syth PHILOLOGVS is nought else, but one that loues to talke,
And common of the worde of God, but hath no further care,   *commune*
According as it teacheth them, in Gods feare for to walk,
If that we practise this in deede, PHILOLOGI we are,
And so by his deserued fault, we may in tyme beware.[30]

Philologus himself outlines the standards by which he ultimately fails. The body of Christ, he explains to Mathetes, is the body of the martyrs, who "must needes suffer, vnlesse that they be dead" (153), because suffering is what unites the community in the love of God. Suffering is therefore the way to discern the true church from the false, "Of the which, the one doth suffer, the other doth torment: / And in the woundes of his Brother is delighted" (158–59). Bale's and Foxe's oppositional image of both churches thus reappears in *The Conflict of Conscience*, and Woodes is no less emphatic than the early Reformers about the importance of discerning "Gods Church from the Diuels" (195).

The difference is that Woodes recalls these early Protestant pieties in the 1570s in order to stress Foxe's point about the difficulty of maintaining them in a time of ease and prosperity. The truth of God, Philologus urges, brings an "incumbrance . . . vpon them that will it professe, / Wherfore, they must arme themselues, to suffer distresse" (197–99). Mathetes rejoins with an emphatic summary of "all your talke": "God doth punnish his elect to keepe their faith in vre," because continuous ease makes people forget God; suffering thus makes believers abjure sin, it proves their constancy, and it makes them instruments to show God's might (238–44). Philologus ultimately fails in each of these standards of faithfulness, and Mathetes' allusion to "all your talke" is a pointed pun on Philologus' name and essence, as in the prologue. Though based on the story of Francesco Spira, an actual Protestant who recanted, Woodes's story is as firmly grounded in a personified abstraction as any other morality play. What has made this point difficult to grasp is not only the fact of Spira's story in the background but the particular abstraction Woodes embodies in Philologus, which involves a failure to maintain the specifically Protestant standards of the new community.

As in pre-Reformation plays, those standards are delineated in part by default in the vices, who are called into the kingdom by Satan. Though Avarice, Tyranny, and Hypocrisy characterize Catholic oppression, they also express essential aspects of Philologus in his failure, because his choice to become Catholic is a connivance with evils perpetrated by a persecuting church. Like Crowley's Philargyrie, Philologus as a Protestant apostate is worse than a Catholic.

Philologus explicates his own condition before recanting by comparing it to Susanna's:

> My case indeede I see most miserable,
> As was *Susanna* betwixt two euyls placed,
> Either to consent to sinne most abhominable:
> Or els in the worldes sight to be vtterly disgraced:
> But as she her chastitie at that time imbraced,
> So will I now spirituall whordom resist,
> And keepe mee a true Virgin to my louing spouse Christ. (1358–64)

Woodes reads Susanna's story in exactly the same way Garter does – as a test of faithfulness in the face of suffering. Philologus is able to withstand interrogation because he is a good talker and verbally defeats his interrogators, as Foxe's martyrs invariably do,[31] but Sensual Suggestion defeats him, not with erotic temptation but with vivid imaginative descriptions of the deprivation he faces if he persists in his Protestant views. Unlike Susanna, Philologus is unable to risk his reputation, preferring social standing and wealth to his Protestant commitment (1496–1500). He is therefore unable to resist the Cardinal's promise of wealth and power if he recants (1579–82).

The Cardinal might as well be named Mundus, because he offers the same temptation to which Worldly Man succumbs in *Enough Is as Good as a Feast* and to which Humanum Genus succumbs long before, in *The Castle of Perseverance*, when the tempter is actually called Mundus. Woodes' play has been described as secular because Philologus is modeled on an actual human being, but the issues are just as "other-worldly" in *The Conflict of Conscience* as they are in *The Castle of Perseverance*, because the ultimate consequence of worldly choices in both cases is spiritual peril, or what Philologus calls "spirituall whordom." "To say trueth," he affirms damningly to his sons, "I doo not care, what to my soul betide, / So long as this prosperitie and wealth by mee abide" (1958–59). This is Humanum Genus' sentiment precisely, when he gives in to Mundus: "What schulde I recknen of domysday, / So that I be riche and of gret aray?"[32] Protestant soteriology offers Philologus no second choice after death, and his care for worldly prosperity therefore dooms him eternally, unlike Humanum Genus, though Woodes' alternative ending, in which Philologus repents before he dies, suggests that Woodes may have felt the tragedy was too harsh. In any case, the point about spiritual destiny remains: in this latest of Protestant morality plays, published after the opening of the first commercial theatres near London, the critical issues are identical to those in one of the first extant moralities, from the early fifteenth century. Despite the great divide of the Reformation, both playwrights understand moral issues – including issues of social justice – in the context of ultimate human destiny, and the function of stage devils in both plays is to clarify what ultimately counts.

THE DEVIL AND THE VICE IN PROTESTANT PLAYS

An objection to the argument that later Protestant devils mark a resurgence of pre-Reformation tradition is that they are less interesting, and less frequently staged, than the Vice. Even in plays where devils do appear, they usually do so only briefly, at the beginning or end of a play, leaving the most visible and effective work of evil to the Vice. An influential comparison of these two traditional stage characters is Bernard Spivack's negative assessment of the devil in Protestant plays:

> In none of these . . . plays is he anything more than the functionless and undifferentiated source of all evil, whose deputies in the real action of the plot are the vices . . . In all these plays he is for the most part a grotesque and lugubrious figure, without verve or alacrity – a lumbering, helpless target at whom the Vice shoots his scurrilous jests. He never has any part in the intrigue itself and never associates with its human victims. His sole, easily dispensable, business is to commission the Vice, without whose aid he is helpless.[33]

Spivack's commitment to a story of secular evolution in early drama explains this generalization but also weakens it. He slants his account to favor the Vice, because he sees the Vice as a transitional figure between "other-worldly" and "this-worldly," or secular, concerns in drama. Unlike the devil, Spivak argues, personified abstractions, of which the Vice was chief, could be made to serve social and political purposes (i.e., secular purposes), and the Vice therefore supplanted the devil. The Vice was eventually supplanted in his own turn, according to the inexorable logic of secular progress, by mimetic human characters, whose concreteness made them the most "this worldly" of all.

Spivack's story of incremental secular change follows earlier critical accounts in its failure to recognize continuity between stage devils before and after the Reformation. In the Protestant plays we have just surveyed, the dichotomy between "this worldly" and "other-worldly" is false, as it is for pre-Reformation plays, because playwrights consistently use the devil to dramatize the situation of those who make morally tragic choices in the context of their ultimate ("spiritual") destiny. In short, the social function of devils in all early religious drama, whether traditional or Protestant, is directly related to their moral and spiritual function, because the secularization of stage devils is reflected in the particular community they threaten (the Protestant godly nation, in contrast to the sacramental social body), not with the issues they represent, which remain constant.

Spivack's assertion that the devil does nothing more than commission the Vice therefore acknowledges a great deal more than the dismissive language suggests, for where the devil and the Vice are concerned, there is never any question about precedence or superiority: the Vice derives his authority and power from the devil. In *The Longer Thou Livest, Like Will to Like*, and *Enough Is as Good as a Feast*, the devil exits with the Vice on his back at the end of the play, a stage device anticipated by Bale in *King Johan*, when he has Usurped Power carry Sedition in the same manner. This is a stage emblem of relative power and authority, for Usurped Power's historical counterpart is the pope, while Sedition is a mere monk. There is no doubt about who serves whom.[34]

Even in plays where the devil does not appear, the language of the Vice makes his subordination clear. *The Tide Tarrieth No Man* (1576) has no devil, but the inspiration for Courage, the Vice, is borrowed in part from *The Ship of Fools*, and Courage is quite clear about where the ship is headed: "we sayle, / To the Diuel of hell," he explains, and he calls on sinners to join him "Tyll hell doe them swallow," for "That is all they do win."[35] Allegorically it is clear that vice leads to hell, but Courage makes no claim to have originated hell in the first place, to be God's principal rival, or to seek to win souls to his own kingdom.

Spivack is right, too, that the Vice often mocks the devil in Protestant plays, but it would be a mistake to assume that the devil is therefore a diminished figure of scorn. Sedition in Bale's *King Johan* mercilessly mocks both King John and Dissimulation, another vice, yet this even-handed treatment does not make King John and Dissimulation merely grotesque, lugubrious, and helpless targets of the Vice's wit. In *Enough Is as Good as a Feast* three lesser vices, called Temerity, Inconsideration, and Precipitation, invoke "Couetouse the Vice" (sig. Bii) and then proceed to mock him, trading insults with him about prisons and hanging. When Covetous calls for his cap, gown, and chain, so he can undertake the rescue of Worldly Man from the influence of Contentation and Enough, he foolishly rejects the gown, mistaking it for a cloak, and Temerity mocks him: "Why my brother is blinde, I holde you a Crown: / Body of me he knoweth not a Cloke from a Gown" (sig. Biv). If the Vice himself is mocked by his henchmen, as in *King Johan* and *Enough*, then being mocked cannot be a sign of a stage figure's evolutionary decline, since these are plays from the height of the Vice's popularity.

The Vice's mockery of the devil needs to be understood in the context of vice mockery in general. When vices taunt and rail at virtues, as they do consistently from *The Castle of Perseverance* on, their mockery is self-defeating – a manifestation of the myopia and self-absorption which constitute destructive moral choices and result in more of the same. Reading vice mockery as subversive social protest does not explain why vices consistently represent concentrated wealth, competitive upward mobility, and upper-class oppression. Examples range from the World and Flesh in *The Castle of Perseverance*, who are repeatedly identified as kings, to Ambidexter in *Cambises* (1558–69), who connives at Sisamnes' exploitation of Commons Complaint and Commons Cry. A vicious commitment to social privilege is also shared by Mischief in *Mankind*, who exploits country priests and laboring peasants with scurrilous jibes and practical jokes. This is not to deny that when vices mock virtues they are irresistibly funny, indulging an impressive repertory of scatalogical and bawdy jokes, pratfalls, and stage buffoonery that accounts as much as anything does for the enduring quality of early drama in performance. The point is that risibility per se does not determine social function, especially when explicit indicators point to the vices as a way of satirically enacting upper-class pretension, arrogant upward mobility, or the concentration of wealth and power.

When pre-Reformation vices mock each other, or when vices mock devils, they embody another kind of moral self-defeat, and it is also designed to be funny. As we noticed in chapter 4, devils and vices serve the purpose of social satire in pre-Reformation drama in their inevitable and vicious infighting, which reflects the realities of baronial civil war, because civil war reflects the broader collapse of social cohesion that resulted from the failure of charity. This moral insight continues to shape vice conflict in Protestant drama – including conflict between the Vice and the devil. When Hypocrisy first meets Tyranny and Avarice in *The Conflict of Conscience*, he mocks them in asides that are set off marginally by the printer in different type, as if to try to capture visually on the page what is meant to go on in the theatre. The Vice in fact mocks the devil in only four extant plays: *Lusty Juventus, Virtuous and Godly Susanna, Like Will to Like*, and *All for Money*, and it is a gesture that needs to be compared to other examples of vice mockery in Protestant plays, as well as in their predecessors. The Vice's mockery of the devil is not a sign that the devil was obsolete or was giving way to the vitality of the Vice. Conflict between the devil and the Vice is a perpetuation of Vice conflict from the pre-Reformation morality play, and it continues to have the same significance in Protestant plays.

This point of continuity is complemented by other indications of traditional stage devilry that occur in later Protestant plays. Lupton stages two of the seven deadly sins in *All for Money*, even though the tradition of the seven sins is non-biblical in origin and should therefore be technically objectionable to Protestants. In *Susanna*, Ill Report boasts in soliloquy about his great antiquity and his ubiquitous influence, which he attributes to "The pollicy of the Deuill" (147). He explains that that policy is motivated by the devil's envy, which has prompted him to call on five of the seven deadly sins in his attempt to corrupt Susanna: pride, gluttony, envy, sloth, and covetousness (153–71).

Satan himself mentions six of the seven deadly sins in *The Disobedient Child* (Fiiiᵛ), and his doctrinal correctness is so retrograde that he even invokes the World, Flesh, and Devil, though this infernal trinity is also not biblical:

> The worlde is my Sonne, and I ame his Father
> And also the fleshe, is a doughter of myne
> It is I alone, that taught them to gather,
> Both Golde and Syluer that is so fyne.   ([Fivᵛ])

Indeed, the devil in this play is likely one reason why Spivack leaves *The Disobedient Child* out of his study altogether. The play contains no personified abstractions and therefore disqualifies itself as a morality play by Spivack's definition, yet its prodigal-son plot is the basis of other contemporary plays which are also concerned with the appropriate rearing of young people.[36] Moreover, Ingelend's Satan makes havoc of evolutionary schemes by combining in himself characteristics of both the devil and the Vice, as devils sometimes do in the mystery plays. He enters by demanding room, exulting in his cleverness, and taking the audience into his confidence, in the manner of the Vice, but his boasting is unmistakably that of the devil: he has a kingdom opposite to God's, but he complains it should be grander than it is, because it attracts those of every degree from every nation (sig. Fiv). This boasting is wholly traditional; it does not single out Catholics as the Enemy, and its explicit concern is how spiritual destiny is manifested in moral choice – in this play, the "secular" choice of a young man to neglect his education and marry a woman who is interested only in his wealth.

One of the most traditional stage images of the devil in Reformation drama appears in the fragment W. W. Greg called *Processus Satanae* and dated to the decade of the 1570s, which makes it contemporary with *The Conflict of Conscience*.[37] In addition to the devil, this play also stages God, Christ, the archangel Michael, and the Four Daughters of God. Indeed, the subject would seem to be appropriate to the cosmic scale of the mystery plays, though the particular subject of this play is not treated in any extant cycle. The fragment is an actor's part, containing only God's lines, from which the rest of the play must be inferred. What is important is its conformity to traditional religious expectation as late as the second decade of Elizabeth's reign. Nothing about the fragment is obviously Protestant, either in favor of Protestant doctrine or opposed to traditional religion. If the fragment is as late as Greg thinks it is, it exemplifies the residual strength of traditional religion in stage plays.

The perpetuation of the major mystery cycles into the decade of the 1570s in fact makes clear that "secular progress" is a misleading concept for drama of the sixteenth century. The cycles may well have ceased performance for more reasons than official suppression and resistance.[38] The eventual recovery of a pre-Reformation tradition of stage devils parallels other cultural changes in Protestant England. While national identity was becoming increasingly Protestant, and radical Protestants (eventually called "Puritans") called for ever stricter reform in church and society, the reality of most people's daily lives seems to have been relatively undisturbed by the upheavals of mid century. What Ronald Hutton has recently called a "merry equilibrium" gradually emerged, marked by the retention of many features of popular culture that had been formed by centuries of parish life before the Reformation.[39] That equilibrium was far from being achieved in the sixteenth century, but the elements that eventually constituted it were in place, and the perpetuation of popular stage devils with traditional moral meaning is one such element.

CHAPTER SIX

The devils of "Dr. Faustus"

Chambers found the evolutionary goal of early drama in the London commercial theatre, for in his view Marlowe and Shakespeare threw off the rusty shackles of religious tradition so that drama could flourish as fully secular. He was surely right that what happened in the late sixteenth century was different from what preceded it, but incremental secular evolution is not the only possible explanation. We have just seen that devils in Protestant plays retain the same kind of moral and spiritual vitality as traditional stage devils until well into the 1570s, and many elements of traditional dramaturgy, including specific features of the morality play, persisted into the commercial theatres. Richard Tarlton, the famous clown, is thought to have written two plays about the seven deadly sins in the mid-1580s, and shortly afterwards Robert Greene and Thomas Lodge used biblical characters and a "ruffian" disguised as a devil in a moral diatribe against urban vice in *A Looking Glass for London and England*. For the most part, however, it is clear that playwrights favor mimetic human characters, rather than personified abstractions, and the stories in which the characters are caught up seldom emphasize the state of one's immortal soul; they are stories of mundane destiny.

The question, then, is not whether drama was secular, but how to evaluate its secularity and how to describe the process of secularization. The received response to these questions – that the process was gradual and developmental – takes an "early form" of secular drama or a "hybrid" combination of the traditional and the secular as a rhetorical point of an evolutionary argument, rather than real evidence that an incremental process of secularization was at work over the course of more than two centuries of vernacular drama. Terms like "medieval" and "renaissance" are used loosely in making the evolutionary argument: depending on what account one is reading (and sometimes even different parts of the same account), English "renaissance" drama begins anywhere from 1490 to 1590. I have argued instead that stage devils enact oppositional assumptions in English plays before the 1580s – as devils do in the wider culture – whether they are shaped by traditional religion or by the Protestant reaction against traditional religion. In this view, stage devils are therefore not secular anticipations of drama at the end of the century.

In contrast to an evolutionary process of secularization over the entire course of early drama, change seems to have been more like the result of a geological cataclysm in biological evolution, with the factors causing it being contingent and unpredictable. The mystery plays were systematically suppressed by the Elizabethan regime, as Harold Gardiner has shown, in a process that directly parallels the secularization of ecclesiastical real estate, church government, liturgy, time, and language.[1] Legislation also likely affected saints' plays for the same reason that it affected the mysteries, but official opposition does not explain the replacement of Protestant moralities and their lively devils with the drama of Marlowe and others who are the admired flowers of secular drama. To understand this process, we need to consider other factors that emerged for the first time late in the sixteenth century.

Most important was the establishment of permanent commercial theatres near London, beginning with John Brayne's Red Lion in 1567, about which we know very little, followed in 1576 by the Theatre, built by James Burbage in the same year that the Blackfriars opened.[2] The advent of fixed commercial acting locations changed the nature of drama in profound ways. To succeed, acting companies now had to have a constantly changing repertory: they could no longer perform the same limited number of plays in varying locations as they traveled, nor could they make money by repeating the same play annually on a ritually significant occasion.[3] The result was intense commercial pressure for new plays and new subjects, including secular subjects. The establishment of commercial theatres was not inevitable or obvious; it depended on the initiative of an entrepreneurial grocer at the Red Lion and a joiner at the Theatre, who had the idea of doing theatrical business differently from the way it had been done before them. They must have been inspired in part by the rapid increase in London's population and the wealth created by thriving commerce in the capital, but they could not have been certain their ventures would succeed (indeed, Brayne's apparently didn't), nor could they possibly have foreseen all the consequences of their bold move.

A second contingent reason for the rapid secularization of play subjects is the development of religious opposition to the stage per se. Both before the Reformation and during its early years, the authors of drama were mostly priests and schoolmasters. As the commercial theatres thrived, however, they invited opposition to their repertory and to the lifestyle of the players. For the first time, serious moral and religious opposition to the stage itself appeared in the 1580s, thus discouraging those who had been the principal suppliers of plays hitherto (including Puritan divines like Nathaniel Woodes, who published *The Conflict of Conscience* in 1581, fourteen years after Brayne established the Red Lion) and further widening the gap between the theatre and religious culture.[4]

At the same time that preachers and teachers withdrew from play-writing because of the increasing stigma attached to it, other playwrights took their place with different motives and priorities – and this too was a contingent development. Most important among these were recent university graduates, the so-called university wits, whose upward mobility was frustrated by a static social system, and who therefore turned to play-writing to make a living at just the time the commercial London theatres were establishing themselves. The emulation of these young social hopefuls brought a characteristic innovative edge to drama that is understandable in light of their university training, their social ambition, and their consequent feeling of entrapment in a degrading occupation. As Richard Helgerson puts it, "these men constructed a self-presentational dialectic in which the author was defined by his social superiority to the institution for which he wrote."[5] The intense rivalry among them complemented economic rivalry among the fledgling theatres to create a new commercial motive and context for drama, in place of the ritual and educational context in which drama had largely functioned up to that point. James Shapiro points out that personal and commercial rivalry produced such innovations as dramatic parody, because of parody's usefulness in "prematurely aging a rival's work and confirming the novelty of one's own," as well as "the collapsing of literary generations," as one dramatic fashion rapidly replaced another in the quest for commercial success.[6]

Several factors thus reinforced each other to produce a rapid secularization of dramatic subjects at the end of the sixteenth century, but none of them was predictable or intrinsic in past events, as the evolutionary argument would maintain. They did not "unfold," "grow," or "progress." Moreover, the advent of predominantly secular subject matter in drama does not necessarily indicate a change of mental habit in the culture as a whole. Stuart Clark has documented remarkable continuity in "thinking with demons" throughout the sixteenth and

seventeenth centuries, and that continuity is evident in the way playwrights staged devils.[7]

Probably the first to do so on the commercial stage was Christopher
Marlowe, the most brilliant and successful of the university wits. The
first text of his *Tragical History of Doctor Faustus* (1604) may well have been
written in 1588–89, before Green's *Friar Bacon and Friar Bungay*.[8] In any
case, it was reprinted as a play text and revived on stage many times over
the next half century, and it exerted an incalculable influence on subsequent plays, even when they parody it as old-fashioned. *Dr. Faustus*
assumes the oppositional assumptions that Clark identifies and that we
have seen throughout the stage tradition thus far. At the same time, it is
no exaggeration to say that Marlowe's devils are the second major
change in the history of early dramatic devils, the first being the
Protestant Reformation. For Marlowe is the first playwright who uses
devils to exploit the religious secularization of English life that the
Reformation had produced.

Marlowe himself was highly conscious of theatrical competition,
already distancing his "muse" from the "jigging veins of rhyming mother
wits / And such conceits as clownage keeps in pay" in the Prologue to his
first play, *Tamburlaine*. All his major characters are willfully and aggres-
sively competitive – "overreachers," to use Harry Levin's irreplaceable
term – even though their aggression is never rewarded with unambiguous success.[9] Whether or not the portrait of a young man at Marlowe's
Cambridge college, Corpus Christi, is really of Marlowe, its motto captures the ambiguity of Marlowe's life and that of his heroes as well:
"Quod me nutruit me destruit" ("What nourishes me destroys me").[10]
Where Faustus is concerned, one might even say that what nourishes and
destroys him is his competitive ambition itself, and this ambiguity about
Faustus so affects the world of his play that it is what distinguishes
Marlowe's devils most strikingly from any preceding devils on the English
stage.

To be sure, Marlowe was well aware of the tradition he was borrowing, and he acknowledges it in several ways. His acknowledg-
ments, however, indicate change as well as continuity. Traditionally, for
example, Lucifer was believed to have fallen because of overweening
ambition, and Marlowe acknowledges this tradition when Faustus questions Mephistopheles about Lucifer:

> *Faustus.* Was not that Lucifer an angel once?
> *Mephistopheles.* Yes, Faustus, and most dearly loved of God.
> *Faustus.* How comes it then that he is prince of devils?

Mephistopheles. O, by aspiring pride and insolence,
 For which God threw him from the face of heaven.   (1.1.66–70)

Marlowe may well have encountered the idea of Lucifer's *libido dominandi* in his own reading of Augustine at Cambridge,[11] but he could have found it in innumerable other places as well (there is a hint of it in his source, the English Faustbook), and it is pervasive in early religious drama. Milton's memorable and influential interpretation of Lucifer's lust to dominate in *Paradise Lost* indicates that the idea was still vital almost a century after Marlowe. Whether or not Marlowe saw any of the mystery plays, they were still being staged in some places when he entered Cambridge in 1580, so his earliest audiences might well have imagined easily what Mephistopheles describes, because they had literally seen Lucifer's fall in a pageant performed within ten years of the time *Dr. Faustus* first alluded to it on the public stage.

The archetypal *libido dominandi* that Mephistopheles describes is a central but troubled idea in *Dr. Faustus*. From a traditional point of view, Faustus perpetuates the stage convention by repeating Lucifer's sin in his own turn, as innumerable personified abstractions had done before him. According to Mephistopheles, "pride and insolence" (a strangely orthodox phrase for a devil to use) led to Lucifer's overthrow, and pride is the key concept in Faustus' story: initially he wishes to go beyond the bounds of received knowledge because it is "too servile and illiberal for me" (1.1.36), and he believes the conjuring of devils will afford him "a world of profit and delight, / Of power, of honour, of omnipotence" in which "All things that move between the quiet poles / Shall be at my command" (1.1.55–57). Pride is the first in the pageant of the seven deadly sins, complementing the Evil Angel's temptation to Faustus: "Be thou on earth as Jove is in the sky, / Lord and commander of these elements" (1.1.78–79), a temptation that in turn answers Faustus' own ambition to "gain a deity" (1.1.65). No less than Tamburlaine before him, Faustus is a hero who rises from an inauspicious background ("Now is he born, his parents base of stock" [Pro. 11]), and eventually comes to believe that he can have the means to "reign sole king" over everyone he encounters (1.1.96), including the Duke of Parma, Catholic oppressor of Protestants in the Netherlands.

But aspiring pride and insolence are not as straightforward as they appear to be in *Dr. Faustus*. For one thing, Mephistopheles' account of Lucifer's being thrown from the face of heaven is closely anticipated by the opening Chorus' description of Faustus as "swoll'n with cunning of a self-conceit" and mounting on waxen wings, till "heavens conspired his overthrow" (Pro. 20–22). The Chorus' description is not neutral; it is as strongly slanted as Mephistopheles' language to connote mere power in the "heavens": "God threw him" and "heavens conspired his overthrow." In similar terms, the power-hungry Tamburlaine sees God as a competitor, imagining that the "frame of Heaven" might "conspire my overthrow."[12] Moreover, the emphasis on mere power reappears in the closing Chorus of *Dr. Faustus*, which refers again to "the hellish" fall of Faustus:

> Whose fiendful fortune may exhort the wise
> Only to wonder at unlawful things
> Whose deepness doth entice such forward wits,
> To practise more than heavenly power permits.   (Epi. 5–8)

Traditionally, damnation had been understood as a logical necessity of divine love, yet the defining characteristic of God in *Dr. Faustus* is not love but overwhelming power.[13] And this characteristic cannot be explained as a perception of a guilty conscience, because the Chorus uses the same terms. In Marlowe's rendering of the story, Lucifer and Faustus are not willful rejecters of creative and loving goodness; they are merely losers in a struggle for power.

Marlowe alludes once more to Lucifer's fall in *Dr. Faustus*, introducing still another characteristic ambiguity: homoerotic wit. When Mephistopheles describes the women he can supply to Faustus, he promises that

> She whom thine eye shall like, thine heart shall have,
> Be she as chaste as was Penelope,
> As wise as Saba, or as beautiful
> As was bright Lucifer before his fall.   (2.1.158–61)

The switch from female chastity and wisdom to male beauty is understated in the exotic catalog, which has the same witty quality as a similar catalog in *Hero and Leander*:

> There might you see the gods in sundrie shapes,
> Committing headdie ryots, incest, rapes:
> For know, that vnderneath this radiant floure
> Was *Danaes* statue in a brazen tower,
> *Ioue* slyly stealing from his sisters bed,
> To dallie with *Idalian Ganimed*.[14]

Another gender switch occurs in the intense eroticism of the scene with Helen, whom Faustus apostrophizes:

> O, thou art fairer than the evening air,
> Clad in the beauty of a thousand stars.
> Brighter art thou than flaming Jupiter,
> When he appeared to hapless Semele,
> More lovely than the monarch of the sky
> In wanton Arethusa's azured arms,
> And none but thou shalt be my paramour.   (5.1.104–10)

Orthodox readings of *Dr. Faustus* are severely strained by the rhetorical power of such passages and by their similarity to the undisguised homo-eroticism of *Hero and Leander*.[15] To suggest that the beauty of the unfallen Lucifer was powerfully erotic is to read his fall very differently from the way it had been understood by Augustine or by the tradition indebted to Augustine.[16]

The devils of *Dr. Faustus* are also subversively ambiguous as they inter-act with Faustus in his struggle for power. For if Faustus is "overthrown" on one hand by an absent, punitive, malignant, and merely powerful God, he is destroyed on the other by the lying promises and empty threats of demons. The result is less an opposition of good and evil than of one overwhelming cosmic power and another. Faustus' bid for power is thus hopeless from the outset, and his condition has been aptly described in Constance Kuriyama's clever neologism, "omnimpotence" (*Hammer or Anvil*, pp. 95–135). The devils are the only effective influence on Faustus, and they appear in large numbers in this play: eight out of thirty-five characters in the character list of the A-text are devils, and nine others are personified vices. The most powerful agents who oppose them are the Good Angel and the Old Man, who make brief, inter-mittent, and ineffectual appearances, in contrast to Mephistopheles' ubiquitous presence.[17]

Marlowe thus recreates a simulacrum of familiar oppositional think-ing in order to deconstruct it. He does this, in part, by identifying even the ineffectual Old Man rhetorically with the struggle for power. The Old Man's final speech is a cry of victory with more than a hint of gloat-ing in it, as well as an echo of the Chorus' allusions to the powerful heavens:

> My faith, vile hell, shall triumph over thee.
> Ambitious fiends, see how the heavens smiles
> At your repulse, and laughs your state to scorn!   (5.2.116–18)

This is Marlowe's version of the idealized defiance of tortured and dying martyrs in Foxe's *Acts and Monuments*, including their ready memory for biblical quotations. (The Old Man alludes to Psalm 2:1.) But it is far

removed from precedents in Protestant drama.[18] In context, the Old
Man's declaration of victory culminates a sequence of similar triumphs,
all made by Faustus himself, which begin with a mockery of traditional
ritual in the scurrilous terms that Bale had introduced into virulently
anti-Catholic drama:

> How? Bell, book, and candle, candle, book, and bell,
> Forward and backward, to curse Faustus to hell.
> Anon you shall hear a hog grunt, a calf bleat, and an ass bray,
> Because it is Saint Peter's holy day.   (3.2.84–87)

Protestants were accustomed to believing that traditional religion was an
instrument of Satan, but *Dr. Faustus* is a rare (if not unique) Elizabethan
instance of the devil intervening explicitly on the Protestant side. Faustus
appropriates a power superior to the Pope's to make the Pope look like
a gull and an asshead, just as the Old Man will appropriate a power
apparently superior to the devil's to smile at hell's repulse and laugh its
state to scorn. Marlowe's implicit reduction of the reformation to a
struggle for power is an acute response to the secularization introduced
by the Tudors, not because struggles for power were invented by
Protestants but because Protestants made religion a matter of crown
policy and thus, comparatively, a matter of mere power.

Staged between Faustus' victory over the Pope and the Old Man's
over the devil are four more, all won by Faustus in league with
Mephistopheles. The first vindicates learning against courtly arrogance
(4.1.1–99); the second similarly vindicates learning against clownish
aspiration (4.1.100–89); the third demonstrates intellectual prowess
before a duke (4.2); the fourth demonstrates similar prowess before fellow
academics (5.1.100–10). Like the sequence of victories in *1 Tamburlaine*,
all of Faustus' victories are sympathetic but ambiguous, beginning with
his victory over the Pope: he is courted by the most powerful ruler in
Europe and demonstrates his invulnerability to courtly detraction; he
vanquishes lower-class demands for justice with an ease that might have
made Martin Luther envious;[19] he handily wins the unfeigned admiration of the powerful and the learned. In short, his career embodies a
fantasy of upwardly mobile Protestant power in the sixteenth century,
and the demonic motivation of this career is one of the play's most subversive ironies.

Viewed in the context of the sequential victories that make up the
second half of the play, the Old Man's ultimate victory has less to do
with a triumph of faith over despair (or of cosmic goodness over evil)

than it does with making sure one joins the winning side from the outset – provided, that is, that one can know what the winning side is going to be. When Faustus torments and humiliates an anonymous knight, for example (4.1), it is because the knight refuses to believe in the power of Faustus' magic. But the refusal to believe in a certain kind of super-human power is precisely what the Old Man, the Good Angel, and the Chorus say is Faustus' problem, and his torment of the anonymous knight is therefore a direct parallel to his own torment at the hands of heavenly power as the play ends. If devils are the means of torment in Faustus' case (as he seems to believe), then his case parallels the anony-mous knight's even more closely, since Mephistopheles is also the means of the knight's torment at Faustus' hands.

The deconstructive ambiguity of traditional oppositions in *Dr. Faustus* is enhanced by Marlowe's secularization of the fiend's traditional equivocation. Faustus' determination to enhance his power leads him naturally to reject traditional affirmations of human limitation, because to acknowledge them would be to give up before he begins. Having rec-ognized the cosmic determinism of traditional theology, as he sees it, Faustus scorns the theological truisms he hears from Mephistopheles:

> What, is great Mephistopheles so passionate
> For being deprivèd of the joys of heaven?
> Learn thou of Faustus manly fortitude,
> And scorn those joys thou never shalt possess.   (1.3.85–88)

If one's dominion that exceeds in magic is to stretch as far as does the mind of man, it will have to stretch farther than traditional hopes and fears about the human condition, even when those are voiced in appar-ent sincerity by the devil himself. In retrospect and from an orthodox perspective, Faustus' refusal to listen to what Mephistopheles tells him is fatal and ironic.[20] In context, however, it is an affirmation of the manly fortitude that set him on his course in the first place. Given the triumph he enjoys as a consequence of his choice, he appears to have chosen rightly, despite occasional doubts, because he is clearly on the winning side: successful, admired, powerful, Protestant, and fully aware of his deserving superiority.

Yet the devils who seem to offer Faustus a means to escape traditional limitations are apparently the means of his undoing in the end, the duplicitous source of his "omnipotence." The demons play a role in *Dr. Faustus* that is analogous to the Vice of the morality play and that therefore parallels the role of Vice-derived characters in other plays by

Marlowe, such as Barabas in *The Jew of Malta* or Mortimer in *Edward II*.[21] The point of contact for all these characters is their essential hypocrisy and their *libido dominandi*, which is the origin of both devils and vices in English stage tradition. But as in other points where Marlowe deconstructs the tradition, the effect of his equating devils in *Dr. Faustus* with the Vice is strikingly different from anything in earlier drama. The defeat of Faustus in the cosmic power struggle offers no evidence of a good and loving God who opposes evil with redemptive power, any more than Barabas' defeat in the human power struggle is proof of justice in human affairs. For all Marlowe lets us know in *Dr. Faustus*, God is no better than Ferneze: what both indubitably have in common is that they win in the end, and in a struggle for power, winning is all that counts. The difference in *Dr. Faustus* is that Barabas' dramaturgical analogues (i.e., the devils) are not defeated either, or at least not in the short term. Despite allusions to their one-time defeat by God, they triumph maliciously over the only character who is defeated in this play – a mortal loser in the stakes for cosmic dominance.

To be sure, Mephistopheles as a tempter does not seem like an equivocating Vice, because he is so solemn and seldom takes us into his confidence.[22] His method of temptation is actually more like that of the devil in the mystery plays, who tends to be less comical than the Vice and infrequently reveals his purpose. Lucifer's temptation of Eve in the cycle plays is closer to Mephistopheles' temptation of Faustus than, say, to Titivillus' temptation of Mankind. Mephistopheles seldom uses dramatic asides, but he does so once with telling effect: "O, what will I not do to obtain his soul?" (2.1.73). Otherwise, Marlowe's devil presents the same face to us that he presents to Faustus, thus creating uncertainty about when he is lying and when he is not.

The focus of demonic dissimulation in *Dr. Faustus* is the bargain itself. That the pact is really a means to make Faustus *submit* (rather than giving him the means to dominate, as he hopes to do) seems apparent from the moment Mephistopheles explains blasphemy as a sign of potential interest in submission to demons (1.3.47–55). Yet even this claim may merely be a demonic feint in Mephistopheles' incessant battle to control Faustus, because Mephistopheles always seeks to dominate Faustus rhetorically and always succeeds. Like Tamburlaine, he is a master of "working words" by which he overpowers his victim, and he serves a power-seeker, as Theridamas does, whose sole aim is to "enlarge his kingdom" (2.1.40).

Take Mephistopheles' phrase to describe the motive for Lucifer's rebellion, for example: "aspiring pride and insolence" (1.3.69), which captures God's view of the matter, as it had been traditionally understood. Since Mephistopheles presumably does not hope to convert Faustus to God's view, his use of traditional diction is presumably to tempt Faustus to persevere in "manly fortitude," because that kind of perseverance is really a submission to the devil. The rhetorical effect of this reverse psychology on the audience is the same as it is on Faustus: to make us feel the limiting restrictions of orthodoxy.

The bargain thus appears to be another demonic feint, as the Good Angel and the Old Man suggest in their assurance of divine mercy long after Faustus has signed. For their assurance clarifies one point: we can assume that the devil is telling the truth about the bargain only if we assume that the Good Angel and the Old Man are lying. If the bargain were indeed what Mephistopheles claims it is, he would not pursue his victim after the signing but would expend his energy elsewhere, confident that he could abandon Faustus to his already accomplished damnation.[23] Mephistopheles "serves" Faustus not in good faith according to a bargain but because he is vigilant to "obtain his soul," that is, to dominate him by pretending to serve him.

This is why Mephistopheles' threats are empty but effective. Threats (including the bond) are the stick in his approach; temptations to power, the carrot. If the devils literally harmed Faustus, they would be less likely to obtain his soul, that is, to secure his unswerving allegiance, because physical pain could break the victim but not "turn" him, and the threat of torture is useful in persuading him when he wavers, because it convinces him of the threateners' power. This is why the Old Man does not fear the "sifting" of Satan: secure in his allegiance to the other side, the Old Man knows the devils can torture and destroy him, but they cannot "obtain his soul," as Mephistopheles admits:

> His faith is great. I cannot touch his soul.
> But what I may afflict his body with
> I will attempt, which is but little worth. (5.1.79–81)

The Old Man even sees the "furnace" of demonic torture as God's hand trying his faith (5.1.115) – a telling comment on divine and demonic instrumentality in the destruction of Faustus as well, and a deconstructive view of martyrdom.

At the same time, as long as Faustus still thinks he has something to gain from Mephistopheles, he does not want to abandon the opportunity to gain it. Lies and truth thus become intermingled and difficult to distinguish:

> *Faustus.* Come, I think hell's a fable.
> *Mephistopheles.* Ay, think so still, till experience change thy mind.
> *Faustus.* Why, think'st thou then that Faustus shall be damned?
> *Mephistopheles.* Ay, of necessity, for here's the scroll
>   Wherein thou hast given thy soul to Lucifer.   (2.1.130–34)

Mephistopheles seems to take one step backward, as he affirms the real existence of hell, in order to take two steps forward in lying about the efficacy of the bargain in Faustus' domination. But if the reality, as Marlowe presents it, is that God and Lucifer are locked in a power struggle, then the truth of what opposes the devil is not guaranteed either, any more than Ferneze's truth is guaranteed simply because he is a Christian. If the aim of both sides is to catch Faustus' soul, what will they not do to obtain it? In *Dr. Faustus* Marlowe reproduces the effect of ubiquitous dissimulation in the quest for power that he also creates in *The Jew of Malta*, but the effect appears on a cosmic scale, and the stakes are correspondingly higher.[24]

Marlowe's deconstruction of traditional stage devils is matched by his treatment of traditional social cohesion as well. Stage devils were originally conceived oppositionally as threats to community, whether it was the sacramental social body in traditional religion or the body of the suffering martyrs that Protestants regarded as the true church. But Marlowe's devils seemingly oppose only another version of the *libido dominandi* that they represent themselves, except that their opposite seems to be more successful than they are and therefore, presumably, more powerful. When Mephistopheles asserts that "this is hell, nor am I out of it" (1.3.78), he may be making an orthodox point about *poena damni*, as he goes on to suggest:

> Think'st thou that I, who saw the face of God
> And tasted the eternal joys of heaven,
> Am not tormented with ten thousand hells
> In being deprived of everlasting bliss?   (1.3.79–82)

But Mephistopheles' equivocation makes the point doubtful, for how can we tell that he is not using reverse psychology, as he does elsewhere, to assert traditional ideas of human limitation in order to tempt Faustus to reject them and thereby choose the devil's side? What better way to obtain Faustus' soul? Nothing in the play enables us to determine the truth of Mephistopheles' assertions, and nothing therefore alleviates the impression that this is hell and nothing can escape it. In short, the society Marlowe creates in *Dr. Faustus* is defined by aggressive and unremitting competition, equivocation, and dissimulation – precisely the kind of society that had traditionally been identified as demonic.

We do not have to look far to find models for this imagined social world. The newly commercial theatres were inherently competitive, like the young men who wrote for them. But in the late sixteenth century, commercial competition was nothing compared to the court, which was the center of power, the only means of gaining the kind of social recognition that counted in Elizabethan England, and the real impetus to competition among the university wits. As a university education became a principal route to success at court, even for sons of the aristocracy, dense networks of patronage quickly developed around the universities. The Archbishop Parker scholarship that took Marlowe to Cambridge was his entrée to a world of social contacts that a mere shoemaker's son could never have dreamed of entering otherwise. In this world, one acted the part of privilege, if one could, whether one had it or not. "I'll have [devils] fill the public schools with silk," dreams Faustus, "Wherewith the students shall be bravely clad" (1.1.92–93). This was in direct violation of dress regulations at Cambridge, whose effect was to obscure social differences.[25] If a poor "sizar" like Marlowe could wear silk, he could make himself look like the noblemen's sons who flouted the dress regulations.

Dissimulation was therefore a lesson one learned early in the competition for place and power, because it was a lesson that was essential to success at court, as Puttenham asserts. He identifies *allegoria* as "the Courtly figure," because we use it "when we speake one thing and thinke another, and that our wordes and our meanings meet not":

no man can pleasantly utter and perswade without it, but in effect is sure never or very seldome to thrive and prosper in the world, that cannot put it in ure, in somuch as not only every common Courtier, but also the gravest Counsellour, yea and the most noble and wisest Prince of them all are many times enforced to use it, by example (say they) of the great Emperour who had it usually in his mouth to say *Qui nescit dissimulare nescit regnare*. Of this figure therefore which for his duplicitie we call the figure of *false semblant or dissimulation* we will speake first as of the chief ringleader and captaine of all other figures, either in the poetical or oratorie science.[26]

Given Puttenham's evaluation of dissimulation, Marlowe did not need to turn to an authority as foreign and exotic as Machiavelli in perpetuating the lust for power as the source of native dramatic diablerie. "Policy" had long been recognized as a vice in the morality play,[27] and Puttenham's *Arte*, published in 1589, offered an extensive English vocabulary for many of the same courtly insights that earned Machiavelli condemnation and rejection. As Marlowe's Machevil incisively observes, "To some perhaps my name is odious, / But such as love me guard me from their tongues" (*Jew of Malta*, Pro. 5). Harry Levin is surely right that Marlowe was drawn to hyperbole, or what Puttenham calls the "over reacher" and the "loud liar," but hyperbole is a species of "allegoria" for Puttenham, and Mephistopheles follows Puttenham's advice precisely in using dissimulation as the chief ringleader and captain of all other figures in rhetorical science.

That the court is the model for such social cohesion as we find in *Dr. Faustus* is also suggested by Faustus' social negotiation in the court itself, a process that repeatedly hints at the ambiguous bargain between Faustus and the devil. That bargain involves Faustus' submission to the devils, by means of the bond, in order to win their submission to him, but the bond appears to be a demonic strategy – a show of submission that is designed to "turn" Faustus, or win his irreversible submission to them in the long run. As Mephistopheles tells Faustus, Lucifer approves a plan whereby Mephistopheles "shall wait on Faustus while he lives, / So he will buy my service with his soul" (2.1.31–32).

This bargain enacts the dynamics of courtly power, echoed in the pleasantries of courtly discourse as Faustus converses with those for whom he conjures. "I am content to do whatsoever your Majesty shall command me," Faustus tells the Emperor (4.1.17–18), in response to the Emperor's request. A complex social negotiation is involved in this exchange, whereby both understand that Faustus' service exacts the Emperor's implicit admission that Faustus can do more than the Emperor can do himself.[28] The parallel with Mephistopheles' submission-in-order-to-dominate is reinforced by the constant presence of the mysterious friar at Faustus' side, always ready to "serve" him and always the means by which the magician exercises his superior skill. Faustus' easy victory over the anonymous knight in the same scene is another example of courtly rivalry in which Faustus dominates, though the dominance is again ambiguous, because Mephistopheles is the one who places horns on the knight's head and removes them again at Faustus' command. Faustus adds insult to injury by informing the Emperor that he humiliated the knight only "to delight you with some mirth" (4.1.91), but the self-serving reality is revealed in Faustus' comment to the knight: "And, sir knight, hereafter speak well of scholars" (4.1.94).

The ambiguous pattern of courtly service repeats itself when the Duchess of Vanholt requests grapes. "For I see your courteous intent to pleasure me," the Duchess says to Faustus, "I will not hide from you the thing my heart desires" (4.2.8–10). By revealing the desire of her heart to one who serves her, the noble lady acknowledges his power, because he can fulfill the desire that no one else can, and she is thereby indebted to him. After Mephistopheles supplies the grapes, the Duchess concedes that while she lives she will "Rest beholding for this courtesy" (4.2.35–36). "Courteous intent" and "courtesy" make clear where this kind of social negotiation was most at home. Both the Emperor and the Duke promise Faustus a rich reward for his service (4.1.99 and 4.2.38), thus underscoring the obligation they have incurred to him and implicitly assenting to his dominance in superhuman and illicit power, which he always describes in the language of service and submission.

The final appearance of this courtly pattern involves the scholars' request that Faustus make Helen of Troy appear. The scholars are not Faustus' superiors to begin with, but he responds to them with the same similitude of courtly submission that he had used with the Emperor and the Duchess:

> For that I know your friendship is unfeigned,
> And Faustus' custom is not to deny
> The just requests of those that wish him well,
> You shall behold that peerless dame of Greece.   (5.1.18–21)

The parallel between courtly favors and the devilish bargain is manifest when Faustus in his own turn asks Mephistopheles to let him have Helen as his paramour. Echoing the Duchess, he frames his request in courtly elegance: "One thing, good servant, let me crave of thee / To glut the longing of my heart's desire" (5.1.82–83), and Mephistopheles accedes to his request in the same manner but with profound ambiguity and barely disguised rapacity: "Faustus, this or what else thou shalt desire, / Shall be performed in twinkling of an eye" (5.1.89–90). This courteous exchange between Faustus and his "good servant" definitively explicates the courteous exchanges that precede it.

Closely related to the court itself as a model for the society Marlowe imagines in *Dr. Faustus* is the world of espionage that he had been drawn into by his involvement with the fringes of the court.[29] In the 1580s, espionage carried out by the Protestant regime in England and by its Catholic competitors on the continent inevitably involved duplicity in covertly questing for advantage over an adversary in matters of religious affirmation. This is also the situation in *Dr. Faustus*, especially when it concerns efforts to "turn" a prospect who might serve one's cause.

Nothing more effectively deconstructed traditional oppositional thinking than espionage, for in this murky world all affirmations were suspect,
no matter how persuasive, sincere, or candid their language seemed to
be, because their purpose and motive were difficult to determine.
Marlowe's representation of this world in *Dr. Faustus* is his most incisive
response to the secularization of English life in the sixteenth century, for
the extent to which religion had become the focus of a struggle for power
was most evident in the spying games played by the Elizabethan regime.

Take the "confession" of Richard Baines in 1583, for example – the
same Baines who would accuse Marlowe of atheism to the Privy Council
ten years later.[30] Baines had been planted in the Catholic seminary for
English priests at Rheims to do what he could: gather information,
destroy morale, possibly even murder. (As Nicholl and Kendall point out,
Baines' plot to destroy everyone at the seminary by poisoning their well
parallels a strategy that Barabas puts into effect in *The Jew of Malta*.)
When he confided his plots to a fellow seminarian whom he hoped to
turn, however, the man reported him, and Baines was confronted with
evidence of his duplicity. In response, he confessed in a traditional
Catholic manner, and the seminary published his confession, presumably in order to take maximum advantage of its unsettling effect in
England. Baines' Catholic affirmation, in other words, has all the marks
of profound moral and spiritual self-examination, yet it turned out to be
a device to buy time while he considered his next move. He might in fact
have made his confession good by going over to the Catholic cause.
Alternatively, if advantage served him, he could explain the confession
back in England (as in fact he did) as a ploy to save his life and future
career as a government informer.

In his published confession, Baines inverts the terms of Protestant
truth by portraying it as a heresy inspired by the devil, in keeping with
the traditional view depicted, among other places, in the Chester play of
Antichrist. Baines refers to his conversations with a hoped-for accom-
plice as "deuilish communication" and wonders rhetorically "how farre
the deuil would haue driuen me, who now holy occupied my hart in
hope of aduauncement in England" (sig. 26). He identifies his "practices" against the seminary as "detestable treasons" against God and the
church, and rejects his "abhominable periurie dissimulation & fiction"
in taking mass and swearing "an oth vpon the Euangelists that I
beleeued al points of the Catholick faith" (sig. 27) while undermining the
seminary. He acknowledges the sins of pride, sloth, and gluttony, "an
immoderat desire of more ease, welth, and (which I specially also

respected) of more delicacie of diet and carnal delits then this place of banishment was like to yeld vnto me" (sig. 24ᵛ). He confesses to intellectual pride, omitting the divine service, jesting and scoffing at it, then mocking "the lesser points of religion, which is the high way to Heresie, Infidelitie & Athisme [sic]," until he was close to "this heresie of Protestants and that the next dore, yea the next steape of this staire is atheisme and no beleefe at al" (sig. 25ᵛ).

Information and disinformation are difficult to disentangle in this confession. Cardinal Allen, who published it, presumably hoped it was sincere, because he wanted to believe that Baines, who had been ordained a Catholic priest two years earlier, had returned to the fold and was safe against Protestant suborning. Baines certainly tells the truth about his ambition, since ambition was implicit in government service, and his allusions to gluttony and sloth may also be partly true while simultaneously aiming to titillate his hearers and readers and thus undermine their own ascetic commitment, as Nicholl suggests. But what are we to make of his confessed apostasy – the very thing of which he accused Marlowe ten years later?[31] Is he describing his own mental processes here too, or is he incriminating himself falsely in order to impress his Catholic inquisitors with the sincerity of his repentance? Did he himself know whether he believed what he was saying? Reading Baines' confession, we are in the same mental world that Marlowe creates in *Dr. Faustus*, where someone is caught between competing allegiances in a struggle for power, where his ambition is used against him by both sides (by God to condemn him; by the devil, to obtain his soul), where the terms of allegiance are the terms of religious belief or unbelief, where the stakes are hard to determine (worldly success or eternal damnation?), and where it is difficult to find a statement that can be taken at face value.

What makes *Dr. Faustus* so stark is that it offers no alternative: as with the world of courtly social negotiation, this is hell, nor are we out of it. Moreover, if we go to the opposite end of the social scale from the court, we find the same thing; in fact, the play's treatment of commoners (whether Marlowe's or some other's) is one of its most important departures from the sense of charitable social cohesion that devils oppose in traditional drama. One of the hallmarks of traditional devils is their consistent identification with those who have the greatest wealth and power, because the socially elevated are most vulnerable to the sin of pride and therefore most capable of inflicting damage on the sacred social body. Demonic power thus manifests itself by analogy to social oppression (from above), rather than social subversion (from below), and a disproportionate number of the faithful whom devils victimize are those, like Jesus himself, who were least privileged in a hierarchical society: peasants, farmers, shepherds, women. Even personified protagonists like Magnificence, who is imagined as a king surrounded by vicious courtiers, discover their true nobility only in the process of affirming adversity, humility, and the need for grace, which are qualities that commoners are imagined to achieve more easily, because less prevents them.

The commoners of *Dr. Faustus* are very different. They acquire no mysterious dignity as God's "freindes deare, / such as poore and naked weare," but are mere hapless gulls in the ubiquitous struggle for power.[32] Theirs is the world above which Faustus successfully rises ("Now is he born, his parents base of stock" [Pro. 11]) by virtue of his brilliance at Wittenberg, and it is also the world from which he dreams of liberating students, in his fantasy of dressing them in silk. Robin the ostler is startled when Mephistopheles actually appears in response to Robin's conjuring, but Mephistopheles is disgusted that he responded to mere "damnèd slaves" (3.2.34), a revealing indication that human social status matters as much to the demons of this play as it does to human beings. Traditionally, social worth had never been an indicator of spiritual worth; indeed, the two often appeared in an inverse proportion to each other. Yet in *Dr. Faustus* Mephistopheles thinks no better of commoners than Faustus himself does.

Faustus' own scorn of those at the bottom of the social hierarchy is evident in all his dealings with them, even though he comes from a "base" social origin himself. His advice to the horse courser not to ride his horse into the water uses the same kind of reverse psychology that Mephistopheles uses with Faustus, encouraging the very behavior it appears to prohibit. The stage device that makes the vengeful horse courser believe that he has indeed pulled off Faustus' leg is the pivotal illusion in a confidence trick set up by Faustus and Mephistopheles, whose design is to double the money they milk from the gullible horse courser: "Well, this trick shall cost him forty dollars more," remarks Faustus with satisfaction (4.1.188).[33] Critics have often noticed that Faustus demeans himself increasingly as the play progresses, and this is the culminating example. What has gone unremarked is that this example reinforces an analogy between the Faustian bargain, courtly negotiation, espionage, and confidence trickery. Mephistopheles' dealings with Faustus are echoed in his dealings with Robin and in Faustus' own dealings with the horse courser, where he is actually assisted by

Mephistopheles, as he is in his ambiguous service to the socially elevated. Social worth is therefore definitive in *Dr. Faustus*, and nothing is worth less than common status, even to the devil, yet the competition for place is inevitably degrading in itself and terrifyingly uncertain in its outcome.

Marlowe thus uses the terms of social contest to redefine a world traditionally defined by moral and spiritual worth, and it is therefore tempting to say that *Dr. Faustus* is a fully secular play, even a "material-ist" play, and that its devils are fully secularized as well.[34] This claim is accurate insofar as it responds to the play's depiction of religion as mere power and to devils as instruments of a cosmic power struggle. But nothing in *Dr. Faustus* is as straightforward as it appears to be, and its deconstructive devils need to be weighed against reports of its contem-porary impact, which depended on the traditional assumption that devils are a malignant spiritual reality with potent material effect. As early as 1594, stories surfaced that an extra devil appeared in a produc-tion of *Dr. Faustus* at the Theatre, terrifying actors and audience alike.[35] William Prynne tells the story again in 1633, including a detail that may help to date the play to 1588, because he locates the production in the Belsavage playhouse, which seems not to have been used after 1589. At least one other seventeenth-century version of the story is extant before its appeareance again in John Aubrey's *Natural History and Antiquities of Surrey* (begun 1673), which locates the performance in Exeter.

The deliciously terrifying effect of the extra devil on stage depends in large part on the ambiguity of staged ritual. Common in anti-Catholic drama is the reduction of traditional ritual to mere "jugglery," as in Bale's *King Johan* and even more pointedly in the anonymous *Jack Juggler*.[36] Parodying ritual on stage had a deliberately demystifying effect, attempting to prove the Protestant point that sacraments were not effectual in themselves, because if they were, they would be just as effective when performed in a play as when they were performed in the liturgy. Despite its slapstick anti-Catholicism, *Dr. Faustus* is not openly skeptical about ritual in the accustomed Protestant manner (even though the ritual it stages is demonic rather than sacred), because when Faustus utters his blasphemous charm, the devil indeed appears. The fact that he "indeed" appears only in a play is irrelevant in a context where the effectiveness of ritual had long been established in plays for the edifica-tion of the faithful. The stage miracle of blood pouring from the side of the ascended Christ in the Chester play of the Ascension has a close parallel in *Dr. Faustus* when Faustus' blood ceases to flow during the signing of the bargain. That it commences to flow again when

Mephistopheles fetches a chafer of coals to warm it raises skeptical and reductive doubts, as if the problem were merely physiological, but the *frisson* of Faustus' terror is not necessarily diminished, for the devil is a liar, and it is in his interest to explain away the power of ritual, as the Protestants were wont to do. Moreover, Faustus' panicky question, "Why streams it not, that I may write afresh" (2.1.66), is echoed in his final agonizing plea, "See, see, where Christ's blood streams in the firmament! / One drop would save my soul, half a drop. Ah, my Christ!" (5.2.78–79), and the second cry is harder to explain away.

In similar terms, Mephistopheles has a sophisticated explanation for his coming in response to Faustus' conjuring, namely, that he hoped to obtain the soul of a blasphemer, not because a ritual invoked him, and this explanation also moves in the direction of explaining away the compelling power of ritual. But Mephistopheles' explanations are deeply suspect, as we have seen, because he is a subtle equivocator. Are his appearance and the drying up of Faustus' blood mere stage effects, the necessary illusions of a demonic confidence trick (as when the horse courser pulls off Faustus' leg), or are they examples of ritual power, as in traditional drama? The fact that we cannot be entirely sure is what makes *Dr. Faustus* so provocative. The play was written in a world where a self-proclaimed "atheist" (as Marlowe was reputed to be), Thomas Fineux of Dover, attempted to prove that the devil did not exist by going into a forest at night to pray to the devil, a gesture that buys heavily into the very reality it attempts to disprove.[37] For all its reductiveness, *Dr. Faustus* is skeptical in a different way from Protestant anti-Catholic drama, because it leaves so much room for metaphysical terror, and its devils are therefore hard to dismiss definitively as symbols of secular power. While Marlowe renders cosmic strife in terms that recall Elizabethan social and political tensions, he retains something of the power of traditional cosmic drama at the same time, even if the staged ritual in *Dr. Faustus* is blasphemous rather than blessed. In effect, the play's ritual, too, is hell, nor are we out of it, but hell is a potent reality, which equivocates, like the juggling fiends of *Macbeth*, to the inevitable destruction of those who palter with it.

CHAPTER SEVEN

Reacting to Marlowe

Dr. Faustus had both an immediate and lasting impact on the London commercial theatre. The lasting impact was general and diffuse, involving the advent of modern tragedy, the portrayal of a despairing protagonist, the atmospheric sense of an irredeemably evil world, the compelling exploration of interiority. The immediate impact can be described in terms of a handful of plays that responded to Marlowe's play over the dozen years after its first appearance in the way they staged devils. For Marlowe's play is, so to speak, the conduit through which this stage device made its way from religious drama to the commercial stage. From the building of the Theatre in 1576 to the advent of *Dr. Faustus* some twelve years later, no extant commercial play stages devils, yet several plays in the late 1580s and throughout the 1590s include devils, and all of them react to Marlowe in one way or another.[1]

Imitation involves interpretation, as Peter Berek has argued in the case of *Tamburlaine*,[2] and the first imitators of *Dr. Faustus* tell us a good deal about how they understood it, and incidentally how they understood stage devils. That understanding, as we shall see, is remarkably traditional, often deliberately recalling pre-Reformation assumptions in sympathetic ways, as if to exorcise or at least diminish the potent threat of Marlowe's ambiguous fiends. At the same time, however, playwrights who staged devils in direct reaction to *Dr. Faustus* often seem admiring about it, as well as disapproving, and they sometimes secularize the tradition in ways that Marlowe had not anticipated.

A consistent feature of these plays is the placement of their action in pre-Reformation England. In this, they all contrast with *Dr. Faustus*, which is located in Germany and focuses on a heroic Protestant, even if he also happens to be a necromancer. Though only Shakespeare's *1* and *2 Henry VI* (1590) are "history" plays, all five of the plays that stage devils in reaction to *Dr. Faustus* explicitly recall a distant English past, from before the Norman conquest to the fifteenth century, and they use the past to comment implicitly on the present. The mid-sixteenth-century Protestant Germany of *Dr. Faustus* is also, in some sense, a version of late sixteenth-century Protestant England, and the plays that react to Marlowe seem designed to present a different England from his – in general a more hopeful one.

In the 1590s, setting a play before the Reformation would seem to be an excuse for anti-Catholicism, especially in view of the threat from Spain. Yet none of these plays is as strongly anti-Catholic as *Dr. Faustus* or even *Edward II*, which is also set in pre-Reformation England,[3] and only *1 Henry VI* manifests the characteristic Protestant identification of devils with traditional religion. In Greene's *Friar Bacon* (1589–90) the conjurer is the thirteenth-century Oxford philosopher, Roger Bacon, whom Marlowe briefly mentions as a precursor to Faustus.[4] If Greene acted on this hint, he had plenty of material from which to draw, most importantly a prose romance that had been published at mid-century called *The Famous Historie of Fryer Bacon*.[5] Regardless of his sources, however, Greene treated both devils and the conjurer in ways that reflect on *Dr. Faustus*, primarily by challenging its bleak assumptions.

Most striking is Bacon's repentance. In contrast to Faustus, Bacon eventually acknowledges that his necromancy is wrong, and he rejects it in terms that restate the theological origin of stage devils before the Reformation. Repenting that he meddled "in this art," he remembers tossing fearfully at night from "Conjuring and adjuring devils and fiends." Fearful that he risked damnation "For using devils to countervail his God," he nonetheless refuses to despair, confident that repentance is effectual, and that

> Mercy sits where Justice holds her seat,
> And from those wounds those bloody Jews did pierce,
> Which by thy magic oft did bleed afresh,
> From thence for thee the dew of mercy drops
> To wash the wrath of high Jehovah's ire,
> And make thee as a new-born babe from sin. (13.85–105)

Traditional here is the invoking of Christ's passion as the effective antidote for evil, the triumph of mercy over justice, the penitential humility of the speaker, the certainty of forgiveness, which is both the mark and consequence of repentance, and the exclusion of Jews from the Christian social body because of their part in the crucifixion.[6]

The orthodoxy of Bacon's repentance is reinforced by other features of the play that are indebted to traditional religion. Albert Wertheim argues that Bacon commits each of the seven deadly sins before his repentance, and that his championing of Prince Edward against Lacy explains the frequent allusions to Prince Edward's disguise as a green man when he courted Margaret of Fressingfield, since green was a favorite color for the devil to wear.[7] These symbolic links between the friar and the prince complement the explicit link between them in their repentance, respectively, of magic and tyrannical passion. Greene uses still another traditional device in *Friar Bacon* when a devil carries someone on his back: the mistress of the Bell at Henley (2.116 SD and 2.157 SD), Friar Bungay (6.170 SD), Vandermast (9.161 SD), and Miles (16.63–64). This was a venerable stage picture by the time Greene used it, anticipated not only by the numerous instances of the devil carrying the Vice on his back in Protestant plays but also by the devil carrying the despairing and the wicked to hell in the graphic arts and in plays from before the Reformation, including Latin liturgical drama.

While Greene thus reacts to Marlowe by recalling orthodox traditions about the devil, he also introduces ambiguities that betray the unresolved impact of Marlowe's bold and iconoclastic dramaturgy. What Greene does to *Dr. Faustus* in *Friar Bacon* therefore parallels what he does to *Tamburlaine* in *Alphonsus*. With regard to Friar Bacon's repentance, for example, Greene tries to have it both ways: Bacon needs to repent (thus correcting Faustus' despair), but at the same time he reaps such gains from his sorcery that by means of it he becomes the most powerful and admired character in the play, just as the conjuror does in *Dr. Faustus*. In keeping with Protestant tradition, Greene celebrates England and English destiny, but the preserver of both is Friar Bacon, and he achieves his reputation through black magic, just as Faustus wins worldly approbation through his league with Mephistopheles. King Henry himself twice refers to Bacon in this role (5.59–60, 9.165–66). Bacon enjoys a series of triumphs in the manner of Tamburlaine or Faustus: over Burden, whose peccadilloes he exposes (2), over Prince Edward, whose disguise he penetrates (5), over Bungay, whose assistance of Lacy and Margaret he prevents (6), and over the German scholar Vandermast (possibly Greene's most explicit response to Faustus), whom Bacon so despises that he will not even dispute with him (9). All of these triumphs are made possible by Bacon's skill in conjuring devils, and in that respect they are identical to the ambiguous triumphs of Faustus. The sympathy Greene generates for Bacon's impressive victories is at odds with the conjuror's repentance.

This ambiguity continues to the end of the play, when Bacon flatters Queen Elizabeth as a future monarch who will bring peace and prosperity to England (16.42–62). This vision constitutes, in effect, an

updated version of the prayer for the monarch that Protestant playwrights had introduced as a substitute for the sacraments – an inevitably
secularizing device, as we saw in chapter 5. What is surprising about
Bacon's vision is that he attributes it to the conjuring skill that he has
since repented: "I find by deep prescience of mine art, / *Which once I tem-
per'd in my secret cell* . . ." (16.42–43, my emphasis). The play's mystical
nationalism is not a mistaken product of Bacon's magic, since Bacon
enunciates the play's climactic vision by means of his "art," and King
Henry endorses it: "Thus glories England over all the west" (16.76).

Greene's devils may be ambiguous in part because he was imprecise
in accommodating learned theories of magic.[8] Burden initially accuses
Bacon of "pyromancy," "hydroman[cy]," and "aeromancy" (2.15–17), or
in other words, of commerce with elemental spirits of fire, water, and
air. Though Bacon himself has already referred to "necromantia" (2.3)
and does so repeatedly thereafter, what Burden mentions is white magic
rather than traditional demonism, and it is not clear, therefore, why he
is so indignant with Bacon for practicing it.

The same confusion arises later, in Bungay's dispute with Vandermast
– "whether the spirits of pyromancy or geomancy be most predominant
in magic" (9.24–25) – and the authorities Vandermast cites are all, for
Greene and his contemporaries, mainstream philosophers, not black
magicians: "Hermes, Melchie, and Pythagoras" (9.29). Yet Vandermast
mixes magical theory with traditional theology, expressly identifying elemental spirits as fallen angels: "when proud Lucifer fell from the
heavens," those who fell with him "Retain'd their local essence as their
faults," so that some fell into fire, and "second faults did rest within the
air," but Lucifer and others

> Were thrown into the center of the earth,
> Having less understanding than the rest,
> As having greater sin and lesser grace.
> Therefore such gross and earthy spirits do serve
> For jugglers, witches, and vild sorcerers;
> Whereas the pyromantic genii
> Are mighty, swift, and of far-reaching power.   (9.58–71)

Using splendid stage spectacles Vandermast goes on to prove the
superior power of pyromantic spirits in the contest that follows. He
therefore vindicates his theodicy, with its absolute assertion that all spirit
magic involves fallen angels. Since Vandermast himself is defeated with
scornful ease by Bacon, the spirits Bacon uses must be even more potent
than Vandermast's, and by the logic of Vandermast's analysis, they

should therefore be less evil, originating in some sphere above the air and fire, rather than in hell. Yet Bacon repeatedly refers to his servants as necromantic fiends, they appear on stage as traditional devils from hell, and Bacon's repentance is orthodox. Greene may well have been striving for theatrical effect, rather than theoretical accuracy, but his confusing devils nonetheless reinforce the impression that he had not entirely shaken off Marlowe's focus on mere power.

This ambiguity affects the love plot as well. Greene parallels magic and love, as William Empson incisively noticed,[9] yet Bacon's art also disrupts Margaret's and Lacy's romantic quest. If Bacon's magic were unambiguously evil, then his interruption of Bungay's marriage of Lacy and Margaret would be consistent, because it could be construed as one of the evils for which he eventually has to repent. In fact, however, Bacon's victory over Bungay is one of his series of triumphs, comically reducing Bungay to crying "Hud, hud" (6.151 SD), as he is carried off by a devil at Bacon's command (6.170 SD) – a demonstration of power on Bacon's part that later climaxes his victory over the hapless Vandermast. This kind of ambiguity is characteristic of Marlowe's bleak and equivocal play worlds, from which it almost certainly derives, yet its function in Greene's romance of repentance and reconciliation is not clear. Morally the play seems at odds with itself.

Marlowe's lingering influence on the ambiguity of *Friar Bacon* appears not only among the better sort but also in Greene's treatment of commoners. Rafe and Miles sometimes manifest the mysterious dignity often accorded to peasants in traditional drama, as they comment with gnomic prescience on the follies of their betters (1.24–35; 2.20–22), speak satirically in Skeltonic rhyme (7.40–42, 63–68), or allude pointedly to Barclay's *Ship of Fools* (7.69–74, 82–87). Though Bacon refers exasperatedly to Miles as "gross dunce" and beats him (5.36 and SD), it is not clear that Miles' comments are really stupid; on the contrary, they may well be satirical, and if they are, then Bacon is the one who looks foolish when he loses patience and beats a servant who has just mocked him. Miles easily perceives that Rafe is disguised as Prince Edward when they come to Oxford: "One wise man, I think, would spring you all" (5.48–49), and when Prince Edward boxes him on the ear, the gesture has precisely the same effect that Bacon's beating has: it makes the prince look merely intemperate and overbearing. These instances of wise folly on the part of clowns in *Friar Bacon* recall the inversion that often occurs in traditional drama, where peasants are graced with greater insight than their overbearing social superiors.

Greene's failure to sustain this inversion may be due to the influence of Marlowe's emphasis on mere power in cross-class social relationships. Rafe's suggestion that he and Prince Edward exchange clothing appears to be morally emblematic in the time-honored manner of traditional drama, and the "hurly-burly" that erupts when Rafe actually dons the prince's clothes (7.32ff.) seems to be an instance of hell literally breaking loose because the prince has become a fool. Yet the effect is to identify Rafe with the devil, not because he has done anything evil but because he has stepped out of his appointed social place by means of his disguise ("These are my lords, and I the Prince of Wales" [7.48–49]). We are thus left with a conflicting image of Rafe as both an expounder of wise folly and a disruptive and devilish commoner.

By the end of the play, a similar unresolved ambiguity surrounds Miles as well. Miles' failure to pay adequate attention to Bacon's experiment with the brazen head results in the failure of the magician's most ambitious experiment, and Bacon furiously curses him as a consequence: "Some fiend or ghost haunt on thy weary steps, / Until they do transport thee quick to hell" (12.129). Bacon's greatest feat is arguably his greatest folly too, of course, as suggested by his repentance and the breaking of his "prospective glass." Yet the last devil to appear in *Friar Bacon* enters long after the magician's repentance, and his mission is to find and punish Miles, in keeping with Bacon's earlier curse. This devil complains that "every charmer with his magic spells / Calls us from nine-fold trenched Phlegiton," just as Bacon has now called this one "To search about the world for Miles his man, / For Miles, and to torment his lazy bones" (15.1–10). This episode complements Bacon's final encomium for the queen in showing how the magician profits from his magic after he has renounced it, and in Miles' case the profit feeds Bacon's vengeance, which contrasts starkly with his earlier expression of penitential humility. Though Miles' joking with the devil serves the purpose of social satire (15.21–44), in the end the devil carries Miles to hell on his back (15.63–64). The play's final verdict on Miles is thus the same as it is on Rafe: uppity servants belong to the devil.

The anonymous author of *A Knack to Know a Knave* (1592) eradicates Greene's ambivalence and answers *Dr. Faustus* forthrightly by reverting to a remarkably archaic dramaturgy. *Knack* pointedly replaces Marlowe's necromancer with the heroic English archbishop, St. Dunstan. Flourishing a century before the Norman conquest, Dunstan won his greatest hagiographical fame for his apotropaic power over devils, spectacularly recorded in Caxton's *Golden Legend* (1483). The author of *Knack* thus chose a hero who contrasts with both Faustus and Bacon in controlling devils without having to repent of it. Dunstan's best known feat is his seizing the devil's nose with a pair of red hot tongs, celebrated with a statue in the Henry VII chapel of Westminster Abbey that remained untouched by the iconoclastic fervor of the mid-sixteenth century.[10] Despite the debunking of Dunstan's miracles by both Foxe's *Acts and Monuments* and Archbishop Parker's *De Antiquitate Britannicae Ecclesiae* (1572), the author of *A Knack to Know a Knave* reverted to a distinctly pre-Reformation hagiography, apparently unimpressed by the weight of Protestant cultural authorities (Parker was the first Elizabethan archbishop of Canterbury).[11]

Though *Knack* omits the favorite episode of Dunstan's seizing the devil's nose, the playwright strongly emphasizes Dunstan's apotropaic power. Dunstan functions psychomachially as Edgar's good angel, in opposition to the corrupt courtier Perin. When Dunstan leaves the king briefly, Perin seizes his chance to influence Edgar toward evil by informing him of Ethenwald's dissembling about his love for Alfrida.[12] The playwright almost certainly borrowed the Ethenwald/Alfrida plot from *Friar Bacon*, since it is not reported in the sources but closely parallels Greene's plot of Lacy and Margaret, and Perin's informing on Ethenwald thus becomes an oppositional action, while Dunstan protects those whom King Edgar threatens in his tyrannical passion. Moreover, Dunstan's intervention to save Ethenwald from destruction by the enraged king is a direct contrast to Bacon's intervention on behalf of Prince Edward. Dunstan calls up a devil called Astoroth, who tells him that Edgar intends to execute Ethenwald; in response, Dunstan resorts to virtuous trickery, sending Astoroth to the king in the form of Ethenwald, to deflect Edgar's murderous anger away from Ethenwald and onto the disguised devil. In the event, however, the ruse is unnecessary, because Dunstan's direct intervention with Edgar successfully persuades the king to repent of his lust and rage, to forgive Ethenwald's dissembling, and to permit the marriage of Ethenwald and Alfrida. Dunstan's successful persuasion of King Edgar also helps to make *Knack* more traditional and psychomachic than *Friar Bacon*, where Prince Edward anguishes and reasons with himself in soliloquy, finally deciding on his own to be merciful (*Friar Bacon*, 8.112–21).

Dunstan's conjuring of Astoroth alludes to Faustus' conjuring of Mephistopheles, for the sake of contrast. Dunstan invokes the devil with a single line: "Astoroth, ascende! Veni, Astoroth, Astoroth, veni!" (p. 576), echoing Marlowe's "Veni, veni, Mephistopheli," but demystifying the necromantic ritual by replacing it with a simple, direct command. The saint's orthodox control of demons is clear in his order to Astoroth to speak, though the devil had initially refused:

> I charge thee, by the eternal living God,
> That keeps the prince of darkness bound in chains,
> And by that sun that thou wouldst gladly see,
> By heaven and earth, and every living thing,
> Tell me that which I did demand of thee.   (p. 577)

While the devil obeys Dunstan unhesitatingly, it is a case of good effectively opposing evil, as the playwright makes clear when Perin attends his dying father, the Bailiff of Hexham. The scene is emblematic, since Perin is one of the Bailiff's four sons, and the other three are Cuthbert the Coney-catcher, Walter Would-have-more, a wealthy and grasping farmer, and John the Precise, who is repeatedly described as "precise" and "pure," and whose diction gives him away as a stage caricature of Elizabethan Puritanism (pp. 578–80).[13] The Bailiff is the "old man" of Pauline theology, whose grasping self-centeredness opposes the communal ideal that Protestant England inherited from the social expectations of parish life that had been shaped by sacramental theology in a predominantly rural context. He commends his sons "for your forward minds, / That in your lives bewray whose sons ye are," as he encourages them not only to make themselves wealthy at others' expense, but to "care not what they say, / That bid you fear the fearful judgment-day" (p. 519). The Bailiff dies unrepentant, and his evil is rewarded when a devil carries him away (p. 520). In contrast to the ambiguity surrounding similar images in *Friar Bacon*, this devil draws attention to the eschatalogical destiny that results from particular moral choices, including choices about how one ought to live in society, and he therefore recalls the devils in earlier Protestant plays and in traditional sacred drama.

Dunstan's "guiling the beguiler" by disguising Astoroth as Ethenwald is a motif from traditional dramaturgy that explains Dunstan's peasant ally in his struggle to purge the kingdom. This ally is Honesty, "a plain man of the country" (p. 508), who is commissioned by the king "To stifle such caterpillars as corrupt the commonwealth" (p. 510), and who therefore performs the same function in his social role as a lay commoner that Dunstan performs at a more exalted social level as a noble cleric. Honesty is the "one that hath *a knack to know a knave*" (p. 507), and he uses his knack to detect the knavery of the Bailiff of Hexham's sons, whom the king turns over to him in the end for grizzly sentencing (p. 590). This image of the commoner is more impressive and positive than Greene's in *Friar Bacon* or Marlowe's in *Dr. Faustus*, and the source of the anonymous author's moderate populism is in moral tradition from before the Reformation. Honesty is actually assisted at one point by Piers the Plowman in bringing a complaint against Walter Would-have-more, the grasping farmer. Acknowledging early tradition, the author has the king exclaim: "Alas, poor Piers! I have heard my father say, / That Piers Plowman was one of the best members in a commonwealth" (p. 560). The archaism of this social ideal is indicated by Robert Aske's complaint after being arrested for leading the Pilgrimage of Grace in 1536: "non hospitalite [is] now in thos places [the former abbeys] kept, but the fermers for the most parte lettes and taverns out the fermes of the same houses to other fermers, for lucre and advauntage to them selfes."[14] Aske complained about a crown policy, the secularization of ecclesiastical property, whose effects continued to rankle, as *Knack to Know* makes clear, well after the Protestant regime had been firmly established and several generations had passed.

A Knack to Know a Knave is in fact a good example of how the mainstream of Elizabethan Protestantism came to depend increasingly on pre-Reformation tradition and eventually eschewed the most radical innovations of its founders as the church adopted a centrist position. The author's rejection of official Elizabethan attitudes toward Dunstan in favor of pre-Reformation hagiography is consistent with his caricature of venal priests as Puritan rather than Catholic. The economic thinking behind the play is religiously inspired and simplistic in its idealism, manifesting the same assumptions that govern the sense of charitable sociability in the mystery plays. The Knight is unfailingly generous, assisting the poor with their debts (p. 549) and lending as much as he can when the king needs to borrow from him (p. 550), though he can lend only a tenth as much as Walter, who calculatingly regards such loans as investments (p. 551). When John the Precise admonishes a beggar by reminding him of St. Paul's saying that "he that will not labour is not worthy to eat," Honesty comments, "Ay, but he remembers not where Christ saith, He that giveth a cup of cold water in my name shall be blessed" (p. 579). The reference is to Matthew 10:42, cited here in the same spirit that Matthew 25 is cited in pageants of the Last Judgment, where charity is the criterion for distinguishing the blessed from the damned. "Good deeds do not justify a man; therefore, I count it sin to give thee anything," rationalizes John the Precise. His first statement is a principal point of Protestant theology, and it is contrasted unsympathetically in this play with the tradition of charity to one's neighbor. "He remembers not where Christ say'th, He that giveth to the poor lendeth unto the Lord," remarks Honesty (p. 579), again referring to a biblical saying (Proverbs 19:17) in a moral injunction that parallels the apocalyptic scenes of the mystery plays.

Indeed, the devil and his influence in *A Knack to Know a Knave* are hardly distinguishable from devils in religious drama that had been staged until shortly before the play was written. The social issues addressed in *Knack* do not make it secular, for they are the same social issues, addressed in the same manner, that appear in the earliest vernacular drama, and the devils that oppose a good society are the same as those that oppose it in pre-Reformation drama. The principal difference is the importance of royal power. *Knack* tacitly accepts the Tudor centralization of power by focusing on King Edgar, rather than Humanum Genus. Yet the psychomachic shape of Edgar's story makes its traditional origin clear.

Less traditional than *A Knack to Know a Knave* is the anonymous *Merry Devil of Edmonton*, originally produced by the Chamberlain's/King's Men in 1599–1604, but eventually becoming one of the most popular plays in the seventeenth century and therefore one of the company's most reliable alternatives to *Dr. Faustus*, which it both imitates and corrects.[15] Peter Fabell is the conjuror in this play, and he is more like Bacon or Faustus than Dunstan, for he is identified as a "renowned Scholler" at Cambridge University (Pro. 9). In fact, the source of Fabell's story is a chapter in the same prose romance that Greene consulted for *Friar Bacon*, but the anonymous author follows his source in making Fabell a champion of young love and therefore a significant contrast to Bacon, whose role in the source is reversed by Greene, when he has Bacon interfere in the romance between Lacy and Margaret at the behest of Prince Edward.

The initial contrast in *Merry Devil*, however, is not with *Friar Bacon* but with *Dr. Faustus*, which the anonymous author imitates at the outset for contrast rather than comparison. For *Merry Devil* begins where *Faustus* ends – with the arrival of a devil to collect his due at the end of a specified time and in keeping with an agreement that the magician had signed with his blood. Fabell contrasts with Faustus in showing no concern at his imminent doom, calmly asking Corbell, the devil, to have a seat while Fabell dispatches some necessary business, then making the "business" an orthodox repentance. Fabell regrets that "this soule, that cost so great a price / As the deere pretious blood of her redeemer" should err through pride, seeking knowledge that leads to hell (Ind. 41–48). "For this alone God cast the Angelles downe" (49). "Man . . . / Seeking to be a God, becomes a Deuill" (58–59). Fabell's repentance, however, is followed by still another surprise, for the magician escapes Corbell's demand as much by comic coercion as by repentance. Fabell, it turns out, has imprisoned Corbell in a magic chair, and Fabell only releases the devil when Corbell swears to allow Fabell seven more years of life. Corbell's comment on this comic reversal of the Faustian bargain is also a sly commendation of this play's cleverness: "Neuer did man thus ouer-reach the Deuill" (Ind. 76–78).

Stage devils are inevitably secularized when they are used to gain commercial advantage in the theatre by crossing audience expectation, as happens repeatedly in *Merry Devil*. Corbell is the only literal devil in the play, and he appears only in its opening scene, but Fabell's magic remains potent and triumphs in the end by being transformed into a metaphor that governs the main plot. What Fabell the magician opposes with "art," "wit," "skill," and "slights" is the scheming of greedy parents who attempt to direct the romantic fortunes of their children.[16] In effect, the pecunious motives of the older generation become the "devil" of the play, and they are opposed by the resourcefulness of young lovers, assisted at crucial junctures by the beneficent magician, who is himself, ironically, "the merry devil of Edmonton." The anonymous playwright not only reverses Greene's association of magic and passion, then, but secularizes a centuries-old stage device by transforming moral and spiritual conflict into social conflict. The latter involves competing generations as well as competing conceptions of family formation – the "open lineage family," as Lawrence Stone calls it, and "companionate marriage."[17] "For age and craft with wit and Art haue met," as Fabell remarks (1.3.133). These conflicts animate much of Elizabethan comedy, of course, including some of the best-known comedies by Shakespeare, but in no other play are they associated so closely or so consistently with vestiges of traditional religion that were imported into London commercial plays by the continuing vitality of stage devils.[18]

The language of traditional religion is used by Sir Arthur Clare, scheming father of Millicent, to describe his daughter's opposition to the match he plans for her: reminding his wife of "crosses" in Waltham, Cheshunt Abbey, and Cheston, he remarks that "tis ominous to passe / Any of these without a pater-noster," but his point is the parallel he then draws:

> Crosses of loue still thwart this marriage,
> Whilst that we two, like spirits, walke the night
> About these stony and hard hearted plots.   (1.1.55–61)

Clare describes the contest between himself and his daughter over her marital destiny in a metaphor of funerary crosses and spirits that haunt graveyards. His allegorization of his plans in the terms of traditional faith is intentionally witty on his part, but it also links the play's induction metaphorically to its action.

Fabell uses "cross" in a similar way to describe the play's generational conflict, but from the opposite perspective: "We may perhaps be crost, but, if we be, / He shall crosse the deuill, that but crosses me" (1.3.27–28). The young lover, Raymond Mounchensey, borrows explicitly moral and eschatalogical terms to lament Clare's greed: "O thou base world, how leprous is that soule / That is once lim'd in that polluted mudde!" (2.2.64–65), and Raymond's father, Sir Richard, rejects Clare to his face in similar terms: "Churle, hell consume thee, and thy pelfe and all!" (2.2.81). The metaphoric "consuming" of "pelfe," in Sir Richard's terms, is what the play is about, from its induction to its triumphant romantic conclusion.

Clare's plan to sequester Millicent in a convent thus serves a symbolic purpose as well, like the one Theseus uses to threaten Hermia in a similar situation at the beginning of *A Midsummer Night's Dream*:

> For aye to be in shady cloister mewed,
> To live a barren sister all your life,
> Chanting faint hymns to the cold fruitless moon.   (1.1.71–73)

But in *The Merry Devil of Edmonton* the threat is realized, and Millicent's escape from the convent where her father secludes her is a major focus of the action, as well as a symbol of her transformation from virginal daughter to loving wife. Following Fabell's advice (2.3.68–72), young Raymond disguises himself as a novice, so he can enter Cheshunt Abbey and liberate Millicent under the noses of her guardians. In a remarkable scene of displaced stage ritual, he blesses the abbey with holy water:

> Peace and charity within,
> Neuer touch't with deadly sin;
> I cast my holy water pure
> On this wall and on this doore,
> That from euill shall defend,
> And keepe you from the vgly fiend:
> Euill spirit, by night nor day,

> Shall approach or come this way;
> Elfe nor Fary, by this grace,
> Day nor night shall haunt this place. (3.2.26–35)

The scene is mildly anti-Catholic in its comic displacement of traditional ritual and its depiction of a passionate "novice" meeting an equally passionate "nun," especially when they embrace on stage in their distinctive religious costumes (3.2.109–21). But the satire is much less virulent than in early Protestant staging of traditional ritual (or for that matter in *Dr. Faustus*), and the point of Raymond's staged ritual has less to do with satire of the old faith than with the refashioning of traditional exorcism's spiritual function into the disempowering of parental opposition to young love. While this way of staging ritual is more benign than Marlowe's, it is also more secular, in that it substitutes entirely different content for traditional ritual. Something like the same symbolic quality appears in *Much Ado about Nothing*, where a friar assists the beleaguered Hero, a Vice-like figure opposes virtuous youthful passion, and the sense of community is strongly identified with romantic love and companionate marriage.

Unlike the main plot, the deer-stealing subplot in *Merry Devil* is not directly related to Fabell's defeat of Corbell in the induction, yet the subplot complements the main plot's focus on a comic magician and his defeat of "devilish" parental authority. For one thing, the subplot strongly reinforces the transition of Millicent from daughter to wife by its parallels between stealing a deer and conducting a romantic courtship.[19] (This is another point it shares with *Friar Bacon*, where Prince Edward enters hunting and frustrated by his obsession with Margaret [1.3.29], just as young Raymond enters "disconsolate & sad" because of his frustrated courtship of Millicent.) The two plots come together in the forest at night, after Millicent has escaped from the convent, when Brian the keeper detains the pursuing fathers long enough for the young people to escape and be married at the George. "I have killed the greatest buck in Brian's walk," declares Smug (4.1.66–67), just after Millicent has rejoined young Mounchensey in the forest.

Second, and more important, the subplot expands the play's social vision. Everyone in it is a commoner, in contrast to the gentry who dominate the main action. Moreover, these commoners violate social privilege by stealing deer, and their carnivalesque violation of royal entitlement thus parallels the young people's violation of the older generation's privilege in the main plot. "But wend we merrily to the forrest, to steale some of the kings Deere," urges Blague, the host of the George

(2.2.52–53). Their populist idealism is akin to the vision of Duke Senior in Shakespeare's *As You Like It*, who is no deer-stealer, because privilege entitles him to the deer on which he subsists, but whose vision of "co-mates and brothers in exile" from the "envious court" expresses the same leveling sentiments as the subplot in *Merry Devil*.

These sentiments are less radical than their class antagonism may seem to suggest, for they belong to the same archaic social vision, contrasting time-honored communal sociability with newfangled greed, that we have seen in *A Knack to Know a Knave*. The carnival atmosphere of *Merry Devil's* subplot has a counterpart in the main plot, when Sir Arthur Clare speaks slightingly of Sir Richard Mounchesney: "the riotous old knight / Hath o'rerun his annual reuenue / In keeping iolly Christmas all the yeere" (1.1.63–65). A more favorable interpretation is offered in soliloquy by Fabell, who asks rhetorically why a marriage alliance with Mounchensey is scorned, despite "thy bounty and thy royall parts,"

> Onely because thy Reuenues cannot reach
> To make her dowage of so rich a ioynture
> As can the heire of wealthy Ierningham?   (1.3.1–8)

Fabell describes here the social virtue of *Merry Devil*, which consists of the same generosity that also appears in *As You Like It*, when old Adam offers Orlando his life savings, and in *A Knack to Know a Knave*, when the beneficent but impoverished knight is contrasted with Walter Would-have-more, the grasping and newly rich farmer. Walter and Sir Arthur Clare could as easily be called "Covetous," given their function in their respective play worlds, because they serve the same social vision that informs *The Castle of Perseverance* two centuries before. What is striking in the later plays is that they link the traditional sense of social virtue to vestiges of its original eschatalogical context, in the form of devils, even if the devil in *Merry Devil* is so attenuated as to be almost entirely identified with the deadly sin of covetousness.

The most strongly secular response to Marlowe's devils appears a good deal earlier than *The Merry Devil of Edmonton*, in two of Shakespeare's early history plays, *1* and *2 Henry VI* (1590). These plays focus on the literal struggle for political power, in contrast to Marlowe's symbolic focus on it in *Dr. Faustus*, where devils belong literally to the cosmic scope of human action. Writing in the early 1590s, Shakespeare seems to respond to the failed Armada invasion of 1588 as confirmation of the Protestant secularizing of community in the form of the independent English church under the crown. In popular culture, as well as in official proclamations, the defeat of the Armada confirmed the new community's providential sense of itself and its oppositional demonizing of the would-be invaders. A popular ballad, whose refrain was "*Kyrye eleison, Christe eleison,*" declares, "We will not change owre *Credo* for Pope, nor boke, nor bell; / And yf the Devil come him self, we'll hounde him back to hell."[20] Thomas Deloney, who contributed the source plot for Dekker's *Shoemaker's Holiday,* wrote at least four ballads about the Armada. One title proposes that the victory was achieved "through the mightie power and prouidence of God, being a speciall token of his gracious and fatherly goodness towards vs, to the great encouragement of all those that willingly fight in the defence of his gospel, and our good Queen of England." In this highly charged atmosphere, Shakespeare's choice to stage a demonically inspired character who represents foreign interests against the godly English nation would seem to respond to post-Armada popular euphoria, placing the first of the *Henry VI* plays in a tradition of Protestant stage devils that extends back to Bale in the 1530s.

Yet Shakespeare marginalizes this tradition even as he appeals to it, in what amounts to a political analysis that goes well beyond the religious secularism of the early reformation. In *1 Henry VI*, the French peasant woman who consorts with "fiends" is also duped by them, as Faustus is, but the point is not that such things are the making of human tragedy; rather, her defeat is a small eddy in the maelstrom of human politics, the source of whose chaotic energy is a contention for political dominance that has no discernible eschatalogical implications. In *2 Henry VI*, the English noblewoman who consults a "spirit" is gulled not by it but by those who arrange the conjuring, because they also arrange for her to be caught in the act of resorting to black magic, thus providing the means for emulous nobles to destroy her husband.

Marlowe's impression on Shakespeare is evident everywhere in the early plays, and it illuminates Shakespeare's innovative reaction to the devils of *Dr. Faustus.* Marlowe's influence appears even in a casual taunt like the one that Lady Anne hurls at Richard of Gloucester, when she first sees him: "What black magician conjures up this fiend?" (*Richard III,* 1.2.34). In *1 Henry VI* Joan la Pucelle literally consorts with fiends and repeatedly invites comparison with the Marlovian overreacher. She is a shepherd's daughter, like Tamburlaine, and she shares her humble social status with Faustus as well, achieving her sudden astounding rise to power and preeminence not only by her unaccountable military success but by her irresistible rhetorical ability. As Tamburlaine persuades

Theridamas to desert Mycetes and join him, Joan persuades Burgundy to desert the English, in a thirty-line speech of patriotic appeal (3.3.41–77), whose force he keenly feels, though earlier he had dismissed her as the dauphin's "trull" (2.2.28). "She hath bewitched me with her words" (3.3.58), he later admits, nonplussed by how

> these haughty words of hers
> Have battered me like roaring cannon-shot
> And made me almost yield upon my knees.   (3.3.78–80)

Joan's cynical response, "Done like a Frenchman: turn and turn again" (3.3.85), recalls Tamburlaine's aside to Techelles, after his powerful speech to Zenocrate: "Techelles, women must be flattered" (*1 Tamburlaine*, 1.2.303).[21]

But Joan is like Faustus as well, in that she achieves her astonishing worldly success through the agency of hell, though she dissimulates the source of her strength, hypocritically attributing it to heaven in lines that are inspired by the satirical Vice of anti-Catholic morality plays. Acknowledging that she is a mere shepherd's daughter, "My wit untrained in any kind of art," she claims to have been enabled by "Heaven and our Lady gracious," who appeared to her while she was watching her sheep,

> And, in a vision full of majesty
> Willed me to leave my base vocation
> And free my country from calamity.   (1.2.72–81)

Shakespeare's anti-Catholicism is closer to Elizabethan expectation than Marlowe's: Joan's hypocrisy and hellish inspiration as a Catholic saint derive directly from the anti-French and anachronistically Protestant bias of Hall and Holinshed.[22] Joan's sexual avidity parallels Faustus' concupiscence, though hints of this trait in Joan are offered by Hall. By the end of *1 Henry VI* Joan claims to have seduced two French noblemen besides the dauphin (5.4.72–82), but he is her first and easiest conquest (1.2.65–150). In contrast to the gullible French prince, Talbot is a heroic English warrior who stoutly resists Joan, because he immediately perceives her demonic motivation: "Devil or devil's dam, I'll conjure three: / Blood will I draw on thee – thou art a witch" (1.5.5–6). Even Talbot is daunted by Joan as long as her derivative power is ascendant, but he never ceases to believe that she is a pious fraud and therefore an unsettling challenge to providential assumptions: "Heavens, can you suffer hell so to prevail?" (1.5.9; cf. 2.1.25–27; 3.2.38–40, 52, 64, 122).

Joan and Talbot would appear to be two sides of a warrior portrait in *1 Henry VI* that effectively corrects the portrait in *Tamburlaine*.[23] A paragon of feudal piety, Talbot kneels before the king with "submissive loyalty of heart" (3.4.10), ascribing "the glory of his conquest got / First to my God, and next unto your grace" (3.4.11–12). He makes no claims to self-derived virtue, as Tamburlaine does, and his allusion to Icarus, a favorite Marlovian image, is not the boast of an overweening aspirer but the courageous determination of a father to fight beside his son against overwhelming odds (4.6.54–57).[24] As it turns out, young John Talbot is killed first, and his father again compares him to Icarus for his courage:

> Dizzy-eyed fury and great rage of heart
> Suddenly made him from my side to start
> Into the clust'ring battle of the French;
> And in that sea of blood my boy did drench
> His over-mounting spirit; and there died
> My Icarus, my blossom, in his pride.   (4.7.11–16)

Talbot's heroism is marked by two seemingly contrary traits: the ambition proper to a soldier, in contrast to the cowardice of the French, and "submissive loyalty of heart" that directs his energy into channels of service to God and king. That these traditional feudal obligations also include the national interest of England in opposition to French Catholics is one of the play's strongest indications of its distinctively Protestant heritage.[25]

Talbot's heroic qualities contrast not only with Tamburlaine but with Joan, who effectively acquires the negative qualities of Tamburlaine with little or none of his ambiguity, and who thus becomes a demonic parody of Talbot.[26] Following Hall, Shakespeare emphasizes the impropriety of a female warrior: Joan's promise to "exceed my sex" (1.2.90) is not merely descriptive but an implicit self-condemnation for exceeding presumably natural limitations.[27] Her meteoric social rise is not, as she claims, the work of heaven, but of hell, ultimately producing the willful self-deception that goes with deception by fiends, as in *Faustus* and later plays such as *Macbeth* and Barnabe Barnes' *The Devil's Charter* (1606). Her over-weening pride is evident in her rejection of her father as a "Decrepit miser, base ignoble wretch" and her claim to be "descended of a gentler blood" (5.4.7–9). She is a liar, in denying not only her parenthood but her league with hell (5.4.42), a hypocrite, a sexual and social overreacher, and a dupe of the spirits to whom she resorts for temporary dominance. At the height of her success, after the destruction of Talbot, her fiendish assistants abandon her. Appearing in response to her conjuration, they mutely refuse to serve her further and eventually depart (5.3.1–29). "My ancient incantations are too weak," laments Joan, "And hell too strong for me to buckle with" (5.3.27–28). The bawdy suggestion in "buckle" (used earlier to describe her encounter with the dauphin [1.2.95]) is a canny gloss on the erotic suggestions of Faustus' involvement with Mephistopheles. Like Faustus, Joan discovers the predatory power of hell to her undoing.

Shakespeare thus offers a portrait of demonic involvement with human beings that is closer to orthodox expectation than Marlowe's, but while *1 Henry VI* eradicates Marlowe's cosmic ambiguities, it adds new complexities about the merely human struggle for power that Marlowe never implies. Though Joan and Talbot are undoubtedly the most heroic characters in *1 Henry VI*, neither of them ultimately makes any difference to the outcome of events. Talbot is defeated by the secular struggle for power – manifested in the factionalism of the English court – not by Joan's recourse to demons. Factional strife, in the form of the erupting quarrel between York and Lancaster, prevents relief from reaching Talbot, allowing the French to defeat him with superior numbers. Each side blames the other for England's defeat, as the choric Sir William Lucy recognizes: "Whiles they each other cross, / Lives, honors, lands, and all, hurry to loss" (4.3.52–53). The providential clarity of England's war with France is a vestige of the heroic past that dies with Henry V: the properly "submissive" Talbot opposes overweening Joan, obedience to heaven opposes alliance with hell, England opposes France, cosmic order opposes disorder. But the clear bifurcation of this struggle does not apply to the play's principal action, which involves endless infighting at the English court. Lacking effective central authority, England is adrift in a chaos of competing political interests: Winchester vs. Gloucester (1.3), Somerset vs. Suffolk (2.4), York vs. the king himself (2.5), Suffolk vs. Gloucester (5.3 and 5.5), and potentially, Suffolk and Margaret vs. the king (5.5).[28]

Relegating stage devils to the margins of *1 Henry VI* contrasts strikingly with *Dr. Faustus*, for Shakespeare thereby marginalizes the cosmic frame of human action. Both playwrights acknowledge *libido dominandi* as the motive for demonic activity, but whereas Marlowe recalls the ancient doctrine in order to subvert it, Shakespeare takes it for granted and de-emphasizes it in favor of the struggle for power among human beings themselves, quite apart from overt demonic motivation.[29] The cosmic implications of this secular struggle are difficult to discern. We cannot even be certain that Joan's fiends abandon her because Providence has overruled their power. To what end? York captures and destroys Joan, to be sure, but York is a principal contributor to English political chaos, even though he is the immediate instrument of the French witch's undoing. Moreover, in the same scene where York finally achieves what Talbot could not, Suffolk and Margaret of Anjou seduce each other, with consequences that clearly portend disaster for England: the loss of Maine and Anjou without a blow being struck and the elevation of an overbearing French woman to the English throne. Demons contribute little or nothing to the distress of human political life, in comparison to what human beings contribute on their own. *1 Henry VI* does not deny the lust for power as the root of evil, but it does seem to question whether demonic motivation can always be assigned to particular human actions and especially to those that most seriously threaten the national community.

The marginal fiends of *1 Henry VI* are complemented by a single marginal "spirit" in *2 Henry VI*, whose name, "Asnath," is a transparent anagram of "Sathan." This spirit appears in a context that again recalls the Luciferian archetype: Asnath is evoked by Bolingbroke, a conjuror, and Margery Jourdain, a witch, at the behest of Eleanor Cobham, who hopes to enlist supernatural aid in gaining the throne for her husband, Humphrey Duke of Gloucester. Eleanor's overweening ambition makes her a successor to Joan la Pucelle and, like Joan, a spiritual and rhetorical successor to Tamburlaine. She asks Gloucester why his eyes are "fixed to the sullen earth," as if that is where he could find the crown. Instead, she urges,

> Put forth thy hand; reach for the glorious gold.
> What, is't too short? I'll lengthen it with mine;
> We'll both together lift our heads to heaven
> And nevermore abase our sight so low
> As to vouchsafe one glance unto the ground.   (1.2.5–15)

Like Lucifer and Tamburlaine, Eleanor longs for power and a crown that are not rightly hers, and her determination to have them is her undoing, as it was Lucifer's before her.

Shakespeare complicates this picture, however, in ways that make Eleanor more sympathetic than Joan and that make Asnath even less important than Joan's fiends. Indeed, Asnath is Shakespeare's invention. In Hall's account, no one conjures, but Margery Jourdain makes a wax image of the king for Eleanor, "whiche by their sorcery, a litle and litle consumed, entendyng therby in conclusion to waist, and destroy the kynges person, and so to bryng hym death."[30] Nothing in the conjuring scene in *2 Henry VI* involves a direct threat to the king, as the wax image does in Hall's history. Asnath utters a series of ambiguous prophecies, including one about the king that might be construed as favoring Gloucester, at least in the mind of someone like Eleanor, who desperately wants him to succeed, but this prophecy works in the same way as the prophecies of the equivocating fiends in *Macbeth*, for its grammatical ambiguity makes it apply with equal truth – depending on how one construes it – to the present duke of Gloucester and to his successor in the title: "The duke yet lives that Henry shall depose, / But him outlive and die a violent death" (1.4.31–32).

The most serious threat in the conjuring scene is not Eleanor or even Asnath but Hume, a priest whose aid Eleanor seeks in securing the services of Bolingbroke and Jourdain. Hume may evoke the sense of espionage that pervades *Dr. Faustus*, for Shakespeare departs from Hall in making Hume a double agent: having been hired by Eleanor, he also accepts payment from Winchester and Suffolk to inform on her, because they wish to destroy Gloucester (1.2.87–107). Though Hume is small fry, like many of those in Elizabeth's secret service, he nonetheless succeeds in destroying the good duke, yet his destructiveness has nothing to do with demonic power. In *2 Henry VI*, the impenetrable duplicity of secret agency is not a cosmic metaphor, as it is in *Dr. Faustus*. Rather, it is just another manifestation of human dissimulation and treachery in the quest for power. The conjuring incident, which *does* involve demonic power, is bracketed on one side by Hume's plotting and on the other by York's surprise interruption of the conjuring. As in *1 Henry VI*, the real peril to the political life of England is not demonic consultation (Eleanor comes across as pathetic rather than wicked) but human self-deception, duplicity, and ambition.

The most striking distinction between demonic and human activity in *2 Henry VI* occurs in the popular insurrection led by Jack Cade. This episode has long been interpreted as an indication of Shakespeare's own attitude toward popular uprising, and recent opinion has divided on the question of whether it also represents his attitude toward popular culture as a whole.[31] At the very least, one can say with certainty that Shakespeare depicts Cade differently from the way Greene depicts Miles and Rafe in *Friar Bacon and Friar Bungay*. Whereas Greene identifies commoners with demonic disorder, Cade is like Shakespeare's other disrupters of public order in the *Henry VI* plays, noble and common alike, in that he has no demonic motivation; whatever he does, he does on his own initiative. This includes his being a secret agent in Ireland, where he disguised himself as a "shag-haired crafty kern" in order to acquire information on York's behalf (3.1.367–70). Though York refers to Cade as a "devil" (3.1.371), it is clear that the power relations between them have nothing literally to do with hell, however hellish they may be. York exploits Cade, who exploits kerns, just as York and others exploit another secret agent, Hume, in his exploitation of Eleanor Cobham. Competitive infighting is an established characteristic of devils and vices in pre-Reformation drama, but what is striking in Shakespeare's early histories is that the young playwright separates this kind of destructive ambition from literal demonic activity. No matter what social prejudice went into his making, Cade is not demonized, unlike the commoners in *Friar Bacon*; like his social betters, Cade is more than able to motivate himself in the quest for power.

The *Henry VI* plays contribute to another characteristic Shakespearean secularization of traditional stage diablerie, in the way they treat the Vice. As Bernard Spivack has argued, Shakespeare adapts traditions of personified abstraction to named human characters in complex and ingenious ways.[32] Shakespeare would appear to be more innovative in this regard than Spivack suggests, however, because earlier Vices do not depart as clearly or as far from pre-Reformation tradition as Spivack alleges.[33] Three male characters in the *Henry VI* plays reflect the influence of Vice tradition, each succeeding the other, even as he exceeds his predecessor in virulence and destructiveness, with the most potent of them being Richard Duke of Gloucester, afterwards King Richard III. Richard's antecedents in the earlier plays are William de la Pole, the Earl of Suffolk, in *1* and *2 Henry VI*, and Richard Plantagenet, afterwards Duke of York, the father of Richard III, in *2* and *3 Henry VI*. What is striking about these Vice characters in the *Henry VI* plays is that they also have nothing literally to do with devils or hell. Even the imagery of hell is less frequently associated with them than with the Vice-like Richard in *Richard III*, which is a different kind of play from its predecessors, despite the continuity of some characters. The dissociation of Vice figures from literal devils in the *Henry VI* plays is consistent with the separation of devils themselves from effective action in *1* and *2 Henry VI*, in that both emphasize the uniquely human derivation of political chaos and thereby sharpen the plays' focus on secular political action.

Suffolk is introduced in *1 Henry VI* as a young nobleman studying at the Inns of Court, a favorite target of pre-Reformation moral satire, and he takes an ominously self-centered view of his profession, determining to "frame the law unto my will," because he "never yet could frame my will to it" (*1 Henry VI*, 2.4.7–9). Suffolk is a major contributor to the outbreak of hostility that issues in the Wars of the Roses, and he seduces Margaret of Anjou at the play's end. As Spivack points out (pp. 386–87), Suffolk's self-serving rationalization in this scene, "She's beautiful, and therefore to be wooed; / She is a woman, therefore to be won" (5.3.78–79), echoes similar sentiments by Aaron the Moor in *Titus Andronicus* and by Richard of Gloucester in *Richard III*. In *2 Henry VI* Suffolk is the principal agent behind the destruction of Humphrey Duke of Gloucester, the only civic-minded character who attempts to prevent a collapse into mere power-seeking. Suffolk has little of the theatrical brilliance that characterizes Richard III, but he anticipates Richard, and also looks back to the Vice, in his inexplicable viciousness and his determination to sow dissent and mistrust.

York is Vice-like in his ambition, his covert manipulation of others, and his soliloquy, quoted above, in which he describes Cade. His exploitation of both Cade and Hume is characteristic of the Vice, who delights maliciously in making others his dupes. From the time that Mortimer tells York (then Richard Plantagenet) why Henry V executed York's father, Richard Earl of Cambridge (*1 Henry VI*, 2.5), York works tirelessly to promote his own interests at the expense of others. Talbot is destroyed by the French because of York's quarrel with Somerset, and York supports Suffolk in the destruction of Humphrey Duke of Gloucester. In two lengthy soliloquies in *2 Henrv VI*, he outlines his plans in the manner of the Vice, describing his potential targets, revealing his strategy, and declaring his ambition (1.1.212–57 and 3.1.331–83).

Yet both Suffolk and York are secular power-seekers, whose ambition is perverse because it is damaging to political cohesion, not because it poses any explicit risk to their own or others' virtue or eternal destiny. The funeral of Henry V at the beginning of *1 Henry VI* is, in effect, a ritual that mourns the declining secular coherence in English national life, for the ideal of centralized monarchical power in these plays is itself a secularization of the ritual social cohesion – the sacramental social body – that informs pre-Reformation drama. The *Henry VI* plays thus effectively assume the values of the nascent Protestant nation, even though their ostensible subject is fifteenth-century baronial civil warfare. Choric laments for "England" are for a political entity that finds its coherence in a powerful centralized monarchy, symbolized by the king "of so much worth," whose untimely death is lamented at the beginning of *1 Henry VI* (1.1.7). The anti-Catholicism embodied in Joan la Pucelle is not gratuitous; it is a vestige of what opposed the Protestant new community, composed of the monarchy and the suffering martyrs, whose stoic and triumphant deaths are recalled in the death of Talbot, voicing his confidence in providential vindication, like the Old Man in *Dr. Faustus* and countless martyrs in Foxe. The fact that Talbot is sacrificed to English ambition and factionalism, rather than to Catholic authority, is a measure of the play's departure from the religious secularity of early Reformation plays.

By the same token, stage demons and the human beings who derive from the Vice in the *Henry VI* plays are vestiges of the cosmic opposition that threatened the sacramental social body and its Protestant successor. Shakespeare's removal of the originating cosmic context that surrounded these characters is telling. The judgments made about them morally are identical to moral judgments made about their vicious originals. Richard of Gloucester's "I am myself alone" (*3 Henry VI*, 5.6.83) expresses the same myopia and self-absorption that innumerable personifications of evil express in pre-Reformation plays, and the stage tradition enriches Richard's declaration, making it darker and more profound.[34] Yet the context of the traditional expressions has changed definitively. Our concern in Shakespeare's early history plays is invariably directed to political success or failure, not to the eschatalogical warrants for moral choice. Though the playwright's political judgment is incisive in these plays, his referring of communal morality to the good of the nation is a strikingly diminished substitute for cosmic destiny.

At the same time that the young Shakespeare acknowledges his debt to Marlowe, then, he also reacts to Marlowe's bleak cosmic outlook by making his devils more orthodox, even as he pushes them to the margin of an action that is more secular than any Marlowe imagined. The histrionic Machiavellianism of Marlowe's *Jew of Malta* is less politically incisive than the struggle for power in Shakespeare's *Henry VI* plays, where the secular spirit of Machiavelli indeed prevails. Not everyone reacted to Marlowe this way, as we have seen, and ambivalence about stage devils continues well into the seventeenth century. The cool secularity of Shakespeare's history plays is unusual in the tradition, but playwrights quickly invented new ways to secularize stage devils, and they learned rapidly from each other, as we shall see, in their treatment of this archaic stage device.

CHAPTER EIGHT

The devil and the sacred on the Shakespearean stage: theatre and belief

Stage devils thrived on what Andrew Gurr calls "the Shakespearean stage," from the 1570s to the end of the London commercial drama's first phase in 1642, when all the theatres were closed by act of parliament.[1] Devils appeared in about forty new plays that we know of during this time, with the latest of them being performed for the first time as late as 1641.[2] This is an average of a little under one new play a year, and that figure does not reckon with the repeated revival of popular plays like *Dr. Faustus* or *The Merry Devil of Edmonton*. It is not unreasonable to assume that in those years one could almost always have found a devil play in performance somewhere in London.

This remarkable record indicates that traditional dramaturgy survived well beyond the time that it is usually assumed to have disappeared. To be sure, playwrights were endlessly inventive, and competition among the commercial theatres produced innovations in stage devilry, as in everything else. Prominent among these was a satirical distance and self-conscious theatricality that has led to almost complete neglect of stage devils in the seventeenth century, on the assumption that no one took them seriously any longer. This assumption fits well into a teleological narrative of accomplished secularization in English drama, and it also reinforces the oppositional thinking that pits enlightened secularity against benighted superstition. On this reading, playwrights in the early seventeenth century were harbingers of the coming age of reason, and their satirical and metadramatically sophisticated rejection of age-old beliefs about the devil and his influence is evidence of their progressive thinking. As Stephen Greenblatt remarks about official claims that exorcism was mere theatre: "Performance kills belief; or rather acknowledging theatricality kills the credibility of the supernatural."[3] If this was true of mainstream opposition to exorcism, it would seem to be all the more true of plays that satirize conjuration, demonic possession, and exorcism by staging them as a mere performance.

The reality, however, was a great deal more complex. How could stage devils have remained popular for so long, if satirical treatment and self-reflexive performativity destroyed their credibility in the theatre? The seventeenth century was preoccupied with demonology, as witch hysteria attests, and this preoccupation should give us pause, for it continued after the Restoration, as did stage devils. Davenant added devils to his adaptation of Shakespeare's *Macbeth* in 1664, and he and Dryden added them again when they collaborated on a revision of *The Tempest* in 1674. Restoration stage devils are not part of the present story, but they are evidence that audiences continued to find devils fascinating on stage for much longer than critical generalizations have suggested.

The ability of early audiences to tolerate inherent ambiguities in theatrical illusion is hard to overestimate. Every stage devil necessarily involves an actor in a costume and thereby produces an unavoidable ambiguity at the heart of what the play presents as an instance of the uncanny. In this respect, stage devils are analogous to stage miracles. The mechanisms that enabled actors to produce Antichrist's false miracles in the fifteenth-century play of *Antichrist* from Chester were the same mechanisms that enabled them to produce true miracles, as when blood pours from Christ's side as proof of his resurrected corporeality in the Chester play of the *Ascension*. Moreover, the demons who enabled Antichrist's false miracles were actors in costume, like the angels who welcomed an actor playing Christ in Chester, when he ascended by means of stage machinery to heaven.

Jonas Barish has documented antitheatrical writers' attempts to condemn theatre as mere illusion from the fourteenth century onwards, but their attempts seem to have been regularly frustrated by auditors' eager credulity.[4] It is not clear, in fact, that the situation had changed very much by the early seventeenth century, when new ambiguities complicated the credibility of theatrical illusion. The most serious complication was introduced by Protestantism, which took elements of heresy for the new gospel and rejected aspects of the old truth as heresy, thereby putting serious strain on the opposition of truth and heresy. From historical hindsight, it is hard to believe that traditional binary thinking did not collapse immediately under this strain, yet it evidently did not. Catholics and Protestants alike shared fundamental assumptions that remained alive throughout the seventeenth century – most fundamental, perhaps, being the opposition of good and evil in the sacred history of cosmic struggle between God and the devil. This opposition was so essential to belief that a commonplace assertion equated the certainty of the devil's existence with that of God.[5]

The opposition of God and the devil is important for drama because it closely parallels the opposition of truth and illusion. The point of Antichrist's false miracles in the Chester *Antichrist* is that they only *seem* to be miracles; Antichrist was enabled to deceive his weakminded auditors because the devil is a deceiver, and the devil enabled Antichrist to perform stunning feats by means of prestidigitation and the manipulation of natural forces. Achieving these feats in a play was troubling, but not for the seemingly obvious reason that truth claims were made by means of actorly skill and theatrical mechanisms. Rather, what troubled contemporaries was the possibility that real devils might be at work on stage. This is one reason why antitheatrical writers condemned the theatre, and it is also why stories circulated about the extra devil in Marlowe's *Dr. Faustus*.[6] The porous boundaries between theatrical and demonic illusion are suggested in John Heywood's *Foure PP* (1520–22), when the Pardoner tells of a visit he made to hell, where he met a devil whom he knew well, "For oft in the play of corpus Cristi / He hath played the deuyll at Couentry."[7] Not only could devils appear in plays, but plays affected the way people responded to devils. One of the earliest published accounts of demonic possession compares the possessed, Alexander Nyndge, to "the picture of the Deuill in a play, with an horrible roaring voyce."[8] According to a 1615 account, performances of *Dr. Faustus* prompted someone attempting a real conjuration to imitate Edward Alleyn in the title role.[9]

Concern about demonic intervention in the theatre, as in real life, is understandable in view of contemporary thinking about the way demons operated. John Cotta rephrased a common assumption, when he asserted in 1616 that "nature is nothing els but the ordinary power of God in all things created, among which the divell being a creature, is constrained, and therefore subject to that universal power."[10] If the devil was part of created nature, then his operations were not different in kind from those of human beings; they were different only in degree, speed, and power. As Stuart Clark points out, "writers on demonology had to explain not one but four categories of extraordinary events: real demonic effects, illusory demonic effects, real non-demonic effects, and illusory non-demonic effects. And among the non-demonic, they had to allow for both the spontaneous workings of nature and those produced by human ingenuity."[11] If the best of intellectual opinion could not distinguish demonic from human illusion, then it is understandable that audiences in the theatre – and perhaps even actors themselves – might regard the illusions they witnessed (or performed) differently from the way a modern audience does.

Protestantism complicated the credibility of theatrical illusion not only by inverting some of the criteria for truth and falsehood but also by rejecting Catholic claims to miracle, on the grounds that "miracles are ceased," as the Archbishop of Canterbury puts it (anachronistically, because he is a pre-Reformation archbishop) in *Henry V* (1.1.68). This position grew out of early Protestant rejection of how traditional religion interpreted the eucharist, but by the early seventeenth century the focus of Protestant demystifying efforts had shifted from the mass to demonic possession and dispossesion. Since demonic actions were natural, not supernatural, possession was not, strictly speaking, a *miraculum*, but it was certainly a superhuman *mirum*, an uncanny wonder that increased the charismatic prestige of the dispossessor, and the English Protestant church resisted it. To be sure, resistance developed gradually. In 1571 no less an establishment figure than John Foxe performed a dispossession, and Edward Nyndge published the account of his brother's possession in 1573, with no apparent embarrassment or concern for official disapproval.[12] Eventually, however, dispossession was officially forbidden in the canons of 1604, which were anticipated by Samuel Harsnett's books, one directed against Puritans in 1599 and another against Catholics in 1603, arguing that dispossession was a non-demonic effect – in fact, an *illusory* non-demonic effect or in other words, a piece of clever theatre. It is important that Harsnett wrote as a churchman (he held multiple livings as secretary to Richard Bancroft, bishop of London, and was later advanced to the archbishopric of York after his patron became archbishop of Canterbury), so he limits his attack to dispossession – or exorcism, as it was called by Catholics, who used sacred objects and a prescribed ritual eschewed by Protestants. In other words, Harsnett's skepticism is limited and strategic, and his treatise is therefore not directed at devils per se, unlike Reginald Scot's *Discoverie of Witchcraft* (1584), from which Harsnett liberally borrowed.[13]

In short, Harsnett is a good example of religious secularization: he demystifies religion in order to purify it, as Bale had done before him. Harsnett may have contributed to the erosion of belief that eventually produced reasoned atheist arguments in place of the skeptical aphorisms attributed to Raleigh and Marlowe, but Harsnett was far from such arguments himself. Something like Harsnett's view is represented by Hotspur's tactless mockery of Glendower for his claims to be able to control devils in Shakespeare's *1 Henry IV*. Despite Hotspur's apparently materialistic skepticism, he defends his attack by claiming that "such a deal of skimble-skamble stuff . . . puts me from my faith" (3.1.150–51). This is the voice of religious secularization, which is skeptical about traffic with demons because it is an offense to faith, not because it is an offense to unbelief. The strength of belief was such that even eighteenth-century atheists spoke with a minority voice. No less a luminary than William Whiston, who studied with Newton and succeeded him in the Lucasian chair of mathematics at Cambridge, defended the credibility of demons, writing as late as 1737 that they were "no more to be denied, because we cannot, at present, give a direct solution of them, than are Mr. Boyle's experiments about the elasticity of the air; or Sir Isaac Newton's demonstrations about the power of gravity, are [sic] to be denied, because neither of them are to be solved by mechanical causes."[14]

Stephen Greenblatt has argued that Shakespeare seems to voice contemporary skepticism by staging fake or misguided possesion or dispossession in three plays: *The Comedy of Errors, Twelfth Night,* and *King Lear*.[15] Greenblatt's argument that religious symbols in *King Lear* are "emptied out" is compelling, though the effect may have more to do with Shakespearean tragedy than with Shakespearean drama as a whole. We depend "upon symbols and symbol systems," Clifford Geertz observes, "with a dependence so great as to be decisive for our creatural viability and, as a result, our sensitivity to even the remotest indication that they may prove unable to cope with one or another aspect of experience raises within us the gravest sort of anxiety."[16] If this sort of anxiety is what makes *Lear* so powerful, then the play's effect depends on its constructing a dependable symbol system in the first place – that is, a system so close to believed symbol that its inability to cope with what happens in the play produces the kind of anxiety that is the tragic effect of *King Lear*. In short, the emptying out of religious symbol would seem to be strategic for *King Lear*; similarly constructed symbolic worlds work very differently in *Macbeth* and the romances.

One difference between *Comedy of Errors* and *Twelfth Night* is that opposition to Puritan dispossession increased in the 1590s, when Darrel began his spectacular campaign, prompting Harsnett to publish his *Discovery of the Fraudulent Practises of One John Darrel* in 1599. The social energy, to borrow Greenblatt's phrase, of the English church's resistance to dispossession would seem to be at work in Shakespeare's satirical portrait of Malvolio. Maria calls him "a kind of puritan" (2.3.139) and then exclaims "The devil a puritan that he is" (2.3.146). Feste's fake dispossession of Malvolio would therefore seem to be a strategic satire aimed at both religious extremes, since Feste disguises himself as Sir Thopas the priest, remarking that "I wish I were the first that ever dissembled in such a gown" (4.2.5–6), and his dispossession of a "kind of puritan" turns the tables on Darrel the dispossessor.

Shakespeare was not alone in staging fake demonic effects and in aiming them at Puritans in particular. Almost certainly in response to the canons of 1604, the anonymous *Puritan Widow* staged a fake conjuration of demons in 1606, and its metatheatricality and demystification of the conjuror's power involve specific strategic satire. By 1606 Puritans were chiefly associated with dispossession because of Darrel, and dissenters continued to be thought of as dispossessors until well into the eighteenth century because they were identified with "enthusiasm" in religion.[17] In *The Puritan Widow*, Lady Plus' extraordinary gullibility becomes, in effect, a satire of the Puritan community's response to charismatic leaders, like Darrel, who practiced dispossession. This explains why those who gull her are charlatans and confidence men – an unemployed scholar, George Pieboard, and a convicted highwayman, Captain Idle, who has to be sprung from prison to pull off the fake conjuration. The conjuring scene itself is as frankly demystifying as anything in early drama.[18] When George tries to persuade the reluctant Captain Idle to do a pretend conjuring, he compares it to a stage conjuration, which of course this is: "haue you neuer seen a stalking-stamping Player, that will raise a tempest with his toung, and thunder with his heeles?" (3.5.84–86). The captain in fact performs in this way, as his comment after the conjuring indicates: "Paine? I protest *George*, my heeles are sorer, then a Whitson Morris-dancer" (4.2.179–80). In the meantime, he laughs so hard about the pretense that he can hardly pull it off (4.2.119–20). In short, the scene does the same cultural work as Harsnett's books: it satirizes theatrical conjuring in order to suggest that trafficking with demons is a theatrical trick.

The metadrama of *The Puritan Widow* is, however, limited, and its purpose is to expose Puritans, thus supporting the demystifying efforts of the English church. Metatheatrical references are not necessarily a comment on the devil himself, let alone on all religious symbols. Rather, they reinforce the play's satire of Puritan fascination with uncanny effects by exposing them as nothing more than theatrical illusion. Captain Idle professes to be concerned about "the Act past in Parliament against Coniurers and Witches" (3.5.160–61), alluding to the witchcraft legislation of 1604, which was not revoked until 1736.[19] But Idle has an ulterior motive for expressing this concern: he wants to do the conjuration privately, inside Lady Plus' house, in order to tempt her brother, Sir Godfrey, to eavesdrop on it and thus overhear what the purported demon has to say about the location of a gold chain that Sir Godfrey thinks he lost but that Pieboard really stole and deliberately hid in order to return it and thereby persuade its owner that Pieboard is trustworthy. In other words, the con men's only expressed concern about a real law against trafficking with demons is to draw someone into their confidence in order to fleece him more effectively – a fine bit of satire against supposed Puritan charlatanism where demonic effects are concerned. Another expressed concern of Captain Idle, however, comes closer to the ambiguity we have noticed in contemporary theatrical illusion. While still in Marshalsea Prison, Idle has severe doubts about fake conjuring, because he fears it might succeed: "But here lyes the fear on't, how <if> in this false conjuration, a true Deuill should pop vp indeed?" (3.5.125–27). George dismisses this concern (3.2.128–31), and no "true" devil appears, but Idle's question remains unanswerable in this play and indeed in the mental world of its auditors. The cynicism of con men coexists with fear of the devil, and nothing in the play suggests that the two might be incongruous.

The fake conjuration in *The Puritan Widow* is paralleled by fake demonic possession and dispossession in two of Jonson's plays: *Volpone* (1605–6) and *The Devil Is an Ass* (1616). For Jonson too, the critique is strategic rather than general, serving the purposes of political and religious satire in the immediate context.[20] In both plays the perpetrators of the trick are characters like Pieboard and Captain Idle: grasping, conniving, exploitative, and finally exposed as frauds – albeit memorably funny and theatrically engaging; in both plays, they are directed by someone even more crafty and grasping than themselves, who acts as a theatrical coach; both plays borrow details from Harsnett's *Discovery of the Fraudulent Practises of One John Darrel*; indeed, Merecraft in *Devil Is an Ass* explicitly commends "little Darrel's tricks" as models for Fitzdotterel to imitate when he fakes his possession.[21] These parallels all point to a particular satirical context that involves Puritan violation of the 1604 canons against exorcism. The situations in both plays, written ten years apart, are similar to those of Darrel's dispossessions, as Harsnett caustically describes them, including a coach (Darrel) and a performer (those whom Darrel claimed to dispossess). The point of metatheatre in Jonson's fake dispossessions is the same as the fake conjuration in *The*

Puritan Widow – not to empty out religious symbols but to expose abuse of them, at least from the point of view of the English church.

In both *Volpone* and *The Devil Is an Ass*, metatheatre is not confined to fake demonic possession. Volpone's extraordinary shape-changing is the very essence of acting, and the de facto limits of his apparently infinite performability are the source of his undoing in the end. But this kind of character was anything but innovative in English drama, as Rainer Pineas argues in comparing Volpone to the Vice of moral drama.[22] "O my fine devil!" exclaims Volpone of Mosca, his equally protean assistant, when Mosca appears to be pulling their irons out of the fire, late in the play.[23] In reality, Mosca is preparing to double-cross Volpone in another time-honored gesture of vicious evil – the characteristic infighting of devils and vices that we noticed in chapter 4. The imagery of hell grows increasingly frequent as the play draws to its close, and the principal vice of all the characters in the main plot is covetousness, the besetting sin of Humanum Genus in *The Castle of Perseverance* in the early fifteenth century. Given the corresponding language of "fool" and "knave," Jonson's diabolical imagery recalls early Tudor morality plays by Skelton and Medwall. The point is that nothing in the diabolism of *Volpone* satirizes devils per se, or is even condescending about them, given the context of knaves, fools, and gulls. Despite Jonson's rejection of stage devils in his Epistle as "antique relics of barbarism," his play is deeply continuous with Vice tradition, so that whatever ambiguities attend the metatheatricality of Volpone's disguises also attend those of the Vice before him.[24]

The Devil Is an Ass is more explicitly self-reflexive than *Volpone*, and it combines this quality with a thoroughgoing satire of the devil and the Vice as old-fashioned theatre, expanding the brief remarks in the Epistle of *Volpone* into a scene that occupies the first 158 lines of the play. Ironically, "Lusty Juventus" here (1.1.50) is a minor devil called Pug, who naively believes he can achieve something to corrupt humankind, despite cautionary remarks from the older and wiser Satan. The actor playing Pug in the first scene doffs his devil suit for most of the play, exchanging it for the street clothes of a newly hanged cutpurse, whose corpse Pug animates in order to join human society. Pug's ineptitude in inciting human beings to vice is a keen satire on the depths of urban depravity, but it is not original with Jonson, as he implicitly acknowledges in alluding to Dekker's *If This Be Not a Good Play, the Devil Is in It*: "If this play do not like, the devil is in't" (Pro. 26).[25] Dekker borrowed the device, in turn, from a lost comedy of 1601, by Day and Haughton, called *Friar*

Rush and the Proud Woman of Antwerp, which is the first English example of the Friar Rush motif, that is, of a devil in human guise whose machinations barely compete with those of human beings.[26] In short, Jonson's explicit satire of popular tradition coexists with his debt to it in *Devil Is an Ass*, and nothing in the play challenges the real existence of devils or their association with human evil.

Support for this point can be found in Jonson's masques. In 1609, three years after *Volpone*, Jonson wrote *The Masque of Queens*, which is highly respectful of contemporary demonology. Twelve witches appear in the first antimasque Jonson wrote, as oppositional parodies of the twelve queens who danced the masque proper. The witches invoke their "Dame," whom Jonson identifies in a learned note as Ate; they urge her to "saddle your goat or your green cock," which Jonson's note identifies as Satan, acknowledging King James' *Daemonologie* as a source for the goat being "the devil himself."[27] The witches also urge their Dame to "Spur, spur upon little Martin" (80), whom Jonson again identifies as "a great buck-goat" or "the devil himself" (80 n.). Had Jonson intended to undercut any of the demonology in *The Masque of Queens*, he had plenty of satirical devices with which to do it, but satire is less evident than immense and serious learning.

Moreover, the metadramatic qualities of the masque support its demonology. The witches were not really female, when the masque was performed in 1609, because they were played by professional male actors in female costumes. Their noisy and sexually ambiguous impersonation contrasted with the still image of female virtue ("still" in the sense of both silent and unmoving) presented by the twelve queens of the masque, who were not professional actors but ladies of the court, led by Queen Anne. The true natures of the ladies were thus expressed by the ancient heroines whom they impersonated by their costumes, just as the preposterous nature of the witches was expressed by the common actors who played their parts.[28]

The oppositional thinking of demonology is expressed again without satire in *Chlorida*, written for Charles and Henrietta-Maria in 1631, twenty-two years after *Queens* and fifteen years after *The Devil Is an Ass*. This is the only masque Jonson wrote in which an image of the devil actually appears, and it does so in the antimasque, when Cupid goes to hell, in Virgilian fashion, to stir up the gods' jealousy. Consequently "*A part of the underground opening, out of it enters a dwarf-post from hell, riding on a curtal, with cloven feet, and two lackeys.*"[29] The dwarf identifies himself as a "cacodemon," and his mission is to report that hell is in an uproar, with all punishments suspended. The dwarf calls up "goblins" personifying courtly evils – Jealousy, Disdain, Fear, and Dissimulation – who dance with Cupid. Their dance is followed by another, involving "The queen's dwarf [the same who had brought the message of hell's uproar], richly apparelled as a prince of hell, attended by six infernal spirits" (140–41). As in *The Masque of Queens*, Jonson contrasts these monstrous images in the antimasque (the cloven-hoofed horse, the dwarf, the goblins, the angry Cupid, hell itself) with the serenity of the masque and its epiphany of heroic royal power.

The satire of Jonson's popular comedies and the serious stage devilry of his masques are not contradictory but complementary. The Stuart kings' position as supreme head of the English church made them the principal depositories of charismatic power, and one way to read Jonson's masques is to see them as symbolic exorcisms performed by the king.[30] The climax in virtually all of Jonson's masques involves a poetic and scenic display of royal power that symbolically banishes the opposition of the antimasque, thus cleansing the body of the kingdom by rejecting the devils that possess it. This is a fitting tribute to the author of *Daemonologie*, which was written to counter the power of witches. "As our Saviour by his comming into the world, did drive away and cast out the Devils," writes Sebastien Michaëlis, "so his pleasure was, that their speciall attendants and worshippers should by earthly Princes be banished out of their Dominions: which action did belong unto the external Seate of Justice."[31] In *The Masque of Queens* and *Chlorida*, the demonic opposition is explicitly identified as such, but the symbolism of Jonson's antimasques always revolves around the same ideal polarities, whether they stage devils or not. As an exposure of false demonic effects, *Volpone* and *The Devil Is an Ass* are therefore presumably doing the same kind of cultural work as Jonson's antimasques, satirically rejecting Puritan rivals to the Stuart kings' privileged charisma. It is not necessary to see Jonson schizophrenically or insincerely defending in his masques what he attacks in his comedy; rather, he would appear to be attacking the same thing in both contexts – namely, religious delusion that threatens the kingdom, because it threatens the king, who alone has the charismatic authority to dispossess the kingdom of its evil, as Jonson's masques repeatedly affirm.

Corroborating the demonology in Jonson's masques is William Davenant's first attempt in the same genre, *The Temple of Love* (1635), which is highly imitative of Jonson. Davenant presents a series of parallel symbolic images that express the mystery of royal power as embodied in Charles I and Henrietta-Maria. Thus the "temple of love" suggests both the court and the church, alike imbued with an explicitly Platonic love which the masque celebrates, thereby turning the court into a drama of purified courtly love, in contrast to non-courtly theatre. This self-reflexive characteristic of the masque imitates Jonson's implicit contrast between the court and theatre, which had profound social implications, as we have seen. Jonson's implications are explicit in *The Temple of Love*, where the principal opposition is a group of evil magicians, the enemies of Divine Poesy, who are variously called "exorcists" and "Magi."[32] They not only corrupt youth through "pleasant arts" in their "false Temple" (p. 290) – suggesting the public theatre, in contrast to the true temple of the court – but also in their championing

> a sect of modern devils;
> Fine precise fiends, that hear the devout close
> At ev'ry virtue but their own, that claim
> Chambers and tenements in heaven, as they
> Had purchas'd there . . .   (p. 295)

These "fiends" are undoubtedly Puritans, linked with the public theatre in their opposition to the court and its sacred rituals, and thus revealing more about Davenant's royalist viewpoint than about either Puritans or the theatre. The magicians are explicitly identified with hell, witches, and fiends (p. 292). Though no literal devil appears in *The Temple of Love*, the Puritans are demonized in the anti-masque: the "seventh entry" "was of a modern devil, a sworn enemy of poesy, music, and all ingenious arts, but a great friend to murmuring, libelling, and all seeds of discord, attended by his factious followers; all which was exprest by their habits and dance" (p. 296). Presumably the "habits" involved a devil costume with Puritan accoutrements.[33]

Though the baffling ambiguities of demonic illusion, especially in the theatre, are at their most sophisticated in Jonsonian comedy, they are evident everywhere on the Shakespearean stage. William Rowley's *The Birth of Merlin* (1597–1621) offers spectacularly staged devils and fighting dragons in conjunction with sleight-of-hand magic as equal demonstrations of "art," that is, of uncanny effects. No less a character than Merlin, who is able to perform prodigious feats of magic, even as a child, is the one who also performs "slights of hand" on stage and then asserts, "'tis all my Art, which shall not offend you, sir, onely I give you a taste of it to show you sport" (4.1.31–32).[34] The actor playing Merlin had to be skilled at prestidigitation – the Clown whom Merlin fools with his hand tricks calls him "my little juggler" (4.1.24) – yet his performance is continuous, as a demonstration of uncanny power, with the play's more spectacular dragons and devils. The incident is a caution against concluding that the revelation of actorly technique necessarily demystified demonic effects, much though Harsnett and the English church hoped and believed that it would.

Where metadrama is concerned, Nathan Field's *A Woman Is a Weathercock*, identified with the Queen's Revels Children in 1609, is at the opposite extreme from *The Birth of Merlin*. Field was an actor himself, and his play is unusually self-reflexive, with allusions to *The Spanish Tragedy*, the closet scene in *Hamlet,* and to play-making in general.[35] A devil costume is used briefly in *A Woman Is a Weathercock*, and though it does not signify a "real" devil, it is designated as an "emblem" that has the same effect as a "real" devil. The character in question, Nevil, uses a double disguise. "This is a Deuill in a Parsons cote," says Nevil's friend, Scudmore (5.2.69), indicating that Nevil is disguised as a parson. The stage direction then reads: *"Neuill puts off the Priests Weeds & has a Diuels robe vnder"* (5.2.70). Everyone exclaims "A prettie Emblem" (71). After a brief speech, Nevil *"Slips off his Diuels weedes"* (5.2.78), to reveal the "real" gentleman beneath. In spite of its theatrical cleverness, the main plot turns on the devil's inability to perform the marriage sacrament, or to be more precise, it turns on the invalidity of a marriage that had been performed in the second act because the character who performed it was not a parson but a gentleman (Nevil) in disguise. The devil's disguise is introduced to make clear, in theatrical shorthand ("a pretty emblem"), that the marriage is invalid and is therefore no impediment to the hoped-for marriage of Nevil and Kate. The point is the audience's ability to read the emblem, as everyone on stage does. Beneath the unusually clever and superficial exterior of this play is a point everyone recognizes to be true – indeed, the plot depends on its being true – namely, that the devil cannot perform a sacrament. "Hart, what a deale a Knauery a Priests cloake can hide," exclaims Count Frederick, when Nevil doffs his parson's robe, "if it be not one of the honestest friendliest Coozenages that ere I saw, I am no Lord" (5.2.80–82). He is indeed no lord, for he is an actor, but this still remains an honest, friendly cozenage, like Field's play itself.

Closely related to *A Woman Is a Weathercock*, in its unusual combination of archness with archaic seriousness, is John Fletcher's *Monsieur Thomas*, identified with Lady Elizabeth's Men at the Whitefriars or the Hope Theatre in about 1610–16. Here too no devil appears, but in Tom's

madcap pursuit of Mary, she arranges for a maid to disguise herself
briefly with a devil's vizard to scare Tom as he is climbing to Mary's
bedroom, making him fall and break his leg.[36] Later, when Tom believes
he has found Mary in bed and proceeds to join her, it turns out she has
tricked him again, this time having conveyed a "blackamoor" in her
place, whom Tom mistakes for a devil (5.5.30–41). Again, he is frightened
off. Mary's trickery gives this play the traditional comic shape of the
guiler beguiled, a pattern that governs many of the mystery pageants –
where the incarnation of Christ is a divine trick that undoes the devil, as
we noticed in chapter 2 – as well as most morality plays. For Tom is
himself an unparalleled trickster: disruptive, frightening, outrageously
duplicitous, a shape-changer, a mocker of sober expectation, and frequently associated verbally with the Devil.[37] His role requires bravura
acting so as to keep the audience (as well as characters in the play) uncertain as to what Tom is "really" doing. Has he really learned discretion,
as he seems to have done more than once? Has he really broken his leg?
Does he really marry his sister to his lecherous friend (a question still
indeterminate at the end)? Mary is no fool, but she loves Tom, in spite
of her misgivings about his foolery. The fact that she is behind both
successful attempts to fool *him* reinforces the archaic pattern and makes
it significant in a romantic context, for it makes her his romantic equal.

Fletcher rings similar significant changes on traditional stage devils in
The Chances, associated with the King's Men in about 1617, but again it
is not clear that the thrust of skepticism is as broad as Greenblatt suggests. This play is as frankly demystifying about conjuration as *The
Puritan Widow*, and the target again appears to be Puritans, despite
Fletcher's working closely from a Spanish original. As in *The Puritan
Widow*, the sole purpose of the conjuring scene is to expose the falseness
of conjuring, and sophisticated effects are therefore produced by metadramatic ironies. Two characters thus pretend to be devils pretending to
be the characters themselves, and a third character pretends to be a devil
in order to play a deliberate hoax. In masterminding these effects, the
conjuror, Peter Vechio, explains his misdirection to the one he has
deceived, openly acknowledging that he uses what he overhears to make
it appear that he is capable of extraordinary knowledge.[38] Fletcher may
well have borrowed this effect from Scot's *Discoverie of Witches*, where Scot
explains how a magician secretly prepares an inevitable result, then
offers his audience a different (magical) explanation for the event when
it occurs.[39] The play complements these revelations with an argument
between two Spanish gentlemen, Don John and Don Frederick,
concerning the efficacy of conjuring (5.2). John is skeptical, but

Frederick is a firm believer. The action not only vindicates John's skepticism; it also makes him the play's spokesman for anti-Puritan satire. Can the conjuror, asks John, make devils "eate a bawling Puritan, / Whose sanctified zeale shall rumble like an Earthquake?" (5.2.7–8). In the same vein, John asks a question that may be an allusion to *The Devil Is an Ass*:[40]

> does thou thinke
> The devill such an Asse as people make him?
> Such a poore coxcomb? such a penny foot post?
> Compel'd with crosse and pile to run of errands?   (5.2.9–12)

The specific targeting of Puritans in a play that exposes conjuring as a fraud is reminiscent of *The Puritan Widow* and suggests how readily anti-Puritanism became a gloss on skepticism about trafficking with demons on the Shakespearean stage. Skepticism in *The Chances* is therefore another instance of religious secularization, because it functions as a weapon in religious rivalry rather than as an expression of disbelief per se.

Perhaps the most complex treatment of devils in a self-consciously theatrical context is *The Two Merry Milkmaids*, which is attributed to an unidentified "J.C." on the title page. It was performed by the Players of the Revels – a shortlived company associated with the Red Bull Theatre – and published in 1620. It is clear from the outset that this play is as much about magic-as-stagecraft as it is about magic itself, for it begins with a long conjuring scene, which it treats archly by having the devil turn out to be Landoff in disguise – a doctor at Wittenberg University and himself an experienced conjuror. This "devil" is conjured by Landoff's student and apprentice, Bernard, who is unsure of himself as he conjures and therefore fearful, an attitude that raises tension and increases suspense, thus reinvigorating a stage convention much used since Marlowe first invented it in *Dr. Faustus*. Despite the stage direction ("Enter Landoff his Tutor like a Spirit"),[41] no one in the theatre can tell that the devil Asmody is really Landoff disguised until Landoff announces the fact in soliloquy (1.1.112–31). Even when he reveals his disguise, he reaffirms the uncanny terror of conjuring (1.1.114–17), thus reinforcing the mood of Bernard's conjuration, which is fearful and hair-raising. Yet the scene is also arch and metadramatic, as Landoff declares when the scene closes:

> Ile follow him, attending still vpon him
> As if I were the Spirit he guesses me;
> And if there shall be cause, Ile play my part
> So well, that men shall prayse the Magic Art.   (1.1.128–31)

Despite the fact that this is a Red Bull play, J.C. had clearly absorbed the commonplaces of self-reflexive tragicomedy, and he includes them frequently, as when Cornelius, a courtier, comments disapprovingly about two milkmaids' flirtation with the Duke, who is attracted to one of them: "But what is this intended for trow; a Pastorall, or a Comedie?" (1.3.511–12).[42]

Bernard's inept conjuring (which succeeds in raising only his tutor in disguise) is improved later, offstage, by Landoff himself, with substantial effect on the plot of the play and renewed attention to the ambiguities of theatrical illusion. The first time Landoff conjures, he obtains a magic garland, which the self-important Bernard has offered to fetch, believing that he indeed controls a devil, who is, of course, really Landoff, still in disguise as Asmody, though now additionally disguised as a servant to Bernard. When the garland appears (made up, no doubt, of artifical flowers in theatrical reality), it is imagined indeed to have magic properties and must therefore have been obtained through Landoff's conjuration of the "real" Asmody off stage. More telling and spectacular is a ring of invisibility that Asmody produces at Landof's request. The ring is a striking metadramatic device, for it enables the actors to act out "invisibility" while remaining visible, i.e., to display their acting skills in a highly unusual manner. Though we can see they are plainly visible, their actions tell us differently, as in mime, and in order to believe what happens, we therefore believe what we know to be untrue. This is, of course, the very essence of theatre, and it is achieved in *The Two Merry Milkmaids* by a magic ring fetched by a devil.

The metadramatic slyness of *Two Merry Milkmaids* is explained in part by J.C.'s extensive borrowing – including the name "Asmody" – from Scot's *Discoverie*.[43] For Scot is the most corrosive demonological skeptic of the entire period, offering explanations of the kind that Fletcher borrows in *The Chances* and that Harsnett borrows in his exposure of religious fraud. With Scot too, however, it is important to avoid the oppositional thinking of the Enlightenment by reading him as a heroic explorer of progressive skepticism lost in a sea of superstition. Scot affirms the English Protestant commonplace that miracles ceased with the apostolic age, and he therefore undertakes to explain the natural sources of what others took to be demonic; this is what Harsnett borrowed from him. But as Stuart Clark points out, Scot's strategy achieved little, because his adversaries (among them, King James) agreed that demons operated by natural means, and they therefore disagreed that explaining one kind of natural means (i.e., illusory non-demonic effects) excluded others (i.e., real demonic effects).[44] Moreover, Scot's denial that miracles have occurred since the apostolic age coexisted with his affirmation of miracles in the Bible – an inconsistency that later skepticism would not tolerate.[45] His ambivalence is therefore another instance of the religious skepticism that we have seen in various forms on the Shakespearean stage. Whether the ambiguous illusions of these plays reduce the devil and magic to tawdry theatre, or whether they elevate theatre to uncanny expressiveness is more than an esthetic question; it is also a cultural question, and it cannot therefore be answered simply by assuming that satiric or metadramatic stage devils must be reductive because they appear to be reductive to us. On the Shakespearean stage, I would argue, the impact of metadrama on stage devils was more likely to be expressive than reductive, repeatedly calling attention to the permeable boundaries between reality and illusion because no one knew precisely where they were.

CHAPTER NINE

Traditional morality and magical thinking

Seventeenth-century belief about demonic illusion provides a context that helps to explain devils on the Shakespearean stage, as we have just seen, but more than demonological theories are involved in dramaturgical continuity. The moral and eschatalogical story that informed English drama from the beginning remained remarkably vital, in spite of the Reformation and increasing secularization. Remnants of the oppositional moral assumptions that shaped stage devils in the first place thus continue to appear in seventeenth-century plays, just as those assumptions remained active in English culture as a whole. Despite the increasing commercialization of London life – particularly in the theatre[1] – playwrights and audiences continued to think in traditional moral terms, as we noticed in Jonson's targeting of covetousness in *Volpone*, and those terms often complement devils on the Shakespearean stage.

For most of its citizens, London social and commercial life still revolved around parishes and craft guilds, as it had before the Reformation. The joint stock company that owned the Globe Theatre was a commercial innovation, but its members lived in particular London parishes which governed much of their social interaction, from birth to death, and which compelled conformity to the English church's two remaining sacraments, baptism and communion.[2] Despite the growing discrepancy between rich and poor and the competition and disorder of life for most citizens of London, the city was officially ruled by a magistracy whose rhetoric was "essentially paternalist" and "inculcated order, piety, charity" in ceremonies sometimes written by the very playwrights who satirized the city's vices – Dekker, Middleton, and Webster.[3] The incongruity of these diverse activities is analogous to the incongruity between Jonson's satirical comedies and his masques, and in both cases the incongruity would seem to be more consistent with religious secularization than with materialist skepticism.

A relevant example of ritual continuity that also implies moral continuity is the annual church festival called Rogation, which was the only religious procession retained by the reformed English church. Rogation had originally involved an annual exorcism of the parish: the procession that walked the parish boundaries on three successive days was designed to drive away the devil, thus helping to make the fields fertile. The English church eradicated this aspect of the procession, as it forbade literal demonic dispossession, emphasizing instead the blessing of God as the source of fertility and stressing the importance of establishing boundaries and reconciling neighbors in the procession that came to be called "beating the bounds."[4] This is a theme that George Herbert emphasizes in describing how "the country parson" views Rogation:

Particularly he loves procession, and maintains it, because there are contained therin 4 distinct advantages: first, a blessing of God for the fruits of the field; secondly, justice in the preservation of bounds; thirdly, charity and loving walking and neighbourly accompanying one another, with reconciling of differences at that time, if there be any; fourthly, mercy in releeving the poor by a liberall distribution and largesse, which at that time is or ought to be used. Wherefore he exacts of all to bee present at the perambulation, and those that withdraw and sever themselves from it he mislikes, and reproves as uncharitable and unneighbourly.[5]

Herbert's contrast between the Rogation community and "those that withdraw and sever themselves from it" involves the same oppositional thinking that distinguishes the community of Christians from those who belong to the devil. Charity is the normative social virtue, the principal object of the devil's attack, both in *The Castle of Perseverance* and the mystery plays' *Creation and Fall of the Angels*. For Herbert, "charity" thus retains some of its traditional significance from the narrative of salvation history; it had not yet diminished to a synonym for generosity. In Coventry, Rogation was paralleled by the annual oath-taking ceremony, when newly appointed city officers took communion publicly to demonstrate that charity was the essential source of the city's social cohesion.[6] While the Rogation procession would seem to be relevant only to country parishes, it was practiced widely in cities as well; in fact, some London parishes continued beating their bounds until well into the twentieth century.[7]

The continued affirmation of charity as a normative social virtue in seventeenth-century English life frequently accompanies devils on the Shakespearean stage, especially when devils are identified literally or metaphorically with Puritans. In the tough-minded *Puritan Widow* of 1606, for example, with its satirical demystification of conjuring and its exposure of covetous rascals, Pieboard and Idle are reduced to confidence tricks because of high unemployment and the covetousness of moneylenders. "I would eyther some of vs were employde, or might pitch our Tents at Vsurers doores, to kill the slaues as they peepe out at the Wicket," muses Skirmish (1.2.150–53). Pieboard emphatically agrees, turning Skirmish's critique into a contrast between charity and grasping Puritans: "a charitable Knaue is better then a soothing Puritaine" (1.2.160–61). Pieboard's contrast reappears in a conversation between Idle and Nicholas, the Puritan servingman, whom Idle eventually persuades to steal Sir Godfrey's chain. Nicholas objects at first, appealing to the ninth commandment ("Thou shalt not steal"), but Idle cunningly refers to the law of love: "*thou shalt loue thy Neighbour*, and helpe him in extremities" (1.4.145–46). Impressed with Idle's biblical knowledge, Nicholas demands to know the reference. "Why, in the first of Charity, the 2. Verse" replies Idle (149–50). "The first of Charity," scoffs Nicholas, "there is no such Chapter in my booke!" to which Idle quickly retorts, "No, I knew twas torne out of thy Booke, & that makes so little in thy heart" (151–55). Pieboard's own lack of charity is in fact what finally does him in, when he fails to make Skirmish a beneficiary of the plot to which Skirmish had contributed, and Skirmish therefore reveals the plot. One of the endearing features of the con men in this play is that they have charity on their side, yet they are also the over-clever guilers who are bound to be beguiled in the end, and charity as a social virtue in *The Puritan Widow* has no oppositional relation to the play's devils, who are, after all, only an open theatrical trick.

Charity is closer to tradition in three devil plays by Thomas Dekker, *If This Be Not a Good Play, the Devil Is in It* (1611–12), *The Virgin Martyr* (1620), and *The Witch of Edmonton* (1621). The moral cast of Dekker's mind is evident in satirical pamphlets of London vice like *The Seven Deadly Sins* (1606) and *A Knight's Conjuring* (1607), where Dekker recognizes that "t'is [sic] out of fashion to bring a Divell upon the Stage."[8] Despite this admission, he is like Jonson in nodding to fashion and simultaneously defying it in no fewer than three plays. *If This Be Not* is one source of inspiration, as we noticed, for Jonson's device in *The Devil Is an Ass* of having a devil disguise himself as a human being, only to find himself outdone by those he is supposed to tempt. Dekker identifies the folk source of the device by naming one of his disguised devils Friar Rush, but he triples the motif, sending a devil into each of three social contexts (the church, the court, and the city), and generating three interwoven plots in the process. He thus recreates traditional dramatic satire of social vice by associating it with devils, as in pre-Reformation morality plays and their Elizabethan successors, like *A Knack to Know a Knave*. Pluto's complaint about wage inflation by boatmen in the prologue reflects a concern about contemporary covetousness, and the representation of the three tempters in this play as apprentices is another way of suggesting what is demonic, in Dekker's view, about modern London. This impulse to explain contemporary social abuses in archetypal moral terms is as old as English drama, appearing as early as the late-fourteenth-century *Pride of Life*.

Like *A Knack to Know a Knave* and the psychomachic drama it imitates, *If This Be Not* includes both a tempter and a preserver for King Alphonso in the court plot and for the prior in the church plot, whereas the merchant Bartervile's deeper depravity is measured by the absence of a positive voice at his elbow. "Braue *Shalcon-Bohor*, all this while / Our eye has followed yours," exclaims King Alphonso to his new favorite, the devil Rufman, disguised as Bohor.[9] In the end, the king is preserved from Bohor's destructive influence only by penitence and a prayer for forgiveness (5.1.71–72). This comic pattern is one Shakespeare uses several times, as R. G. Hunter has argued, and both Shakespeare and Dekker were indebted for it to pre-Reformation drama.[10]

Charity as a normative social virtue is defended by both of the play's psychomachic "good angels," the nobleman Octavio at court and the subprior Clement in the monastery. Bartervile's urban commercial world is devoid of charity, because of his irredeemable vice, which his tempter Lurchall can hardly improve upon (2.2.11–14). Charity is likewise opposed by the devils. Friar Rush thus urges the prior not to feed two wandering pilgrims, because doing so merely nourishes idle vagabonds (1.3.164–70). William Carroll has recently analyzed contemporary rationalizations for treating beggars harshly, including arguments to that effect by Dekker himself.[11] In *If This Be Not*, however, Dekker attributes such rationalization to the devil and identifies it as the enemy of charity, whose defeat by three of the deadly sins (gluttony, lechery, and avarice) is celebrated gloatingly by Friar Rush after the prior has yielded to temptation and driven away the begging pilgrims (1.3.197–200).[12] Clement, in contrast, is incorruptible, refusing a gift of found gold and urging the priory cook to take it for himself only if he agrees to dispense with half of it as the subprior directs:

> Looke not to prosper; if thou dealst amisse;
> Good workes are keyes opening the gates of blisse;
> That golden key, thou in that heape maist find,
> If with it thou relieue the lame, sick, blind,
> And hungry.   (3.2.128–32)

That good works are keys to the gate of bliss is a pre-Reformation moral assumption, strongly opposed by the early Protestant church, but presented here as a standard of communal charity that the devil corrupts. The court plot and the friary plot come together when Octavio meets Clement and pleads the subprior's case to King Alfonso:

> ô I beseeke
> Thy attention to this Reuerend sub-Prior
> Who plaines against disorders of this House;
> Where once Deuotion dwelt and Charitie,
> Ther's Drunkennesse now, Gluttonie, and Lecherie.   (3.3.102–6)

Unfortunately for Clement, the same thing has happened to the court as well, where the corrupted king harshly orders the monastery disbanded and its proceeds given to one of his young favorites.

This explicit evocation of the dissolution of the monasteries is presented with such sympathy to the religious house in question that it seems hard to reconcile with occasional anti-Catholic jibes (1.1.112–14) and with Dekker's authorship of *The Whore of Babylon* five years before (1606), which idealizes Elizabethan opposition to the pope and virulently satirizes the papacy. Kathleen McLuskie argues that a "complex of popular Protestantism and a 'culture of honour' in relation to the expectations of the artistocracy, combined with antipopery to form the bedrock" of Dekker's political drama.[13] This is a useful observation, particularly if "popular Protestantism" is represented by a play like *A Knack to Know a Knave* (1592), which idealizes a pre-Reformation archbishop of Canterbury, satirizes Puritans, rejects covetous commercial practices, and includes a plain-speaking commoner, Honesty, who is very much like Plain Dealing in *The Whore of Babylon*: both are commoners who are privileged to speak frankly to their social betters, both identify knaves in the same way, and both allude to the ship of fools. The centrist position of *Knack* also involves a celebration of charity, as we saw in chapter 7, and anticipates the end of *If This Be Not*, where both "Guy Faulx" and a Puritan are tormented by the devils in hell. The Puritan intends to "chastize and correct the foule Fiend," as Darrel had done (5.4.263–64), but he is so insufferable that the devils reject him, fearing he will indeed confound hell, as he has confounded the church on earth.

Surprisingly, Dekker's collaboration with Philip Massinger on *The Virgin Martyr* (1620) perpetuates centrist religious and political assumptions about demonology, for Massinger may have had Catholic inclinations, and *The Virgin Martyr* has affinities with the Baroque idealism of Counter Reformation *tragedia sacra* on the continent.[14] This late-Jacobean revival of the pre-Reformation saint's play is actually a prime example of how adaptable oppositional thinking could be. While it is true, as Louise Clubb points out, that "the Catholic in England was in the position of Dorothea in Roman-governed Caesaria" (p. 120), it is also true that Dorothea's martyrdom is mentioned by John Foxe in the *Acts and Monuments*.[15]

Moreover, in at least three episodes of the play, the dynamics of martyrdom would have seemed Protestant to Dekker's audience – and probably to Dekker himself – as a result of reading Foxe. These include a staged scene of Christian iconoclasm, when Theophilus' daughters, Caliste and Christeta, newly reconverted to Christianity, refuse to pay their vows to an image of Jupiter, spitting at it, throwing it down, and spurning it instead (3.2.53 SD).[16] In fact, they have just been reconverted by the virgin martyr's iconoclastic arguments (3.1.162–86). Also reminiscent of Foxe in *The Virgin Martyr* is the ambiguous process of conversion and reconversion, with absolute binary distinctions between truth and falsehood, faithfulness and apostasy, even though the language of truth and fidelity is used persuasively by both sides, and the persecutors repeatedly offer complete amnesty to those who are willing to recant. Third, Dekker's and Massinger's play embodies a contrast between the suffering that necessarily follows true belief and the material prosperity that is possible for pagans and apostates (3.1.79–89), and this contrast is not only in Foxe but also in late Tudor morality plays, as we noticed in chapter 5. The heroine of *Virtuous and Godly Susanna* (1563–69) anticipates Dorothea in this regard, while the earlier apostasy of Caliste and Christeta recalls that of Philologus in *The Conflict of Conscience* (1570–81). As Dorothea faces torture and death, her "good angel," Angelo, urges her that "Thy glorious crown must come / Not from soft pleasure, but by martyrdome" (4.2.100).

Opposing Angelo and Dorothea throughout *The Virgin Martyr* is Harpax, a stage devil who consistently impersonates a human being, in contrast to the three tempters of *If This Be Not*, who begin and end the play in their devilish form. By means of Harpax, the playwrights literally demonize the persecution of true believers, and Harpax's closest stage analogues are therefore the devils of late Tudor morality plays.

Harpax offers plenty of hints that he is a devil without openly saying so, but only at the end, after the death of Dorothea, does he appear "*in a fearefull shape*" (5.1.122 SD) as he rapidly exits Theophilus' study. Harpax's hurry is due to Theophilus' conversion to Christianity and the arrival of a miraculous gift of delectable fruit, following Dorothea's death. The fruit is literal in the play and its sources, appearing in tacit response to Theophilus' mocking challenge to Dorothea, before she died, to send him fruit from the heavenly country where she was going (4.3.104–7). In *The Virgin Martyr*, however, the fruit is also an allusion to the biblical "fruit of the Spirit," the first of which is charity (Gal. 5:22), as suggested in Dorothea's final request of Angelo before she dies:

> For proofe that I forgiue
> My persecutor, who in scorne desir'd
> To tast of that most sacred fruite I go to,
> After my death as sent from me, be pleasd
> To giue him of it.   (4.3.155–59)

Angelo's fulfillment of this request, with its consequent effect on Theophilus' conversion, is the play's culminating symbolic contrast between charity and the devil, for Harpax is Theophilus' constant companion throughout the play and only abandons him when the fruit appears.

In a play where abstractions sometimes identify characters, as in personification allegory, Dorothea might well be called Charity, a word that is frequently associated with her. She suffers not only at the hands of her noble persecutors, but also from two commoners, Hircius, whom Angelo identifies as lust (2.1.124) and Spungius, whose name is explicated by his drunkenness and gluttony. These two illustrate the willful violation of charity, recalling the torturers of Christ in the mystery plays. In a clear allusion to Christian redemption, Dorothea had preserved them from the gallows to be her servants before the play begins (2.1.143–46), but as true representatives of original sin, they misspend the money she gives them for relieving the suffering of other prisoners, using it instead to buy women and wine. Moreover Harpax corrupts them to betray Dorothea to the authorities, in a parallel to the betrayal of Christ, and then pays them to cudgel her to death, a punishment that only fails because miraculous intervention makes their efforts unavailing.

Harpax is an unusual devil because he appears to be thoroughly human, but Dekker opposed charity with an even more unusual devil, when he wrote *The Witch of Edmonton* in 1621 with John Ford and William

Rowley, following a sensational London witch trial in the same year. Whereas *If This Be Not* divides into three plots with a devil each, *The Witch of Edmonton* has three plots that are united primarily by the common presence of one devil. This takes the form of a dog named Tom, who is required to say a good deal and therefore had to be played by a human actor, leaving considerable scope for theatrical invention. Tom comes from the source of the witch-trial plot, a pamphlet written by Henry Goodcole, chaplain of Newgate prison, detailing Mother Sawyer's confession to him after her conviction and sentencing.[17] But Tom is the playwrights' most inspired invention, as he interacts with each of the principals in the play's three plots.

The main plot is not Sawyer's story but one from a higher social elevation, involving the landed gentry, so the evil that overtakes a destitute old woman is the same evil that overtakes her social betters.[18] The gentry plot begins with a portrait of loving commitment that suggests charity in the marital relationship, when Frank Thorney declares he will care for Winnifred by marrying her, having conceived a child with her. They have already plighted troth, and he vows never to "falsifie that Bridal-Oath / That bindes me thine."[19] The innocence of this declaration is complicated by Frank's request that his master, Sir Arthur Clarington, sign a statement that Frank is *not* married, so Frank can receive his father's portion, and Frank's position is deeply undercut by the revelation that Clarington himself has seduced Winnifred and escaped taking responsibility for it by deceiving Frank. This effective opening, where a master violates charity by exploiting his servants, is established as a parallel to old Banks' exploitation of Mother Sawyer, when he calls her "witch" and "hag" and beats her (2.1.17–30), and the parallel is reinforced by subsequent events, when the social victims in each plot are literally driven to the devil by the dilemmas in which they find themselves.

When Tom appears in these stories of intense spiritual and psychological distress, he reinforces the principals' attempts to escape or ameliorate their social problems by resorting to evil of one sort or another – cursing and a prayer for vengeance in Sawyer's case, and deceit and murder in Frank's. Tom describes the limits of his own power, when he refuses Sawyer's order to kill Banks:

> Though we have power, know, it is circumscrib'd,
> And ti'd in limits: though he be curs'd to thee,
> Yet of himself he is loving to the world,
> And charitable to the poor. Now Men

> That, as he, love goodness, though in smallest measure,
> Live without compass of our reach.   (2.1.152–57)

The incident may be inspired by Mephostophiles' refusal to meet some of Faustus' demands, but *The Witch of Edmonton* is a more traditional play than *Dr. Faustus*, though written thirty years later, and Tom's reply is consistent with the age-old assumption that charity expresses the power of God and therefore opposes the devil. "Ho! have I found thee cursing?" exclaims Tom, when he first appears to Sawyer, "now thou art mine own" (2.1.116). Her hatred and vengefulness puts her in his power, as she "abjure[s] all goodness" (2.1.107). Tom makes the same point about Frank: "We can meet his folly, / But from his Vertues must be Run-aways" (3.1.73–74).

The principle that charity repels the devil partly informs the play's third plot as well, involving young Cuddy Banks and his passion for Katherine Carter. Cuddy is kind to Mother Sawyer when he first meets her, offering her silver to compensate for his father's mistreatment of her (2.1.199–201), and asking her assistance, as a "cunning" woman, in winning Katherine's affection. Sawyer is unmollified, however, determining to avenge herself on Banks by punishing his son. She therefore enlists Tom's aid, which Tom offers by appearing to Cuddy as a phantasm of Katherine and leading him into a pond at night (3.1.63–91). This comic punishment is the most Tom can do to Cuddy, whom he uses "doggedly, not divellishly" (5.1.109), because the devil can only influence those who abjure goodness, as Mother Sawyer does (5.1.127–36). In short, Cuddy too is saved from the devil by charity, specifically the kindness he shows to Sawyer when he first meets her, as old Banks is saved by his goodness to others, despite his misuse of Mother Sawyer.

The tragicomic tone of *The Witch of Edmonton* is established principally in its final scene (5.3), when justice is pronounced against wrongdoers in the gentry plot, and charity is restored through mutual forgiveness. This ambivalent mood of punishment and forgiveness in the conclusion is anticipated by the mingling of crime and forgiveness in the death of Susan, who is Frank's murder victim, for she dies "in charity with all the World," forgiving Frank even as he stabs her to death (3.3.61). While the pattern of restoring charity through forgiveness comes from pre-Reformation drama, the social restoration at the end of *The Witch of Edmonton* is particularly well captured by the phrases George Herbert uses to describe the Rogation procession: "neighbourly accompanying one another, with reconciling of differences."

The fallout of charity at the end of the play, however, is ambiguous, because it is confined to the gentry plot. Mother Sawyer does not repent, as Frank does, and no one forgives her. Instead, she directs her rage at the devil for failing to do all she asks, and he abandons her with moralistic scorn (5.1.28–85). Where the human community is concerned, she lies about her murderous bewitching of Anne Ratcliff, even as she is being led to the gallows (5.3.33).[20] Mother Sawyer is thus denied the grace of repentance, whereas Frank is not, though he too is hanged for murder. No longer merely a hapless victim of village prejudice, as she is at the beginning, Sawyer becomes in the end a dangerous figure, whose demonic power is made terrifying in order to justify the way she is treated. Moreover, the farcical plot involving the "clown" Cuddy also introduces social ambiguities. Tom comes to Cuddy because Cuddy is passionate for Katherine Carter, a "wealthy Yeomans Daughter" (2.1.210), but Cuddy's passion does not parallel the evil that invites the devil in the other two plots, for the norms Cuddy breaches in his longing for a woman above his station are those of social class, not of charity. The playwrights may well have been influenced by social class prejudice in the farcical subplot of *Dr. Faustus*, where Faustus treats a countryman vengefully by selling him a demon horse that disappears from under him when he rides it into the water. As Mephistopheles scorns Wagner, so Tom scorns Cuddy for his social insignificance:

> Nor will I serve for such a silly Soul.
> I am for greatness now, corrupted greatness;
> There I'll shug in, and get a noble countenance:
> Serve some Briarean Footcloth-strider,
> That has an hundred hands to catch at Bribes,
> But not a Fingers nayl of Charity.
> . . . .
>   hence silly fool,
> I scorn to prey on such an Atome soul.   (5.1.179–90)

As in Greene's *Friar Bacon and Friar Bungay*, this kind of social scorn on the devil's part confuses the play's contrast in moral value with a contrast in social class.

Real as these social ambiguities are in *The Witch of Edmonton*, they do not outweigh the playwrights' achievement in extending the narrow moralism of Henry Goodcole's pamphlet to a wider social sphere than that of an elderly indigent witch. Mother Sawyer makes the point herself in an exchange with the justice who first questions her: "Men in gay clothes, whose Backs are laden with Titles and Honours, are within far more crooked then I am; and if I be a Witch, more Witch-like" (4.1.86–88). She concludes tellingly in heroic couplets:

> What are your painted things in Princes Courts?
> Upon whose Eye-lids Lust sits blowing fires
> To burn Mens Souls in sensual hot desires:
> Upon whose naked Paps a Leachers thought
> Acts Sin in fouler shapes then can be wrought.   (4.1.103–7)

This is her most powerful speech in the play, condemning the court for moral failure that equals or exceeds what she is accused of and attributing the accusations against her to prejudice against the poor.[21] William Rowley probably deserves credit for this extension of the play's moral vision across a broad social range. He told a story of courtly intrigue and murder that is analogous to Frank Thorney's in two plays, *All's Lost by Lust* (1619), written two years before *The Witch of Edmonton*, and a more famous play, *The Changeling* (1622), written just afterwards. Arthur Kirsch's incisive reading of *The Changeling* against a background of psychomachic drama makes sense in light of continuity between early stage devils and the Vice.[22] But one does not have to look as far as sixteenth-century Vice comedy to find illuminating analogues to DeFlores and Beatrice Joanna, because such parallels exist in a contemporary play about the devil, written at least partly by Rowley.

The presence of a devil in *The Witch of Edmonton* literally enacts the moral assumption – usually symbolic or metaphorical in other plays – that a world without charity is hell. This assumption operates in *Macbeth* (1606–7), a play that has no devils but is profoundly influenced by the oppositional thinking of demonology just the same. What Frank Thorney does to his world, with Tom's encouragement, Macbeth also does to his, when he yields to the suggestive witches: he ruins grace, believes illusions and equivocations, stoops to murder, produces despair and self-destruction, otherwise becomes increasingly barren, life-denying, solipsistic. Webster's *The White Devil* (1612) is like *Macbeth* in eschewing literal stage devils, but it is a compelling portrait of the hell human beings make for themselves when committed to pride, lechery, and avarice. "O me, this place is hell," says Vittoria, when her husband Bracciano dies, in a play replete with references to devils and hell.[23] The play's title is an allusion to the proverb, "The white devil is worse than the black," and the dissimulation implied by the proverb marks virtually everyone in the play.

In comedy, too, playwrights satirically evoked hell to score vice on the Shakespearean stage, as they had done for the previous 200 years. In *If*

This Be Not a Good Play, Dekker again makes explicit, with the Friar Rush motif, what other comedies merely imply – the demonic identity of vice. A literal devil in comedy, this time in female shape, appears in Middleton's *A Mad World, My Masters*, performed by Paul's Boys in about 1606. She visits Penitent Brothel in the form of Mistress Harebrain, immediately after he has foresworn an adulterous relationship with the real Mistress Harebrain. The succubus is thus identified with his over-heated sexual imagination, and while Brothel succeeds in driving her away, she seems bound to come back, since he is doomed by his own ingenious trick to keep constant company with the woman he tried to give up. The succubus is morally serious, insofar as Penitent Brothel is a trenchant satire on false repentance, as his name suggests, and his anguished contrition may be part of an anti-Puritan satire that also includes echoes of exorcism in his confrontation with the devil: "I do conjure thee by that dreadful power," he exclaims, when he first sees her.[24] At the end of her seductive presentation, he again tries to exorcise her from his presence:

> Devil! I do conjure thee once again
> By that soul-quaking thunder to depart
> And leave this chamber freed from thy damned art.   (4.2.69–71)

Sir Bounteous Progress identifies the traditional motif of the guiler beguiled, applicable not only to Penitent but to Follywit in the play's main plot, as he pronounces the closing couplet: "Who lives by cunning, mark it, his fate's cast; / When he has gulled all, then is himself the last" (5.2.282–83).[25] This is the same moral world that characterizes Medwall's *Nature* and Skelton's *Magnificence* a century earlier. In the words of Michaelmas Term: "We must be civil now, and match our evil; / Who first made civil black, he pleas'd the devil."[26] The principal difference is that earlier comedy involves a restoration of charity, as Dekker's does, whereas city comedy is content with the satiric punishment of vice.

Jonson's *Volpone* also suggests an unrelieved symbolic descent into hell, but in contrast to Middleton, when Jonson literally stages devils in *The Devil Is an Ass*, he also produces something much closer to a charitable conclusion than he had in *Volpone*. For the first time in a Jonsonian comedy, a foolish character comes to his senses and desists from his folly. Significantly, the character is Fitzdottrel, who had been trying to conjure a devil in order to get rich, and who pretended to be possessed by a demon for the same purpose. He begins to think differently when he discovers that a devil has indeed been active in local society:

> Nay then, 'tis time to leave off counterfeiting.
> Sir, I am not bewitched, nor have a devil:
> No more than you. I do defy him, I,
> And did abuse you. These two gentlemen
> Put me upon it. (I have faith against him.)
> They taught me all my tricks. I will tell truth
> And shame the fiend.   (5.8.137–43)

Fitzdottrel's renunciation of the devil parallels the renunciation in the English church's baptismal liturgy ("Dost thou forsake the devil and all his works? *Answer.* I forsake them all"),[27] reinforcing the play's rejection of Puritan excess from the established church's point of view. Complementing Fitzdottrel's newly discovered self-awareness, Wittipol decides in favor of virtue, in an explicit contest between "virtue" and "vice" (4.6.28–41). Loving Mistress Fitzdottrel's goodness more than her beauty, Wittipol desists from his amorous pursuit of her and instead ensnares her foolish husband in a plot that obliges him to settle his wealth upon his intelligent, resourceful, and beleagured wife. "Fruitful service" (4.6.40) to the lady Wittipol admires thus replaces selfish pursuit of her, as Fitzdottrel replaces folly with self-awareness. For the first time, Jonson thus presents goodness convincingly, including loyalty, trust, charity, and self-recognition. "Trust," as Anne Barton points out, "is the most important word in *The Devil Is an Ass,* even more significant than the two, often reiterated, nouns in the title."[28]

One of the strangest examples of traditional virtue appearing in a devil play is Robert Davenport's *A New Trick to Cheat the Devil* (1624–39), played by Queen Henrietta's Men, who were associated with the Cockpit. The devil in this play is like the one in *The Two Merry Milkmaids,* in that he is a character in disguise – both from other characters in the play and from the audience – so that for all practical purposes he *is* a devil until he unexpectedly reveals his identity. Davenport offers hints, however, as to who this devil really is, and the most important hint turns on the incongruity of a devil who rescues the prodigal Slightall from ruin, thereby, in effect, practicing charity. Since bountiful generosity is the principal quality of Master Changeable, who assumes a devil's disguise, the devil's behavior is a veiled clue to his identity and a clever allusion to the tradition that charity and the devil are incompatible, in much the same fashion that the marriage rite and the devil are incompatible in Field's *A Woman Is a Weathercock.* What makes the devil's charity strange is that it is initially impossible to distinguish from the traditional demonic bargain. Changeable adopts his disguise in response to Slightall's despairing determination to abandon all hope and turn to the devil for assistance, which the "devil" offers him in exchange for his soul. Only in retrospect, when it becomes clear that Changeable has paid off all the debts of his prodigal prospective son-in-law, is it also clear that the "devil" acted with extraordinary charity.

Another clue that Changeable is the devil is a metadramatic reference in his assurance to his daughter Anne that he can foil her mother's and Lord Scales' designs on her and restore her to Slightall:

> Ile crosse thy Mothers workings,
> And foole that Lords attempts; onely be you
> Of a more temperate humour, and more stay'd,
> Observing but *what I shall project for you,*
> *And doubt not my performance.*[29]

The most deeply buried clue to Changeable's disguise is in parallels between the main plot and the fabliau subplot, which would actually seem to be the source of the main plot.[30] Changeable parallels the resourceful Friar John in the subplot, in that both preserve a marriage, discharge an interloper in it, and provide magically for the married pair by a pretense involving devils. The demystification of conjuring in both plots suggests anti-Puritan satire, which is confirmed by the gratuitous apparition of a Puritan who rises in response to Slightall's conjuring and identifies himself satirically:

> I am a Puritan.
> *I am a Puritaine?* One that will eate no Porke,
> Doth use to shut his shop on Saterdayes,
> And open them on Sundayes: A Familist;
> And one of the Arch limbes of *Belzebub,*
> A Jewish Christian, and a Christian *Jew.*   (4.1; p. 251)

Given this explicit satire, it seems odd to describe *A New Trick to Cheat the Devil* as a Puritan play.[31] Mistress Anne's independence and outspokenness would appear to owe more to Shakespeare's heroines than to Puritan ideals of women – a model also recalled by Jonson's Mistress Fitzdottrel, as Anne Barton points out[32] – and the identification of charity as the key to successful social relationships in both plots has less to do with Puritanism than with centrist values that were deeply embedded in English thinking from before the Reformation. "Since Charity late is dead, / How can beggers live?" asks Slightall despairingly in his destitution (4.1, p. 249), just before Changeable charitably relieves him, and the contrast between Slightall's faithful servant Roger and his pragmatic servant Geffrey is a comic version of the contrast between the charitable Edgar and scheming Edmund in *King Lear*.

As a vital element of archaic dramaturgy accompanying stage devils, traditional moral thinking is complemented on the Shakespearean stage by magical thinking. This point may seem redundant, since the devil himself is usually construed as an example of magical thinking.[33] In arguing that early seventeenth-century stage devils perpetuate aspects of traditional sacred culture, however, identifying the category of magical thinking separately is useful, because it helps to clarify distinctive elements of seventeenth-century demonology that pertain to what happened on stage. For one thing, the increasingly urgent effort to clarify the status of devils meant that, as Stuart Clark says of witches, they "came to be seen, even by some contemporaries themselves, as creations of the normal world, not its parodists."[34] If devils were indeed part of the natural order, then their nature, like that of anything else, could presumably be described in itself, rather than as a perversion of angelic nature. A naturalization of the demonic therefore took place that made everything associated with it appear to be "natural" as well, including a host of folk beliefs and practices.

Yet religious authorities continued to maintain a distinction between the mainstream of religious belief and traditions of folklore and popular culture. The devil of theology and the liturgy in the West was not dependent on particular folk beliefs and in fact was defended conceptually in opposition to them, because the devil implied an order created by God, whereas popular magic implied a manichean universe that the church repeatedly resisted.[35] Moreover, the devil of sacramental theology and its ritual expression shaped the earliest devils on the English stage and continued to shape them in the seventeenth century, whenever playwrights associated the devil with traditional moral expectation. The distinction I am making here between magical thinking and the devil is therefore analogous to the broader distinction between a sacred culture and religious secularization.

A good example of ambivalence about magical thinking can be seen in *The Witch of Edmonton*, when a citizen called Hamlac enters with a handful of thatch from Mother Sawyer's house and burns it, "for they say, when 'tis burning, if she be a Witch, she'll come running in" (4.1.17–18). Hamlac's magical thinking seems to be confirmed when Sawyer indeed appears (4.1.18 SD) and someone comments, "This Thatch is as good as a jury to prove she is a witch" (4.1.26). This folk belief is opposed by elite culture, however, when a justice scolds the mob for abusing an aged woman and scorns their proof that she is a witch: "Come, come; firing her Thatch? ridiculous: take heed Sirs what you do: unless your proofs come better arm'd, instead of turning her into a Witch, you'll prove your selves starke Fools" (4.1.40–42). This voice of moderation and reason comes from Henry Goodcole's pamphlet, which also mocks the custom: "And to find out who should be the author of this mischief, an old ridiculous custom was used, which was to pluck the thatch of her house and to burn it, and it being so burned, the author of such mischief should presently then come."[36] In the end, however, the play vindicates popular custom, not the voice of elite skepticism, for Sawyer not only comes when Hamlac burns her thatch, but she is also found guilty of witchcraft by the justice who had doubted the custom in the first place.

A parallel example comes from Heywood's *The Silver Age*, identified with the King's Men in about 1611, the same year they played Shakespeare's *The Tempest*. Following Ovid's *Metamorphoses* (9.281–316), Heywood makes Juno a jealous wife, unable to prevent Jove's seduction of Alcmena but determined to prevent the consequent birth. Heywood's presenter, Homer, introduces the episode dismissively, attributing Juno's power to "*old wiues*" who believe that as long as the goddess sits cross-legged, the birth cannot occur.[37] Homer is like the justice in *The Witch of Edmonton*, however, because the subsequent action vindicates the folk belief and belies his skeptical assessment. Alcmena successfully gives birth, despite Juno's opposition, only when Galantis, the presiding midwife, deceives Juno into rising. If Juno's posture were indeed merely an old wife's tale, Galantis would not have to trick her, and the trick would not be effective. Moreover, whereas Juno's power in Ovid derives from her being the goddess of childbirth, in *The Silver Age* it becomes an example of a witch's *maleficium*. "I suspect witchcraft," remarks Galantis (p. 123), and when Juno stands up in response to Galantis' trick, another midwife exclaims, "The witch is rouz'd" (p. 124). "How the witch storms," remarks another, and when Juno learns she has been tricked, Galantis mocks her: "You are a witch, are you? you sat crosse-leg'd, did you? my Lady could not bee brought to bed, could she? And now *Gallantis* hath gul'd you, hath she?" (p. 124). The mockery is potent. At the same time that it relieves the threat of the witch by making her power laughable, it also puts Galantis into the same position as those who laugh at oracles and omens, thus increasing the uncanny power of the witch. When Juno threatens vengeance, we have no doubt that it will come.

Words of power, like Juno's, are the most common example of magical thinking on the Shakespearean stage, and they are almost always effective.[38] Riddles, oracles, omens, prophecies, spells, oaths, swearing, sometimes mere threats and warnings, all are examples of this kind of magic, and nothing indicates Reginald Scot's misreading of his time more than his belief that arguments against magical language would make people stop believing it.[39] The tide that Scot tried in vain to stem was swollen not only by biblical precedent but also by classical literature. Senecan tragedy included prophecy, oracles, and omens, providing a warrant for them on the Shakespearean stage.

It is therefore no surprise to find words of power frequently associated with devil plays, though they are by no means confined to such plays. The influence of Seneca almost certainly accounts for the ambiguous prophecies of Behemoth, the "spirit" who appears in Chapman's *Bussy D'Ambois* (1604–5), as Senecan influence also accounts for the play's five-act structure, a sword fight reported by a Nuntius, an exclusively high society, a difficult high style, and a presiding "Fate" that is acknowledged at one point to circumscribe the actions of Behemoth.[40] In Barnabe Barnes' *The Devil's Charter*, performed by the King's Men in 1606, the same year they performed *Macbeth*, Pope Alexander VI signs a compact with the devil that turns out to be ambiguous, like the witches' prophecies in *Macbeth*. In both cases, credulous power-seekers find the same thing Buckingham does in *Henry VIII*, when he is presented with similar prophecies:

> that 'twas dangerous
> To ruminate on this so far until
> It forged him some design, which, being believed,
> It was much like to do.   (1.2.179–82)

The Birth of Merlin (1597–1621) revels in magical language as indulgently as it stages devils and dragons. The British king ignores "holy councel" sent by the prophet Anselm, urging him to continue fighting the Saxons; instead, he marries a Saxon princess to his inevitable undoing (1.2.37–42). But the child Merlin, born with a beard and able to discourse rationally, is even more powerful than Anselm. When Proximus prophesies that Vortiger's new castle will be built with young Merlin's blood, Merlin warns Proximus that his own fate hangs over him, at which a stone falls, cutting Proximus off in the midst of his scornful laughter and killing him (4.1.176–91). The clown who mocks Merlin's interpretation of a comet is struck dumb, able only to utter "hum, hum,

hum" (4.5.72–123), as Friar Bungay is forced to cry "hud, hud" in *Friar Bacon and Friar Bungay*.

Stage devils are complemented by a stage omen in response to perjury in Dekker's *If This Be Not a Good Play, the Devil Is in It*. When Barterville the wicked merchant falsely swears that he paid a debt – "Else let that eye, / Which sees me play false, scourge my periury / With fearefull stripes" (3.3.32–34) – he promptly falls down and bleeds at the mouth, while his staff beats itself on the ground until it shatters, "for heauen loues truth" (3.3.37), as a bystander points out. This is the same kind of folk justice that visits Mother Sawyer in *The Witch of Edmonton*, and guilt is presumed to be equally obvious in both cases. The jumping staff that shatters itself must have been a considerable technical challenge for the actors of the play, but it is not more challenging than the miracles performed by Jesus in the mystery plays, and the effect on the audience was presumably the same, no matter how often their pastors and teachers told them that miracles had ceased since the apostolic age.

Dekker's fascination with magical language did not abate in the ten years between *If This Be Not* and *The Witch of Edmonton*, during most of which time he was in prison and wrote no plays. One way that he and his collaborators tied the main plot of Frank Thorney to the secondary plot of Mother Sawyer was by emphasizing words of power. In the first two scenes these are used in the context of Frank Thorney's new marriage to Winnifred. Vowing fidelity to her, he calls down a curse upon himself if he ever violates his oath (1.1.59–68). Sir Arthur Clarington offers verbal assurances of his support for the couple – "yet thou shalt be sure / I will not fail thee"; "trust my bounty" (1.1.120–22) – but these assurances and Clarington's apparent generosity are soon revealed to be a cynical pay-off of Frank, when Clarington talks salaciously to Winnifred about their pre-existing liaison. She responds indignantly, rejecting Clarington's attention now that she is married. Echoing Frank, she curses herself if she ever agrees to see or hear her former lover (1.1.189–91), and she cites Frank's oath to her in equating her oath to him with marriage as a sacrament:

> And shall I then for my part
> Unfile the sacred Oath set on Record
> In Heaven's Book? Sir *Arthur*, do not study
> To add to your lascivious lust, the sin
> Of Sacriledge: for if you but endeavour
> By any unchaste word to tempt my constancy,
> You strive as much as in you lies to ruine

> A Temple hallowed to the purity
> Of holy Marriage.   (1.1.200–8)

Though written in 1621 by a Protestant playwright, Winnifred's declaration identifies a betrothal oath with the traditional affirmation of marriage as a sacrament, and her weighty words hang heavily in the air in the play's second scene, when Frank indignantly tells his father that he is *not* married in order to deceive old Thorney into giving him his portion:

> What do you take me for? an Atheist?
> One that nor hopes the blessedness of life
> Hereafter, neither fears the vengeance due
> To such as make the Marriage-bed an Inne,
> Which Travellers day and night,
> After a toylsome lodging leave at pleasure?
> Am I become so insensible of losing
> The glory of Creations work? My soul!
> O I have liv'd too long.   (1.2.172–80)

To describe these lines merely as tragic irony understates their gravity and importance and misses their revelation of how closely Dekker and his collaborators still tied magical thinking about language to moral and eschatalogical assumptions in 1621. Frank calls down a curse on himself no less certainly than Bartervile does in *If This Be Not*, and the reality of what awaits him as a consequence cannot be doubted.

Complementing the focus on words of power in the first two scenes is Mother Sawyer's opening soliloquy. Analyzing the power of others' words, she wonders to herself why she should

> be made a common sink,
> For all the filth and rubbish of Men's tongues
> To fall and run into? Some call me Witch;
> And being ignorant of my self, they go
> About to teach me how to be one: urging,
> That my bad tongue (by their bad usage made so)
> Forspeaks their Cattle, doth bewitch their Corn,
> Themselves, their Servants, and their Babes at nurse.   (2.1.6–13)

"Forspeak" and "bewitch" both refer to language as a *maleficium*, and Sawyer ambiguously denies that her use of such language is due only to the filth and rubbish directed at her by others. For these lines too are an instance of dramatic irony: although they evoke sympathy for Mother Sawyer when she speaks them, it is not long before she is indeed doing what she says others merely impute to her. No sooner has she voiced her complaint than old Banks enters, calls her a witch, and beats her when she curses him. The play later emphasizes his charity to others, and the effect is to suggest at least a partial vindication of his response to Sawyer in this scene, as if he is justified in responding violently to one who is literally capable of harming him with her words: "Would they [my bones] stuck cross thy throat, thy bowels, thy maw, thy midriff" (2.1.25–26).

Though devils were theologically more serious than popular magic, playwrights sometimes treated the latter more seriously than devils, as in Richard Brome's *The Queen's Exchange*, "acted with generall applause at the Black-Friers by His Majesty's Servants" in about 1630.[41] The only devils in this play are three craftsmen "in Divels habits" who create confusion and knockabout comedy in their clumsy attempt at burglary (5.1, pp. 535–39). On the other hand, six ghosts of Saxon kings appear in Act 3 (p. 505), and a prophecy about the royal succession made by one of the ghosts in dumb show unexpectedly comes true late in the play. A "genius" also appears, whispering in a character's ear to give him essential information (Act 4, pp. 528–29). These benign spirits are real in the play; that is, the ghosts and genius are imagined to be themselves, not another character in costume, as is the case with the play's devils.

Brome's anomalous treatment of ghosts as more credible than devils is not necessarily evidence of growing skepticism about stage devils; rather, it would seem to confirm ambivalence about magical thinking that we have seen elsewhere on the Shakespearean stage. In Cyril Tourneur's *The Atheist's Tragedy*, for example, likely performed by the King's Men at about the same time they staged Shakespeare's *The Tempest*, ghosts are treated with the same metadramatic archness that devils are subjected to in other plays on the Shakespearean stage. D'Amville "counterfeits to take [Charlemont] for a ghost" in order to maintain his lie that Charlemont is dead, thus outfacing Charlemont, as well as others who see the "real" Charlemont when he returns.[42] Hypocritical play-acting is thus indistinguishable from the play-acting of the actor who plays D'Amville, whether hypocrite or not. When Montferrers' ghost appears (3.2.37 SD), Charlemont's reaction is identical to the "false" reaction of D'Amville, even though Montferrers is "truly" a ghost, and D'Amville only feigns to see one. When the candlemaker Languebeau Snuff (who is posing hypocritically as a Puritan minister) uses a ghost disguise to prevent detection of his philandering (4.2.53 SD), his disguise is identical to the ghost disguise used by the actor playing Montferrers as a "real" ghost in other scenes. Snuff discards the ghost disguise in a fright, and Charlemont picks it up and dons it himself

(4.3.69–75), explicitly identifying it as a disguise, even as he puts it on. Charlemont is the play's most upright character, and when he rises with this disguise on, he succeeds unintentionally in frightening D'Amville (4.3.158 SD). The effect of a character disguised as a ghost is thus indistinguishable from the effect of a ghost.

But metadrama functions in this play not to promote disbelief but to condemn it.[43] D'Amville is an "atheist" not only because he denies God but because he discounts an omen (2.4.145ff.), betrays his nobility, and lies and murders without compunction. The idea of a virtuous atheist is a contradiction in terms for this play – as it seems to have been for the culture as a whole – because the providence that sustained the material world was also thought to sustain human society through moral expectation; to deny providence in the first was necessarily, therefore, to deny it in the second. Closely related to D'Amville's atheism is his play-acting, to which he calls attention, especially after murdering his brother, Montferrers (2.4.89, 113, 131, 161–62). This quality associates him with the Vice, to whom he is also allied in his hypocrisy, his gloating, his cynicism, his diabolical machinations, and his defeat in the end.

These elements of traditional dramaturgy in *The Atheist's Tragedy* qualify the seemingly obvious conclusion that its self-conscious play-acting empties out religious symbols. On the contrary, by repeatedly calling attention to the porous boundaries between illusion and reality, Tourneur heightens the uncanny effect of the stage ghost itself, as other playwrights heighten the effect of stage devils, because ghosts and devils both inhabited a realm that was scientifically and theologically liminal.[44] Confronting a forest of ideas about ghosts, Lewes Lavater thus clears the underbrush – melancholy imaginings, fearful fantasies, dull senses, and papists' deliberate hoaxes – to reveal the trees: "testimonies out of the word of God," "testimonies out of the ancient fathers," and arguments that "it is no harde thing for the diuell to appeare in diuers shapes, and to bring to passe straunge things"; that "God by the appearing of Spirits doth exercise the faithful, and punish the unbeleeuers"; and that we ought to take heed "when we heare strange crackes, or when other forewarnings happen."[45] Popish counterfeiting aside, "strange cracks" *are* a forewarning, and Lavater's ambivalence parallels Tourneur's ambivalent ghosts in *The Atheist's Tragedy*, as well as ambivalent devils on the Shakespearean stage. The oppositional thinking behind that ambivalence is the product of a particular historical moment, fraught both with traditional religious thinking and with religious skepticism about some aspects of it. This is clearly different from the oppositional thinking of the Enlightenment, with its confident bifurcation between reason and superstition, and to understand the mental world of the early seventeenth century therefore requires an act of imagination to resist antinomies that are more familiar and more credible because they are more recent.

CHAPTER TEN

New directions

The frequent and regular staging of devils in Jacobean and early Stuart drama belies the prevailing narrative that increasing secularization had effectively killed their credibility in the sixteenth century by reducing them to rare, risible, and empty vestiges of traditional dramaturgy on the Shakespearean stage. On the contrary, acting companies staged devils in ways that are generally consistent, either dramaturgically or morally or both, with the way devils had been staged during the previous two centuries of English drama. This is not to say, however, that nothing changed. The demand for variety in the commercial theatres was a powerful impetus to innovation, and playwrights responded accordingly. To be sure, not every new attempt was successful, and some are represented in only one or two plays. More enduring sources of innovation were Stoicism and Fletcherian tragicomedy, but the most striking change in the seventeenth century involves the social function of stage devils: increasingly, they are identified with those at the lower end of the social scale, in contrast to the formative tradition, which had associated devils almost exclusively with the nobility.

EXPERIMENTS

An early experiment with few imitations is William Haughton's *The Devil and His Dame* (1593–1601), which is extant only in a Restoration edition, renamed *Grim the Collier of Croydon*.[1] New in this play is Machiavelli's influence on stage devils. His antifeminist novella, *Belfagor*, turns on the point that women's resistance to patriarchal authority makes them more devilish than devils themselves. Haughton's debt to Machiavelli is explicit in the name ("Belphegor") and function of the devil who is commissioned in hell to find out if women are as treacherous as their reputation makes them. Cashing in on the popularity of patriotic plays, Haughton incarnates Belphegor as Castiliano, an arrogant Spanish doctor who becomes the object of anti-Spanish satire. The play thus makes almost nothing of Belphegor's real identity as a devil, and it is divided against itself, sometimes invoking sympathy for Castiliano because of his wife's treachery, sometimes invoking laughter at him because he is Spanish. His first effort at courtship is foiled by an independent Englishwoman's refusal:

> Base Alien, mercenary Fugitive,
> Presumptuous *Spaniard*, that with shameless pride
> Dar'st ask an English Lady for thy Wife.   (1.4.104–6)

When Castiliano thinks he has deceived her into sleeping with him anyway, he is himself deceived by a bed trick and forced to marry the woman he really bedded. Haughton does not adapt the traditional motif of the guiler beguiled to the multiple bed tricks in his play, though he conceivably gave Shakespeare the idea for doing so shortly afterwards, in *All's Well That Ends Well* and *Measure for Measure*. When Castiliano surprises his wife making love with another man, he rails at her: "Well may the world call thee the Devil's dame" (3.3.229), but she ably defends herself:

> What, do you think to pin up *Marian*,
> As you were wont to do your Spanish girles?
> No sir, I'le be half Mistriss of my self,
> The other half is yours, if you deserve it.   (3.3.258–61)

Haughton's contrast between Spanish jealousy and English relational freedom repeatedly collides with his attempt to impugn faithless noblewomen by comparing them unfavorably with the devils of hell.

Few dramatists followed Haughton in borrowing directly from Machiavelli, but in Barnabe Barnes' *The Devil's Charter*, performed by the King's Men in 1606, Machiavelli's influence helps to distinguish the play from *Dr. Faustus*, which Barnes otherwise imitates fairly closely, beginning with a conjuror who raises devils only to be undone by them in the end.[2] Barnes is less interested in native tradition than in a fashion set shortly before by John Marston in *Antonio and Mellida* (1599), inspired by Guicciardini's history of early sixteenth-century Italy. Barnes implicitly acknowledges his debt to Geffray Fenton's English translation of Guicciardini and to Machiavelli's *Discorsi* by creating a presenter called "Guichiardine."[3] The effect on the devils of *The Devil's Charter* is profound. Barnes creates a world where the principal motive for action is intimidation, and in this world, devils simply become the most effective intimidators, defeating the pope in the end because they are cleverer than he is and compel him to beg for mercy, as he had himself coerced others to plead before nonchalantly refusing them.[4] While Marston's influence was considerable in subsequent Italianate tragedy by Tourneur, Middleton, and Webster, no one followed Barnes in staging devils according to the pattern of intimidating intrigue that Guicciardini and Machiavelli describe.[5]

About as rare as Machiavelli's direct influence are plays that use stage devils to create spectacle for its own sake. While plays of this kind are a tribute to the continuing popularity of an age-old theatrical device, their very small number cautions against concluding that devils remained popular only because they made for spectacular theatre. The famous stage direction in Thomas Heywood's *The Silver Age* (1610–12), "fire-workes all ouer the house," is remarkable but understandable, because the scene is hell, and devils have just appeared "at euery corner of the stage with seuerall fire-workes."[6] The classical context did not prevent gods of the underworld from being costumed like devils in other plays, where the context is assumed to be Christian. "*Enter* Pluto, *his Chariot drawne in by Diuels*" reads the stage direction for the beginning of the rape of Proserpine (p. 135), and Proserpine's reaction could come from any other devil play: "Yon vgly shape affrights me"; "Hence foule fiend"; "Out on thee Hell-hound"; "Clawes off Diuell" (p. 136). Heywood had ample authority, even including Scot's *Discouerie*, for identifying Pluto with the Christian devil and Juno with a village witch, and the move literally demonizes classical mythology.[7] Still, *The Silver Age* contains no opposition that suggests the Christian God, and it is hard to avoid the impression that the real function of devils in Heywood's play is to create special effects.[8]

John Kirke's *The Seven Champions of Christendom*, whose title page describes it as having been played at the Cockpit and the Red Bull by 1638, appeals equally to theatrical thrill-seekers. Kirke calls on an array of devices associated with stage devils: thunder and lightning, fireworks, stage smoke, elaborate costumes, enchanters, rocks that open and close, ascending thrones, and magically transformed maidens (three swans turn into women before the spectators' eyes). These sensational devices are accompanied by no hint of the narrative and moral legacy that opposed saints against devils on the pre-Reformation stage and that continued to do so in plays like *The Virgin Martyr* (1620) and *St. Patrick for Ireland* (1637–40). Kirke omits social satire entirely and substitutes nationalism for traditional moral and spiritual insight, for George of England is by far the most important and successful of the seven champions, and his success often comes at the expense of the others.

STOICISM

More enduring than Machiavelli or stage spectacle in its effect on stage devils was the influence of Stoicism, which had long been reconciled with Christianity but whose assumptions were different and therefore produced different effects in drama, particularly since Stoicism entered the theatre principally with the influence of Senecan tragedy. Chapman's Stoicism in *Bussy D'Ambois* (1604–5) makes stage devils so ambiguous that their identity is difficult to determine, let alone their significance. On one hand, the play almost certainly responds to Marlowe's continuing influence by including both a conjuror and a spirit he conjures, with the biblical name "Behemoth." The conjuror, Friar Comolet, recalls Mephistopheles (costumed as an "old Franciscan friar" in *Dr. Faustus*) and imports the faint odor of anti-popery into *Bussy D'Ambois* that is overwhelming in Marlowe's play.[9] Comolet refers to conjuring as "exorcising rites" – a loaded phrase to use in the year that ecclesiastical legislation was issued against exorcism and dispossession – and his function is to assist the adulterous affair between Bussy and Tamyra, which he does by bringing them together in the first place and then by giving them information about the jealous plotting of Tamyra's husband.[10] All of this conforms to established Protestant traditions of staging devils to satirize Catholic belief and practice as hypocritical and immoral.

On the other hand, Bussy himself is the play's most sympathetic character, and his affair with Tamyra is the play's most sympathetic relationship. Bussy's character is composed of many different strands, among others being the Stoic "compleat man" (5.4.146), who is impervious to the vicissitudes of fate because of his remarkable self-possession, as King Henry recognizes: "A man so good, that only would uphold / Man in his native noblesse, from whose fall / All our dissentions rise" (3.2.90–92). Bussy is less good than the king's praise suggests, but the play favors him so strongly that Friar Comolet seems more like Friar Laurence in *Romeo and Juliet* than Pandarus in *Troilus and Cressida*. The friar expostulates in Christian terms with Tamyra and her jealous husband, Montsurry, when Montsurry confronts Tamyra in a fit of rage (5.1.30–35), and Comolet assures Tamyra of her safety as he leaves the two alone: "think'st thou him a Pagan? / His honor and his soule lies for thy safety" (5.1.43–44). This is a serious miscalculation, as Montsurry immediately proceeds to hideous abuse when the friar leaves – so hideous that when Comolet re-enters and sees what Montsurry is doing, the friar utters a single horrified exclamation ("What rape of honour and religion? / O wrack of nature!" [5.1.155–56]), and falls dead. But Comolet's Christian mission is not finished, for when he reappears as a ghost, he successfully persuades the dying Bussy to forgive his enemies (5.4.111), and then effects a reconciliation between Tamyra and Montsurry. The end of the play looks strangely like a restoration of charity, achieved by a pandaring friar.

The ambiguous conjuror in *Bussy D'Ambois* convokes no less ambiguous spirits to assist him. Bussy himself calls them "good aeriall spirits" (4.2.9), and neither early edition of the play refers to them as "devils."[11] Behemoth is a biblical monster mentioned once, in Job 40:15, as part of God's creation, but the only other named spirit in *Bussy D'Ambois* is Cartophylax, a Greek name that Chapman seems to have invented. Behemoth is three times referred to as "prince of darkness" or "prince of shades" (4.2.86; 5.3.22 and 42), suggesting something evil in Christian tradition, but the phrase has a different connotation if read in conjunction with Chapman's poem, *The Shadow of Night*, where darkness connotes mystery and therefore impenetrable truth.[12] Behemoth similarly refers to himself as "Emperor / Of that inscrutable darknesse, where are hid / All deepest truths, and secrets never seene" (4.2.68–70). He shares the overwhelming human admiration for Bussy, including admiration for his Stoic freedom, which draws the spirit willingly in response to Bussy's demand without the elaborate incantation used by the friar (5.3.13–54). Suspecting that Behemoth has lied to him in this interview, Bussy concludes, "Why then your prince of spirits may be call'd / The prince of lyers," to which Montsurry replies, "Holy writ so calls him" (5.3.92–93). But Bussy is mistaken, for Montsurry has deceived him by disguising himself as the friar, so the only liar in the scene is the demonic Montsurry, not Behemoth or Comolet. To be sure, Behemoth often speaks evasively and equivocally, but Chapman was well aware of classical traditions of prophecy and oracle, which only "lied" if interpreted incorrectly. As we noticed in chapter 8, Behemoth once refuses to disclose information because he is prohibited by fate (5.3.63), and this too is a Stoic detail, since Stoicism describes fate as the course that no creature can evade.

For Chapman, Stoicism did not always make stage devils ambiguous, for he invented a more traditional devil in *The Tragedy of Caesar and Pompey* (1602–5), even though Stoicism is more influential, both as an ethical ideal and as an explanation for the shape of the action. Millar Maclure observes that *Caesar and Pompey* is "essentially a morality" that illustrates the Stoic maxim printed prominently on the title page: "*Only a iust man is a freeman.*"[13] Pompey is thus presented psychomachically, with Caesar and Cato as his evil and good angels, respectively. The tragedy, then, consists in Pompey's failure to follow Cato's example, not in the apparently horrific death of Cato at the end of the play, when he falls on his sword and pulls out his entrails in order to hasten his end, resisting friends who attempt to sew him up (5.2.175 SD). There is no hint of despair on his part, only transcendent virtue. "Iust men are only free, the rest are slaues," are his dying words (5.2.177). Cato's death is, in effect, a Stoic martyrdom.[14]

Maclure describes the devil scene (2.1) as a "burlesque" prelude to Cato's suicide, which is the play's dramatic and ethical climax (p. 155). In traditional fashion, the scene defines the values upheld in the play's main action by enacting their preposterous opposition, as in the subplots of traditional drama and Jonson's later antimasques. Fronto, "a ruined knave," appears in this scene alone. As an English commoner in an unusually classical and high-minded play, he sports "an ouergrowne red Beard, black head, with a Halter in his hand, looking about" (2.1.0 SD), like desperate vices with halters around their necks in Tudor morality plays. In his opening soliloquy, Fronto admits to being a confidence trickster and determines to kill himself because his tricks no longer serve (2.1.1–24). His suicide is prevented by the sudden appearance of Ophioneus, "with the face, wings, and taile of a Dragon" (2.1.24 SD), who successfully tempts Fronto with the promise of upward mobility (2.1.114–20), as the devil tempts weak-minded Protestants in late Elizabethan moralities. Here, though, the values Fronto offends by his weakness are not reformed doctrines but the world-hating attitudes of Cato, the "just man" whose Stoic suicide this scene anticipates by default. In contrast to the ambiguous "spirits" of *Bussy D'Ambois*, Ophioneus describes himself as "an immortal deuill" (52), who is identified in "the old stoick *Pherecides*" (57), as a "Deuilish Serpent, by interpretation; was generall Captaine of that rebellious host of spirits that wag'd warre with heauen" (2.1.60–62). This is a genuine classical reference (though not a Stoic one), but it could as easily be Christian, especially since Chapman alludes to "spirits," not "giants," who warred with heauen.[15] Ophioneus promises Fronto "Chopines at commandment to any height of life thou canst wish" (156–57), and when Fronto fears he has already fallen too low, Ophioneus is reassuring: "hast thou not heard of *Vulcans* falling out of heauen?" (159–60). "Better goe lame in the fashion with *Pompey*, then neuer so vpright, quite out of the

fashion, with *Cato*" (162–64). Chapman borrows a traditional, and ultimately Christian, dramatic satire of power and ambition as a foil to his
upright Stoic hero.

Stoicism might be expected to influence the devils of Thomas Goffe's
The Courageous Turk, because it is an academic play, associated with Christ
Church, Oxford, in 1619. Yet popular drama is surprisingly influential
in this play as well, for it borrows from both Senecan tragedy and the
Marlovian rhetoric and staging of Shakespeare's *Richard III*. Four devils
who visit Amurath the Turk on the eve of his defeat imitate the ghosts
who appear to Richard III on the eve of Bosworth.[16] The fiends are
"framed like Turkish Kings, but blacke, his supposed predecessors."[17] They dance
about Amurath *"to a kind of hideous noyse"* and warn him that his doom is
near, mentioning his crimes (5.3.29) and asserting that the furies will
resign their snakes to him when he is damned (36–39). They clearly fore-
shadow his fate, and they therefore complement the comets and falling
stars that Amurath observes (5.3.0 SD) before he retires to be visited by
the fiends. These portents are sponsored by the Christian God, as
Amurath himself recognizes, when he invokes Mahomet to

> Command the puny-Christians demi-God
> Put out those flashing sparkes, those *Ignes fatui*,
> Or ile unseate him.   (5.3.5–7)

Since Amurath is overthrown in the end, the play vindicates the Christian
God against Amurath's skepticism about portents, but in deference to the
Senecan conventions that Goffe adapts, God is never named in the play.
The Christians invoke "heaven," not God. "Thou sacred guider of
the arched Heavens" is the first phrase uttered by a Christian in the
play (3.1.1). Christ is not named, nor is any distinctively Christian idea
mentioned.

More important for Goffe's devils, Stoicism provides a distinctive
moral framework for Amurath's story. As his lieutenant Schahin points
out, "in each man we see a Monarchy" (1.2.6): reason should govern the
affections, as a king governs his kingdom. Schahin's point is the conventional one that Amurath is now a subject, not a king, because he is ruled
by passion for Eumorphe (1.2.14). Though Amurath overcomes this
passion through murderous misogyny, he nonetheless regains command
of himself by doing so and therefore achieves Stoic virtue: "for he surely
shall / That conquers first himselfe, soone conquer all" (2.5.84–85). The
fact that a Christian destroys Amurath in the end may suggest that Stoic
virtue is not enough in itself. References to fate and fortune are frequent

in Turkish mouths, but the Christians' reliance on "Heaven" is vindi-cated in the end by the death of Amurath, with its celestial portents and scolding fiends. To be sure, the Christians are all destroyed as well, and their lands are under Turkish control as the play ends, but earthly success or failure is not what counts for the Christian hero who kills Amurath:

> What terror can affright a Christians thoughts
> Who knowes there is a world, at liberty
> To breath in, when this glasse of life is broke?
> Our foes with circling furie are intrencht;
> Pelions of earth and darknesse shall orelade them,
> Whilst we shall mount, and these our spirits light,
> Shall be yet ponderous to depresse them lower.   (5.2.41–47)

In fact, the "world, at liberty / To breath in" seems to be as Stoic as it is Christian, especially in comparison with the motto of Chapman's *Caesar and Pompey*: "*Only a iust man is a freeman*," and with Bussy's equally defiant death. Viewed in this light, Goffe's fiends would appear to be as syncretic as Chapman's.

FLETCHERIAN TRAGICOMEDY

Even more influential than Stoicism, as an innovation affecting stage devils, was the impact of tragicomedy as adapted from Italian drama by John Fletcher. In chapter 8 we noticed a characteristic recourse to self-reflexive dramaturgy in two plays by Fletcher, *Monsieur Thomas* (1610–16) and *The Chances* (1617), and his influence is also apparent in Nathan Field's *A Woman Is a Weathercock* (1609). While the satire involving devils in these plays is limited and strategic, as I have argued, it also has a secularizing effect. In *Monsieur Thomas*, Tom indeed repeats the pattern of the guiler beguiled – reinforced by his tricks, by references to him as the devil, by his bravura acting, and by his being tricked by Mary in his own turn – but he does so in a romantic plot, where the stakes are a lighthearted resolution of the theatrical reversals that have separated him and Mary. Stage devils are similarly transposed from a sacred to a romantic function in *The Merry Devil of Edmonton*, as we saw in chapter 7, and secularization is reinforced in *Monsieur Thomas* by a comic reversal of the prodigal-son motif (the play's subtitle is "the father's own son"). Tom's father is curmudgeonly but whimsical, repeatedly threatening to disown his son if Tom ever becomes serious and gives up his determined folly. The language of stern paternal expectation is thus diverted to the opposite of its expected purpose: Tom fails in Sebastian's eyes when he is most discreet, and wins his father's approval when he behaves most outrageously. The result is a satire of moralistic sternness that probably involves anti-Puritan satire as well, for whenever Sebastian acts like a disappointed father, the reason for his disappointment is Tom's momentary lapse into soberness.

Such reversals of expectation are a hallmark of Fletcher's style, and they contributed to a witty new treatment of stage devils that competed with traditional elements on the Shakespearean stage. While Field's *A Woman Is a Weathercock* depends on the incompatibility of the devil and the sacrament of marriage, as we noticed earlier, the play also delays its over-clever resolution until the last scene, when Nevil reveals his double disguise as both a priest and a devil. The audience is thus prevented from knowing how the action will be resolved, and when the resolution comes, it is a stage trick, the "prettie Emblem" that reveals Nevil not to be a married man after all but an eligible bachelor.[18] The denouement has little to do with the life the play ostensibly imitates and everything to do with theatrical artifice.

Fletcher's influence on stage devils is particularly noticeable in three devil plays, one late Jacobean, the other two late Caroline, and only one of them in part by Fletcher himself. The first of these is *The Prophetess*, which Fletcher and Massinger wrote for the King's Men in 1622. Massinger had collaborated with Dekker two years earlier in *The Virgin Martyr*, and some similarities with that play are apparent in the later one.[19] For the most part, however, *The Prophetess* is a witty palimpsest of the classical and the Christian, evoking elements of both traditions in such a way as to create something that is self-consciously unexpected and strange. The prophetess of the title is Delphia, who combines qualities of several literary characters: the Delphic oracle, the Virgin Mary, and Virgil's Jupiter, Juno, and Cumaean sibyl, from *The Aeneid*. Response to Delphia within the play is ambivalent, inevitably creating a similar response in the audience. Skeptics condemn her as a "juggler" (1.3.69, 98), a conniver with devils (1.3.103), and a village witch whose alliance with the devil enables her to wreak petty wrongs on her neighbors (1.3.113–20).[20] Her admirers call her a "holy *Druid*" (1.3.95), "blessed mother" (3.1.48), and a god (1.3.222), though she eschews the latter title. In addition to being called "blessed mother," she is like the Virgin Mary in being a miracle worker, a powerful intervener in human affairs, an advocate for women, and a "saint" in all but name, who requires people to believe in her power in order for their lives to be blessed. At the same time, she herself speaks incongruously of performing rites to Hecate (2.3.145), and the chorus at one point describes her as having

> free acesse to all the secret counsels
> Which a full Senat of the gods determine
> When they consider man: The brass-leav'd book
> Of Fate lies open to thee, where thou read'st,
> And fashionest the destinies of men
> At thy wished pleasure.   (4.2.73–78)

Though Delphia denies she is divine, she undoubtedly controls the destiny of characters in the play, as Jove does in the *Aeneid*. Yet the values by which the powerful win and retain her favor are not Virgilian but Christian: humility, faithfulness, penitence, and forgiveness. All of these eventually mark Diocles, the common soldier who is elevated to the imperial throne by a prophecy of Delphia, after which he takes the name Dioclesian – ironically one of the severest persecutors of Christians among the Roman emperors. His story compares favorably with English saints' plays that feature the Blessed Virgin, such as the N-Town *Trial of Mary and Joseph* and *The Assumption of the Virgin*.

Delphia's conjuring of a devil at one point is therefore incongruous – a combining of plays about the Blessed Virgin with a well-established tradition of stage conjurors inspired by Faustus. The conjuring occurs in a comic context that echoes Marlowe's *Faustus*. When the foolish Geta accuses Delphia of keeping devils (3.2.89–96), she offers to fetch him one and conjures in response to his wish. A she-devil called Lucifera appears (3.2.108 SD), and Geta asks if he might kiss her. When she sits on his knee and whispers in his ear, he complains that he is "burnt to ashes" with "a kinde of Glass-house in my cod-piece" (3.2.118–19). The episode is clearly farcical, yet it includes Geta, who belongs to the play's Christian pattern. He personifies foolish pride and arrogance, thus providing a comic counterpart to the besetting sin of Dioclesian the emperor in the main plot. When Geta asks Delphia to lend him a devil "That we may daunce a while" (5.3.86), she offers to lend him two. Minutes later, Geta enters accompanied "*with Sprits as* Pan *and* Ceres" (5.4.44 SD). If these are the two devils referred to earlier, then devils and classical gods are implicitly identified, as in Heywood's *The Silver Age*. Whereas the identification in Heywood's play is naive, however, in *The Prophetess* it is another witty device to keep the audience guessing and to create a cleverly kaleidoscopic texture of endless allusions to other plays and other literary traditions.

A similar effect appears in *The Goblins*, written by John Suckling for the King's Men in 1637–41. The trick in Suckling's play is that the identity of the "goblins" is concealed until the very end. They appear and reappear as devils, but they are really noblemen who have been unfairly treated at court and have therefore taken up thievery to survive; they conceal themselves by using devil costumes but reveal their sense of injured justice by acting like Robin Hood. This witty theatrical device is borrowed from Robert Davenport's *A New Trick to Cheat the Devil* (1627), where Master Changeable disguises himself as a devil to perform an act of charity for his prospective son-in-law. In *The Goblins* the noble Samorat contrasts elite and popular views of the goblins in a way that hints at their true identity: "the wiser sort" believe the devils are thieves who disguise themselves "to rob / More powerfully," but "the common people" view them more naively, thinking

> them a race
> Of honest and familiar Devills,
> For they do hurt to none, unlesse resisted;
> They seldome take away, but with exchange;
> And to the poore often give,
> Returne the hurt and sicke recover'd,
> Reward or punish, as they do find cause.[21]

Suckling's "devils" evoke the "fairies" in *The Merry Wives of Windsor*, in that they pinch and mock their victims, eliciting confessions that reveal the ills of the court (3.1.1–43; 3.7.1–39), and at one point echoing Dekker's idea about human depravity exceeding devils' in *If This Be Not* (followed by Jonson in *The Devil Is an Ass*): "Stay! Now I have better thought upon't, he shall to earth agen: for villanie is catching, and will spread: he will enlarge our Empire much, then w'are sure of him at any time" (3.1.50–52). An audience that was aware of devils on the Shakespearean stage could make a reasonable guess that the goblins are disguised human beings; indeed, they were supposed to make that guess.

The Goblins is archly sophisticated, explicitly alluding to Shakespeare and Fletcher, as well as Davenport. The devils capture a character known only as a poet, for the sole purpose of creating allusions to other plays and poetry. Honor is the play's ultimate value, evident in dueling, in satire of the court for its *lack* of honor, in frequent use of "cavalier," an allusion to curled male hair (3.2.1), and a brief debate that anticipates the heroic drama of the Restoration:

> SABRINA. Had'st thou consulted but with love as much
>   As honour, this had never been.
> SAMORAT. I have no love for thee that has not had
>   So strict an union with honour still,
>   That in all things they were concern'd alike.   (2.3.43–47)

Indeed, *The Goblins* looks forward to Restoration drama more than it looks back, and Dryden's judgment about Suckling's play in 1669 is a striking indication of how much Fletcher's style contributed to the loss of what preceded it. After commenting that Fletcher's *Sea-Voyage* imitates the plot of Shakespeare's *The Tempest*, Dryden mentions other imitators as well: "*Sir* John Suckling, *a profess'd admirer of our Authour, has follow'd his footsteps in his* Goblins; *his* Regmella *being an open imitation of* Shakespear's Miranda; *and his Spirits, though counterfeit, yet are copied from* Ariel."[22] Dryden is right that Suckling's goblins are imitative, but his identification of Ariel as their model seems to be a wild guess that suggests he may have lost touch with the continuous tradition of staging devils before 1642.

Fletcher's witty influence remained strong until the closing of the theatres and beyond, as we can see from one of the last devil plays on the Shakespearean stage, a spin-off, of sorts, from Dekker's and Massinger's *The Virgin Martyr*, almost twenty years before. This play is James Shirley's *St. Patrick for Ireland*, performed in Dublin in the late 1630s, when the London theatres were closed because of the plague and some enterprising actors led by John Ogilby attempted to establish a commercial theatre in a colonial outpost.[23] In both this play and *The Virgin Martyr*, the confrontation between Christianity and paganism is an oppositional scheme that is capable of multiple meanings, and Shirley exploits the ambiguities wittily in *St. Patrick* to the point of virtual irresolution. On one hand, Patrick's chief opponent is a conjuror, Archimagus, who owes a great deal to his namesake, Spenser's Archimago, in Book 1 of *The Faerie Queene*. Viewed as a Catholic purveyor of "precious jugling" (2.2.74), Archimagus relates directly to Spenser's character: both consort with and conjure devils, create false images, and personify hypocrisy and double dealing. Indeed, Spenser's character accounts for the devils of *St. Patrick for Ireland* better than native stage tradition does.[24]

At the same time, however, Patrick is accompanied by traditionally habited priests who sing in Latin (1.1.145–56), suggesting a tolerating impulse in the play – a resistance to identifying traditional Christianity with the kind of hypocrisy and duplicity that characterize the pagans. Given Shirley's Catholic allegiance, this seems understandable: all Christians, not just Protestants, are seemingly invited to identify with Patrick, just as all Christians are invited to identify with Dorothea in *The Virgin Martyr*. Shirley's defense of Catholicism (if it can be called that) is severely compromised, however, by the play's attack on the Irish. Patrick comes from Britain (1.1.175), bringing English enlightenment (and specifically religious enlightenment) to benighted Ireland; in this respect,

Shirley's Patrick is a precursor of Spenser and more particularly of Shirley himself, the English stage magician who writes a play about the most powerful magician in Irish history. The Irish native tradition is bankrupt, ignorant, and hypocritical, and therefore easy to identify with seditious Irish Catholicism for the English colonists who saw the play in Dublin. Patrick blesses Conallus, the king's virtuous son, when he repents (5.3.8ff.), predicting a glorious future for the rulers of Ireland, which include the English Lord Governor in 1639. Viewed this way, *St. Patrick for Ireland* is as eager an advocate of English colonization in Ireland as Spenser's *View of the Present State of Ireland*. What looks like toleration dissolves in the ambiguity of theatrical cleverness.

An important difference between *The Virgin Martyr* and *St. Patrick* is Shirley's reduction of oppositional thinking to a contest for power. We have seen this kind of reduction in Marlowe's *Dr. Faustus* as well, but Shirley takes it in a very different direction from Marlowe. Patrick's success in the end is not due to goodness but to stronger magic – another telling appeal to English colonial domination. When Patrick tames the snakes in the play's climactic scene, the Irish King Leogarius acknowledges in an aside that he feels forced to make peace with the invader out of fear, not out of love (5.3.144–45), which presumably says something about his stubbornness but in fact says a good deal about Patrick's dominance. The devils are also afraid of Patrick from the moment Leogarius recounts his fearful dream of Patrick's arrival in the play's first scene. The angel in this play is called "Victor," and he is given no opportunity to demonstrate charity or to counsel it in others, as Angelo does in *The Virgin Martyr*. It is hard to imagine Pepys being as impressed with Victor as he was when he saw Angelo in the theatre: "But that which did please me beyond any thing in the whole world was the wind-musique when the angel comes down, which is so sweet that it ravished me, and indeed, in a word, did wrap up my soul so that it made me really sick, just as I have formerly been when in love with my wife."[25]

The cultivation of ambiguity and triumphant English patriotism in the main plot is complemented in the subplot by an emphasis on farce. Archimagus' assistant, the comical Rodamant, is remarkable only for his risible folly, bringing with him none of the richly suggestive black humor of Hircius and Spongius in *The Virgin Martyr*. Like Cuddy Banks in *The Witch of Edmonton*, Rodamant is infatuated with a woman above his social status – the queen, in fact – and this is why he is so laughable, but his interaction with a devil is not related to his obsession for the queen, which remains irreducibly ridiculous. Patrick's overwhelming power reaches into the subplot as well, affecting Rodamant spectacularly when Patrick resurrects him from the dead, after Rodamant drinks poison that had been intended for Patrick, whom it does not harm (3.1). The episode has a precedent in the N-Town saint's play, *The Trial of Mary and Joseph*, but there the resolution is achieved by Mary's prayer to God to forgive her enemies, and the point is her power to resist evil, not to raise the dead.

THE DEVIL AND SOCIETY

Among new directions that acting companies chose for stage devils in the seventeenth century, the most revealing is the social level at which devils increasingly operated. Traditionally, stage devils had been associated almost exclusively with the nobility, as we noticed in early chapters of this book, because pride, which motivated the archetypal fall of Lucifer, highest in the created order, also beset those at the upper end of the social scale, who potentially inflicted the greatest damage on the sacred social body. This way of evaluating the social hierarchy explains the oppositional narrative symmetry of God defeating the devil by adopting the form of a peasant, and in retrospect it helps to explain why commoners are seldom associated with the devil in pre-Reformation drama, whereas innumerable members of the nobility are caught in the devil's clutches. A dishonest alewife appears briefly in hell in the Chester *Harrowing of Hell*, and the wealthy farmer, Cain, clearly belongs to the devil in the Towneley *Killing of Abel*, but in keeping with the ethics of Jesus, God's "freindes deare" are nearly always "such as poore and naked weare," while God's enemies are usually rich and powerful.[26] This opposition became the foundation of social satire in traditional drama, as I have argued in chapters 2 and 4, and it reasserted itself in later Reformation drama, when the new Protestant regime itself became identified with established wealth and privilege.

No doubt many factors contributed to a gradual shift in drama, from associating the devil primarily with the upper classes to associating him with commoners, but one likely reason is a shifting social attitude toward the indigent. Officially understood before the Reformation as sanctified by their poverty, the poor gradually became the objects of suspicion and rejection. This shift in turn had a number of causes, some relating to religious secularization: the enclosure of common lands that deprived many tenant farmers of their livelihood and increased the number of "sturdy beggars," the dissolution of the monasteries,

Protestant opposition to mendicant clerics, a decline in generosity because of reformed ideas about salvation through faith rather than good deeds. An important symptom of the change is the advent of "rogue pamphlets," designed to expose beggars as confidence tricksters.[27] First in this genre was Martin Luther's *Ordinance for a Common Chest*, whose motivation was both theological and social, but at least two writers for the English commercial stage contributed to the genre: Robert Greene, in his pamphlets on "coney-catching" (1591–92), and Thomas Dekker, in *The Belman of London* (1608). Dekker is the more ambivalent of the two, exposing beggars as dissimulating rascals in his pamphlet but espousing traditional virtues of public charity to the poor in several of his plays, as we noticed in chapter 9.[28]

In any case, as with many other patterns in early drama, the devil's social association began to change with the advent of commercial theatres near London. In Marlowe's *Dr. Faustus* and Greene's *Friar Bacon and Friar Bungay*, social status acquires new value, as we saw in chapters 6 and 7, so that rising above a common origin becomes a good in itself, and the devil despises commoners as much as everyone else does. This is not the same as identifying commoners with the devil, but it realigns the cosmic and social hierarchies that traditional drama had inverted in relation to each other, and that realignment was necessary if commoners were to be demonized because they were commoners.

An example of the latter appears in John Marston's *Histriomastix* (1599), which briefly stages a devil as part of a play-within-the-play presented by a group of traveling actors.[29] In other words, the devil in *Histriomastix* is explicitly presented as a player disguised as a devil, with the intent to satirize common players. The same satire is implicit in Jonson's masques, as we noticed in chapter 8, for the masques required actors from commercial companies to take the preposterous roles of witches, monsters, and commoners in the antimasque. This is a motive for social satire that valorizes the social hierarchy as absolute, rather than emphasizing its moral inconsistencies, as social satire does in pre-Reformation drama.

A similar reinforcement appears in plays where the high-minded assumptions of Stoicism and neo-Platonism are at work. For these assumptions appealed to those who prospered from new social mobility, which had stagnated late in Elizabeth's reign but regained momentum under James. Skill in intellectual labor distinguished those who bettered their minds at university or the inns of court, the apex of the new educational system put in place by the Tudors, and the classical preference for the mind rather than the body, especially favored by Stoicism and Platonism, was an effective way to explain why those who bettered their minds deserved to master those who did not. This is a powerful motive for upward mobility, revealing a social component in the appeal of Renaissance philosophy, if not a social cause for it.

Tudor social change affects the devils of two Elizabethan plays, Lodge's and Greene's *A Looking Glass for London and England* (1587–88) and the anonymous *Pleasant Comedy Called Wily Beguilde*, published in 1606 but likely a reworking of a lost play called *Wily Beguily* from the 1560s. The only devil in *Looking Glass* is a "ruffian" disguised as a devil, and his sole function is to terrify the wife of Adam, a "clown," though Adam himself remains unconvinced.[30] Though the play stages the story of Jonah and Nineveh, it alters the pattern of earlier biblical drama by relegating the devil to a subplot with silly commoners.

As the title of *Wily Beguilde* announces, the play's central motif is the guiler beguiled, familiar to pre-Reformation drama and the Tudor morality play. In this case, those who are undone by their own machinations are a duplicitous lawyer called Churms and a coney-catching confidence man who assists in Churms' knavery. The con man is named Robin Goodfellow, and the play demystifies popular culture by imagining him to be "a boatewrites son of *Hull*," his mother "a refus'd hagge," who conceived him

> Vnder the olde ruines of *Boobies* barne,
> Who as she liu'd, at length she likewlse [sic] died,
> And for her good deedes went vnto the Diuell.[31]

Like the ruffian in *Looking Glass*, Robin is a devil only in disguise, which he uses to frighten the gullible. The successful foiling of a plot by an upstart lawyer and a representative of ignorant popular culture (Robin) vindicates the social ideal of Tudor humanism and is probably a remnant of *Wily Beguily*. The opposition is further vilified by its implicit but consistent identification with the old faith. Several characters swear "barlady" and "bith mas," but Robin does so most consistently and frequently, in the manner of the Vice in Protestant morality plays. The exposure of the guilers is thus an exposure of coney-catching, ignorant popular culture, and the superstitious old faith.

The contrast is reinforced by the erudition and classical learning of the romantic hero, Sophos. He uses the flowers of humanistic rhetoric, referring learnedly to stories of the classical gods and goddesses, borrowing Petrarchan figures of speech, imitating the high style of the 1560s (pp. 10–11). A classical woodland god, Sylvanus, appears to him at the nadir of his fortunes, "Drawne by the sound of Ecchoes sad reports" (p. 40), and offering "Madrigalles and Rowndealyes / To comfort *Sophos*" (p. 41). Sylvanus as a classical woodland healer is thus contrasted with Robin, a native woodland imposter and trouble-maker. The redemptive presence in the play is heroically noble, virtuous, classical, and elite; the malign influence in the form of Robin is native and popular, leagued with a pernicious lawyer, and associated with the devil, if only by means of disguise.

Wily Beguilde's association of the devil with commoners is less explicit, and more closely indebted to Stoicism, in the anonymous *Two Noble Ladies*, performed at the Red Bull Theatre by the Players of the Revels in 1619–23. This play in the popular repertory reproduces a social prejudice that we have seen in Chapman's *Caesar and Pompey*, where Stoicism has the effect of identifying the devil exclusively with a desperate confidence trickster, Fronto, who is a foil to the high-minded Cato. Like Dekker's and Massinger's *Virgin Martyr*, with which it is almost exactly contemporary, *The Two Noble Ladies* is a Jacobean saint's play – in addition to being an interwoven romance involving the two ladies of the title – but whereas Dorothea is martyred, Cyprian is converted, and what he is converted from is Stoicism. Indeed, his high-minded virtue is the principal reason that an angel predicts Cyprian's conversion to Christianity, "since in him vertuous parts / are found."[32] Cyprian the Stoic sage thus offers advice to Lysander, when Lysander is sick in love with the absent Miranda:

> false ffortune cannot lessen a full man.
> Our weaker parts of Earth are only ty'd
> to th' turning wheel of the worlds blindefold guide:
> the minde's aboue her anger. keep thine so.   (2.3.673–76)[33]

Though the devils of *The Two Noble Ladies* have no regard for rank in their assaults, only commoners succumb to them. Cyprian calls devils into the play for the first time to assist him when he falls in love with Justina, a Christian princess. Failing to move her with *carpe diem* sentiments (4.5.1623–29), he resorts to force, invoking the devils to help him rape her, but the devils flee when Justina opens her prayer book, and Cyprian is so amazed that he converts to Christianity (5.2), only to become the object of demonic threats himself, with the devil Cantharides echoing Mephistopheles' threats against Faustus. Cyprian reverses the tragedy of Faustus, however, by accepting the offer of Justina's prayer book, so "*the Devills sinck roaring; a flame of fier riseth after them*" (5.2.1860 SD). With regard to Cyprian's conversion alone, the devils suggest that even Stoic virtue is not enough: as an angel says, when he gives Cyprian the prayer book, "this shews the blindnesse of philosophie" (5.2.1866).

In contrast to Cantharides' frustration in the main plot of *The Two Noble Ladies*, the devil finds easy work in the subplot, where an oppositional counterpart to Stoic rectitude develops as a foil to Cyprian, paralleling the scene with Fronto and Ophioneus in Chapman's *Caesar and Pompey*. The subplot involves four allegorically named commoners who interact with Cantharides: Barebones, Sinew, and Blood compete for the attention of Caro, who is a courtesan, with Cantharides clawing each by turns, in order to incite them to keener sexual competition. Like Chapman's Fronto, the subplot characters of *The Two Noble Ladies* are unable to resist what Cyprian calls "our weaker parts of Earth," and they therefore depict the failure of Stoic virtue by default, as Cyprian himself does when he falls in love with Justina. Confining error to Caro, the flesh, is a marked departure, in a Stoic direction, from the tradition that shaped stage devils in the first place. Caro appears much earlier as a source of moral failure in *The Castle of Perseverance*, but there the personification is male and a king, like his counterparts, Mundus and the Devil, and Caro is less influential in breaching Human Genus' moral defenses than is Mundus, who uses covetousness, not sensuality, as his bait. Covetousness, the besetting sin of concentrated wealth, is not on the moral map of *The Two Noble Ladies*.

Devils tend to be associated principally with commoners in several plays that we have noticed for other reasons. In *The Witch of Edmonton* (1621), the devil's influence increases as one moves lower on the social scale. Though Goody Sawyer is allowed a few lines of trenchant commentary on court depravity, she is herself a pauper, and her failure to repent of her traffic with the devil contrasts strongly with the charity and forgiveness that Frank Thorney wins in the gentry plot, as if grace were dispensed in proportion to social status. In Fletcher's *The Prophetess* (1622), devils appear only in association with the foolish commoner, Geta, who is an unregenerate parallel to Diocles, the repentant convert and future emperor. When devil costumes are used as a disguise in *The Queen's Exchange* (1629–32), those who use them are comic tradesmen, and only a servant is taken in by the disguise; a noble lady who also sees the "devils" knows at once that they are fake. Davenant's first masque, *The Temple of Love* (1635), is constructed oppositionally, in Jonson's manner, identifying opponents of the Platonically idealized court with fiends, hell, and witches. Those opponents include the commercial theatres, with their non-courtly auspices and common actors.

Despite the innovative association of devils with the lower end of the social scale, the influence of new styles and ideas in seventeenth-century drama does not amount to a teleological narrative of decisive departure, by 1642, from the tradition that originated devil plays before the Reformation. This point is borne out by a high-minded association of devils with commoners in Thomas Nabbes' masque, *Microcosmus*, from 1637.[34] Important to this masque is "Malus Genius," whose sophisticated classical name is belied by his appearance, "A divell in a black robe: haire, wreath and wings black" (p. 165), and whose oppositional role is suggested in the decoration of the *frons*: "adorn'd with brasse figures of Angels and Divels . . . The Title in an Escocheon supported by an Angell and a Divell" (p. 166). As its title implies, *Microcosmus* establishes an analogy between the macrocosm and the microcosm, with Nature and Janus ruling over the contending elements in the first, and Physander and Bellamina ruling over the contentious complexions in the second.

The masque's broadly Platonic context helps to account for the particular way in which the central story of moral decline unfolds. For when Malus Genus breaks up the marriage of the body (Physander) and the soul (Bellamina), he is assisted by the five senses, who are all commoners: Seeing, a chambermaid; Smelling, a huntsman; Hearing, an usher of the hall; Taste, a cook; Touch, a lady's gentleman usher. Moreover, in the process of courting Sensuality, Physander dances a country dance with her (p. 191 SD), again associating the senses with what is socially common and most open to the devil's influence. "She's common," complains Bellamina to Physander, when she sees him with Sensuality, "and will mixe her lustfull blood / Even with beasts" (p. 192). An allegory of moral degeneration is also, in effect, an allegory of social decline.

Yet this close analogy between individual microcosm and social macrocosm occurs in a masque which in many other respects is closely akin to the fifteenth-century morality play, *Wisdom*, where personified features of human moral consciousness are also depicted in the process of decline and renewal. Malus Genius' effect on Physander parallels the devil's effect on Anima, whom he tempts away from Wisdom in the fifteenth-century play. Bellamina explains Malus Genius' plan to Physander:

> The other's clad in an infernall robe
> Of mallice to us, and will tempt thy frailty

To loose desires, from her black invention
Forging aspersions on me to divert
Thy love.   (p. 180)

Malus Genius' success is evident when we next see Physander: he is "richly habited" (p. 183 SD), like Humanum Genus after succumbing to the blandishments of Mundus in *The Castle of Perseverance*, and he is now enamored of Sensuality, rather than Bellamina. Following Physander's transformation, the complexions in *Microcosmus* embark on a sensual binge, as the mights do in *Wisdom*, drinking excessively and joking bawdily. The pattern of the morality play continues as Physander falls ill, suffers injury in attempting to part the contending complexions (p. 197), and despairs, blaming Nature for creating him. When Sensuality deserts him, Malus Genius mocks him, laughing at his ruin (p. 199).

Just as Wisdom defeats the devil in *Wisdom*, however, Bellamina's faithfulness defeats Malus Genius in the end. When Sensuality deserts Physander, Bellamina returns, introducing him to a doctor called Temperance, who prescribes restraint and a natural diet. A "miracle" happens (p. 203), and Physander's cure is assured when he is invested with four virtues: Temperance, Justice, Prudence, and Fortitude. The five senses appear in "beggerlike habits" (p. 204 SD), whereas Physander appears in his "first habit," and Malus Genius laments his defeat in terms that recall the traditional devil: "his glory is my shame. / Mischiefe attempted, if it want successe, / Is the contrivers punishment" (p. 204). These words might well be spoken by Milton's Satan in *Paradise Lost*.

The point is that innovative styles and ideas do not necessarily vitiate traditional influence, even in a masque as late as 1637. This is not to say that the archaism of *Microcosmus* is definitive; it obviates neither topical meaning nor the impact of secularization, as in the masque's substitution of four classical virtues for Christian virtues or the redemption of the body by the soul rather than by divine grace. What is nonetheless remarkable about Nabbes' masque is how much remains, even as late as 1637, of the oppositional tradition that gave rise to stage devils in the first place, attributing degeneration and loss to the devil and restoration to what the devil opposes, which is reduced to a "miracle" in *Microcosmus*. This kind of continuity highlights the masque's literal demonization of commoners. The devil is a courtly gallant in the fifteenth-century *Wisdom*, and Anima's mights are transformed into aristocratic retainers, as their livery makes clear, when they yield to the devil's wiles. This is not true in *Microcosmus*, where the five senses are depicted as commoners, and their brief triumph reads like a royalist allegory of parliamentary success. Imagining the devil's influence this way reinforces the masque's platonic ideology, but it marks a definitive difference from the formative tradition of theatrical demons to which both *Wisdom* and *Microcosmus* are otherwise deeply indebted.

Microcosmus is one among several plays, as we have seen, that introduce the same kind of innovation in the social function of stage devils. This innovation is a striking departure from the tradition that gave rise to vernacular stage devils in the fifteenth century, and it convincingly refutes E. K. Chambers' assessment of that tradition. As he read early drama, devils were evidence of salutary secular change that challenged oppressive Christian influence and eventually flowered in the commercial plays of Shakespeare and his contemporaries. This way of telling the story is oppositional, in its contrast between secular enlightenment and religious ignorance, but that kind of binarism prevented Chambers from recognizing another kind of oppositional thinking that introduced stage devils into liturgical drama and continued to animate them in the vernacular drama of the fifteenth, sixteenth, and seventeenth centuries. This traditional conception is what created the formative social function of stage devils, as I have argued, by recognizing God's enemies as those who side with the devil through the sin of pride – a sin to which the nobility were particularly vulnerable. The vitality of this tradition remained strong until the advent of secularizing influences in the commercial theatres. In contrast to Chambers' argument, the devil only becomes identified with commoners late in the tradition, when Christian influence begins to subside, and the motive for that identification is social change and high-minded philosophy, not secular resistance to Christianity or peasant resistance to upper-class abuses. That the upper classes *were* abusive no one doubted, but identifying social abuses with stage devils was consistent with the assumption that the devil was the enemy of the sacred social body, as he was the enemy of individual Christians and of all good things. In that capacity, he was the originator of social oppression, as well as of other kinds of social ills, and it is hard to see why any peasant would seek a social oppressor for a friend.

Appendix. Devil plays in English, 1350–1642

Play		Date	Devil(s)
York	1 *Fall of the Angels*	14th–15th century	I Angelus Deficiens Lucifer/Diabolus, II Angelus Deficiens/Diabolus
	5 *Fall of Man*	"	Satanas
	22 *Temptation*	"	Diabolus
	30 *Pilate's Wife*	"	Diabolus
	37 *Harrowing*	"	I & II Diabolus, Belsabub, Sattan, Bellial
	47 *Judgment*	"	I, II, & III Diabolus
Castle of Perseverance		1380–1425	Belial/Sathanas
Wisdom		1400–50	Lucyfer
N-Town	1 *Creation . . . Angels*	15th century	Lucifer, Angeli Mali
	2 *Creation . . . Man*	"	Serpens, Diabolus
	20 *Slaughter*	"	Diabolus
	23 *Parliament of Hell*	"	Sathan, Belyall, Belsabub
	26 *Passion I*	"	Demon/Lucifer
	27 *Last Supper*	"	Demon
	31 *Pilate's Wife*	"	Sathan, Demon
	33 *Harrowing I*	"	Belyall
	35 *Harrowing II*	"	Beliall
	41 *Assumption*	"	Primus, Secundus Demon
	42 *Judgment*	"	Primus, Secundus, Tertius Diabolus
Towneley	1 *Creation . . . Angels*	1450–1500	Lucifer, Demons
	25 *Harrowing*	"	Ribald, Beelzebub
	30 *Judgment*	"	Tutivillus, Demons
Mankind		1465–70	Titivillus
Digby *Mary Magdalen*		1480–1520	Devil, Bad Angel, Satan, Second Diabolus, Seven Deadly Sins
Chester	1 *Fall of Lucifer*	15th–16th century	Lucifer
	2 *Creation . . . Man*	"	Demon/Serpens

209

10 *Slaughter*	"	Demon
12 *Temptation*	"	Diabolus
17 *Harrowing*	"	Sathan, Secundus & Tertius Daemon
23 *Antichrist*	15th century	Primus & Secundus Demon
24 *Judgment*	15th–16th century	Demon Primus & Secundus
Digby, *Conversion of St. Paul*	1480–1520	Mercury & Belial
Skelton, *Nigramansir* (lost)	1504	Devil
Bale, *Temptation of Our Lord*	1538	Satan
Wever, *Lusty Juventus*	1547–53	Devil
Wager, *The Longer Thou Livest the More Fool Thou Art*	1559–68	Confusion (?) (see Ch. 5, n. 11)
Ingelend, *Disobedient Child*	1559–77	Satan
Lupton, *All for Money*	1559–70	Satan
Fulwell, *Like Will to Like*	1562–68	Lucifer
Garter, *Virtuous and Godly Susanna*	1563–69	Satan
Processus Satanae	1570s	Devil
Woodes, *Conflict of Conscience*	1570–81	Satan
Lodge and Greene, *A Looking Glass for London and England*	1587–88	Ruffian disguised as a devil
Marlowe, *Dr. Faustus*	1588	Mephistopheles, Evil Angel, Lucifer, Belzebub, Devils
Greene, *Friar Bacon and Friar Bungay*	1588–89	Devils, Demonic (?) Voice, Spirit in the Shape of Hercules
Shakespeare, *1 Henry VI*	1590	Fiends
Shakespeare, *2 Henry VI*	1590	Asnath (anagram of Sathan?)
A Knack to Know a Knave	1592	Astoroth
Haughton, *The Devil and His Dame* (prob. same as *Grim the Collier of Croydon*, pub. 1662)	1593–1601	Pluto, Minos, Aeacus, Rhadamantus, Belphegor, Ackercock, devil disguised as Musgrave
Rowley (?), *The Birth of Merlin*	1597–1621	Devils
Marston, *Histriomastix*	1599	Player disguised as a devil
The Merry Devil of Edmonton	1599–1604	Corbell
Chapman, *Caesar and Pompey*	1602–5	Ophioneus
The Puritan Widow	1604	Demonic effects faked by con men
Chapman, *Bussy D'Ambois*	1604–5	Behemoth, Cartophylax, Spirits
Middleton, *Michaelmas Term*	1604–6	Shortyard, Galselight
Jonson, *Volpone*	1605–6	Demonic effects faked by con men

A Pleasant Comedy Called Wiley Beguilde (prob. rev. of *Wily Beguily*)	1606	Robin Goodfellow disguised as a devil
Barnes, *The Devil's Charter*	1606	Devils
Middleton, *A Mad World My Masters*	1606	Succubus in the form of Mistress Harebrain
Field, *A Woman Is a Weathercock*	1609	Nevill disguised as a devil
Fletcher, *Monsieur Thomas*	1610–16	Characters disguised as devils
Heywood, *The Silver Age*	1610–12	Pluto, devils
Dekker et al., *If This Be Not a Good Play, the Devil Is in It*	1611–12	Pluto, Shackle-soul, Rufman, Lurchall
Dekker, *Troia-Nova Triumphans*	1612	Disdain (with a "head Luciferian")
Daborne, *Machiavel and the Devil* (lost)	1613	Devil
Middleton, *The Witch*	1613–16	Malkin
Jonson, *The Devil Is an Ass*	1616	Satan, Pug
Fletcher, *The Chances*	1617	Magician produces fake demonic effects
Goffe, *Courageous Turk*	1619	Fiends
The Two Noble Ladies	1619–23	Cantharides, devils
Dekker et al., *The Virgin Martyr*	1620	Harpax
J.C., *The Two Merry Milkmaids*	1620	Landoff disguised as Asmody, Asmody (off stage)
Dekker et al., *The Witch of Edmonton*	1621	Tom
Fletcher and Massinger, *The Prophetess*	1622	Lucifera
Davenport, *A New Trick to Cheat the Devil*	1624–39	Master Changeable in devil's disguise
Brome, *The Queen's Exchange*	1629–32	Characters disguised as devils
Jonson, *Chlorida*	1631	Cacodemon, goblins, infernal spirits
Davenant, *The Temple of Love*	1635	Puritans in devil costumes
Davenant, *Luminalia*	1637	Devil in the shape of a goat
Nabbes, *Microcosmus*	1637	Malus Genius
Shirley, *St. Patrick for Ireland*	1637–40	Devils
Suckling, *The Goblins*	1637–41	Noblemen disguised as devils
Kirke, *The Seven Champions of Christendom*	1638	Devils
Jonson, *The Sad Shepherd*	1640	Puck-Hairy

For devil plays published during the Interregnum, see Thomas L. Berger, William C. Bradford, Sidney L. Sondergard, *An Index of Characters in Early Modern English Drama: Printed Plays, 1500–1660* (Cambridge University Press, 1998).

Notes

1 STAGE DEVILS AND OPPOSITIONAL THINKING

1 On costumes in general, see Jean MacIntyre and Garrett P. J. Epp, "'Cloathes Worth All the Rest': Costumes and Properties," in *A New History of Early English Drama*, ed. John D. Cox and David Scott Kastan (New York: Columbia University Press, 1997), pp. 269–85.

2 *Records of Early English Drama*, Chester, ed. Lawrence M. Clopper, 2 vols. (University of Toronto Press, 1989), 1:198. The quotation is from the Mayor's List for the Midsummer Show in 1599–1600. "The Deuell in his ffeathers" also appears in the banns for the Chester mystery plays recorded in Rogers' Breviary, 1608–9 (1:244).

3 *Records of Early English Drama*, Coventry, ed. R. W. Ingram (University of Toronto Press, 1981), pp. 163, 167.

4 *Records of Early English Drama*, Cambridge, ed. Alan H. Nelson, 2 vols. (University of Toronto Press, 1989), 1:161.

5 *Dramatic Texts and Records of Britain: A Chronological Topography to 1558*, ed. Ian Lancashire (Cambridge University Press, 1984), p. 271.

6 *Records of Early English Drama*, York, ed. Alexandra F. Johnston and Margaret Rogerson, 2 vols. (University of Toronto Press, 1979), 1:55.

7 *Microcosmus A Morall Maske*, ed. A. H. Bullen, *The Works of Thomas Nabbes*, two volumes in one (1882–89; rep. edn. New York: Benjamin Blom, 1968), 1:165.

8 Stuart Clark, *Thinking with Demons: The Idea of Witchcraft in Early Modern Europe* (Oxford: Clarendon Press, 1997).

9 E. K. Chambers, *The Mediaeval Stage*, 2 vols. (London: Oxford University Press, 1903). The quotation below is from 2:79, and what follows the quotation is a brief summary of the argument in chapter 20, "The Secularization of the Plays" (2:68–105).

10 *Mediaeval Stage*, 2:148. See also 2:91.

11 O. B. Hardison, *Christian Rite and Christian Drama in the Middle Ages* (Baltimore: Johns Hopkins University Press, 1966).

12 The list is Hardison's (p. 15, n. 49), compiled from Chambers.

13 "From the eighteenth century onwards . . . intellectual trends were most hostile to polarity . . . But by the 1790s it was moribund, made obsolete by

the taxonomic sharpness and rational individualism promoted by new philosophies and new models of consciousness and society" (*Thinking with Demons*, p. 35). Elsewhere, however, Clark acknowledges "misleading oppositions" generated by the scientific revolution and describes his book as an effort to destroy them (p. 296).

14 For a detailed study of "how witchcraft moved from the respectability of sermons and treatises, via the ambivalent satire of Defoe, to nineteenth-century embarrassment," see Ian Bostridge, *Witchcraft and Its Transformations c. 1650–c. 1750* (Oxford: Clarendon Press, 1997), quotation from p. 2.

15 James Sharpe, *Instruments of Darkness: Witchcraft in Early Modern England* (Philadelphia: University of Pennsylvania Press, 1997), pp. 1–4.

16 Jules Michelet, *Satanism and Witchcraft: A Study in Medieval Superstition*, trans. A. R. Allinson (New York: Citadel Press, 1939), pp. 98–108. For Michelet's place in the historiography of witchcraft, see Sharpe, *Instruments of Darkness*, p. 7.

17 Bernard Spivack, *Shakespeare and the Allegory of Evil* (New York: Columbia University Press, 1958); David M. Bevington, *From "Mankind" to Marlowe* (Cambridge, Mass.: Harvard University Press, 1962).

18 Robert Weimann, *Shakespeare and the Popular Tradition in the Theater*, ed. Robert Schwartz (Baltimore: Johns Hopkins, 1978) p. 33, quoting Montague Summers' *History of Witchcraft and Demonology*. Among others, see also Rainer Warning, "On the Alterity of Medieval Religious Drama," *New Literary History* 10 (1979), 265–92; Michael Bristol, *Carnival and Theater: Plebian Culture and the Structure of Authority in Renaissance England* (New York: Methuen, 1985), pp. 140–55; Anthony Gash, "Carnival against Lent: the Ambivalence of Medieval Drama," in *Medieval Literature: Criticism, Ideology and History*, ed. David Aers (Brighton: Harvester, 1986), pp. 74–98; Lesley Wade Soule, "Subverting the Mysteries: the Devil as Anti-Character," *European Medieval Drama* 2 (1998), 277–91. For a Marxist view that is much closer to the one represented here, see Walter Cohen, *Drama of a Nation: Public Theater in Renaissance England and Spain* (Ithaca: Cornell University Press, 1985), pp. 65–73, especially the following: "The plays could be radical because they were Christian" (p. 73).

19 Keith Thomas, *Religion and the Decline of Magic* (New York: Scribner's, 1971). Though Thomas asserts that it would "be a gross travesty to suggest that the medieval Church deliberately held out to the laity an organised system of magic designed to bring supernatural remedies to bear upon earthly problems" (p. 46), he entitles his second chapter, "The Magic of the Medieval Church" and repeatedly cites the discrediting reports of the Reformers as evidence for the rituals he describes. This is a Whig liberal argumentative strategy that is very similar to Chambers'.

20 Stephen Greenblatt, "Loudon and London," *Critical Inquiry* 12 (1986), 326–46, and "Shakespeare and the Exorcists," in *Shakespearean Negotiations* (Berkeley and Los Angeles: University of California Press, 1988), pp. 94–128.

21 C. John Sommerville, *The Secularization of Early Modern England* (Oxford University Press, 1992), p. 4.
22 For a similar theory of religion in culture, though it is not one that Sommerville acknowledges, see Clifford Geertz, "Religion as a Cultural System," in *The Interpretation of Cultures* (New York: Basic Books, 1973), pp. 87–125.
23 For the impact of the Reformation on the way people died, see Ralph Houlbrooke, *Death, Religion, and the Family in England 1480–1750* (Oxford University Press, 1998).
24 Sommerville's brief description of how drama was secularized (pp. 82–97) is impressionistic and overly dependent on Harold G. Gardiner's *Mysteries' End* (New Haven: Yale University Press, 1947).
25 In what follows I depend on historians with a lively sense of how traditional religion affected social life. Less useful is a history of ideas like Jeffrey Burton Russell's *Lucifer: The Devil in the Middle Ages* (Ithaca: Cornell University Press, 1984). Though Russell's learning is formidable and informative, he is interested in "the history of a concept," and his "philosophy is unabashedly idealist; it assumes that ideas are important in themselves and the social context in which they arise is more important for understanding the ideas than the other way around" (p. 12). That the devil was much more than an idea is essential to understanding his appearance in early drama, but even as the history of an idea, Russell's discussion of devils in drama (pp. 244–73) is less useful than Rosemary Woolf's in *The English Mystery Plays* (Berkeley and Los Angeles: University of California Press, 1972), pp. 105–31, 159–60, 202–11, 220–23, 239–45, 269–74, 291–99.
26 Henry Ansgar Kelly, *The Devil at Baptism: Ritual, Theology, and Drama* (Ithaca: Cornell University Press, 1985) p. 273.
27 For a description of how a particular infant was baptized in the traditional manner, see Peter Ackroyd, *The Life of Thomas More* (New York: Nan A. Talese, 1998), pp. 3–5.
28 Gerald R. Owst, *Literature and Pulpit in Medieval England* (Oxford: Clarendon Press, 2nd edn., 1961), pp. 287–374.
29 *2 Henry VI*, 3.3.19–23. To be sure, Winchester dies with a heavily burdened conscience and is not therefore representative of all dying Christians, as in traditional religion. His death may in fact recall depictions of evil deaths in the mystery plays, discussed in chapter 2.
30 Eamon Duffy, *The Stripping of the Altars: Traditional Religion in England c. 1400– c. 1580* (New Haven: Yale University Press, 1992), p. 317 and plates 117–19. Hereafter cited as "Duffy" in the text.
31 Unpublished lecture on the early history of Great St. Mary's, delivered at the church on Feb. 6, 1996.
32 Quoted by Owst, *Literature and Pulpit*, p. 297.
33 John Bossy, "The Mass as Social Institution," *Past and Present* 100 (1983), 33.
34 I concur here with Duffy, pp. 46–47, who takes issue with Charles Phythian-Adams' division of the year into "ritual" and "secular" halves, seeing rather

two distinct parts of a single ritual year. For Phythian-Adams, see "Ceremony and the Citizen," in *The Early Modern Town*, ed. Peter Clark (New York: Longman, 1976), pp. 106–28.

35 Duffy concedes that certain festal occasions, such as Plow Monday, "hardly seem religious at all" (*Stripping of the Altars*, p. 13). Even this feast, however, was affected by Jacques de Vitry's thirteenth-century sermon on *Christus agricola*, which identified Christ with a plow and other agricultural implements, in addition to, or instead of, a cross, and influenced a considerable literary and iconographical tradition, including *Piers Plowman*. See Pamela Gradon, "Langland and the Ideology of Dissent," *Proceedings of the British Academy* 66 (1980), 199.

36 E. O. James, *Seasonal Feasts and Festivals* (New York: Barnes and Noble, 1961), p. 220.

37 Alasdair MacIntyre, *Three Rival Versions of Moral Enquiry* (Notre Dame University Press, 1990), p. 191.

38 *The Drama of the Medieval Church*, ed. Karl Young, 2 vols. (Oxford: Clarendon Press, 1933), 1:103. Hereafter cited as "Young" in the text. The play is translated in *Medieval Drama*, ed. David M. Bevington, (Boston: Houghton Mifflin, 1975), pp. 12–13. The north portal undoubtedly was chosen because Satan traditionally dwelt in the north. See Bevington, *Medieval Drama*, pp. 796–97, for example, where the illustration for *The Castle of Perseverance* locates Belial's scaffold in the north.

39 For Diabolus in the *Nativitate*, see Young, *Drama of the Medieval Church*, 1:186–87, trans. Bevington, *Medieval Drama*, pp. 180–201; in the *Passione*, Young, 1:522, trans. Bevington, pp. 202–23.

40 V. A. Kolve, *The Play Called Corpus Christi* (Stanford University Press, 1966), p. 141; Hans-Jürgen Diller, *The Middle English Mystery Play: A Study in Dramatic Speech and Form*, trans. Frances Wessels (Cambridge University Press, 1992), p. 77.

41 *Play Called Corpus Christi*, p. 140. Kolve is summarizing the point of an episode in *The Knight of Tour-Landry*, but his conclusion about the passage makes his position clear: "In the Corpus Christi drama, as in the sources it drew upon, the severance from God is chiefly a result of man's stupidity and his failure to be intelligent." In this view, social subversion cannot be clever and funny, because it is evil.

42 I have argued this point at greater length in an essay that incorporates some of the material from this chapter, "Drama, the Devil, and Social Conflict in Late Medieval England," *American Benedictine Review* 45 (1994), 341–62.

2 THE DEVIL AND THE SACRED IN THE ENGLISH MYSTERY PLAYS

1 For the theology of Lucifer's fall, see Rosemary Woolf, *The English Mystery Plays* (Berkeley and Los Angeles: University of California Press, 1972), pp. 105–13, and R. W. Hanning, "'You Have Begun a Parlous Pleye': the Nature and Limits of Dramatic Mimesis as a Theme in Four Middle English 'Fall

of Lucifer' Cycle Plays," in *Drama in the Middle Ages*, ed. Clifford Davidson et al. (New York: AMS Press, 1982), pp. 140–68. Karl Tamburr points out the theological connection between the Chester cycle's fall of Lucifer and the pageants of the harrowing of hell and of Antichrist, in "The Dethroning of Satan in the Chester Cycle," *Neuphilologische Mitteilungen* 85 (1984), 316–28.

2 *The Towneley Plays*, ed. Martin Stevens and A. C. Cawley, EETS s.s. 13 (Oxford University Press, 1994), 5/67–76. After an initial note with bibliographical information, all the cycles are cited in the text by page and line number.

3 Meg Twycross and Sarah Carpenter reproduce an early seventeenth-century Dutch illustration of devils pursuing bystanders during a religious procession in "Masks in Medieval English Theatre: the Mystery Plays 2," *Medieval English Theatre* 3 (1981), figs. 16 and 17, and commentary, pp. 83–84.

4 Jean Q. Seaton, "Source of Order or Sovereign Lord: God and the Pattern of Relationships in Two Middle English 'Fall of Lucifer' Plays," *Comparative Drama* 18 (1984–85), 202–21, and Norma Kroll, "Dramatic Interaction and Conflict in the Chester Cycle 'Fall of Lucifer,'" *Medieval and Renaissance Drama in England* 2 (1985), 33–50. Both emphasize Chester's attention to personal, social, and political aspects of Lucifer's relationship with God.

5 Contrast Gower's interpretation of the Peasants' Revolt of 1381: "Then at mid-day the devil attacked and his hard-shot arrow flew during that painful day. Satan himself was freed and on hand, together with all the sinful band of servile hell . . . And so when I saw the leaders of hell ruling the world, the rights of heaven were worth nothing." John Gower, *The Major Latin Works of John Gower*, trans. Eric W. Stockton (Seattle: University of Washington Press, 1962), pp. 54–91 (quotation from p. 66). For examples in other chroniclers, see R. B. Dobson, *The Peasants' Revolt of 1381* (London: Macmillan, 1970), pp. 144 and 189 (Jean Froissart), 172–73, 244, 334 (Thomas Walsingham), and 183 (Henry Knighton).

6 *The N-Town Play*, ed. Stephen Spector, 2 vols. EETS s.s. 11 and 12 (Oxford University Press, 1991), 23/44–50.

7 Theodore Lerud, *Social and Political Dimensions of the English Corpus Christi Drama* (New York: Garland Publishing, 1988), p. 44.

8 Arnold Williams, "The Comic in the Cycles," in *Medieval Drama*, ed. Neville Denny (London: Edward Arnold, 1973), p. 120.

9 *Shakespeare and the Popular Tradition in the Theater*, ed. Robert Schwartz (Baltimore: Johns Hopkins, 1978), pp. 20–21, citing E. K. Chambers, *The Mediaeval Stage*, 2 vols. (London: Oxford University Press, 1903), 1:325.

10 For examples of severe social criticism from highly placed ecclesiastics, see G. R. Owst, *Literature and Pulpit in Medieval England* (Oxford: Clarendon Press, 2nd edn., rev. 1961), chapters 5 and 6. Theories of authorship vary widely. Lawrence Clopper argues that the playwrights are likely to have been non-clerical, both because of antagonism between the plays' guild sponsors and local ecclesiastical establishments and because the plays draw so heavily on

vernacular sources. See "Lay and Clerical Impact on Civic Religious Drama and Ceremony," in *Contexts for Early English Drama*, ed. Marianne G. Briscoe and John C. Coldewey (Bloomington: Indiana University Press, 1989), pp. 102–36.

11 L. W. Cushman, *The Devil and the Vice in the English Dramatic Literature before Shakespeare* (Halle: Max Niemeyer, 1900), p. 16.

12 *The Middle English Mystery Play: A Study in Dramatic Speech and Form*, trans. Frances Wessels (Cambridge University Press, 1992), p. 227.

13 For theological explanations of this line, see Woolf, *English Mystery Plays*, p. 111, Hanning, "'You Have Begun a Parlous Pleye,'" p. 150, and John D. Cox, *Shakespeare and the Dramaturgy of Power* (Princeton University Press, 1989), p. 25.

14 See appendix. Manuscript leaves are missing that likely contained the Towneley *Fall of Adam and Eve*, where Satan would have appeared, and Towneley lacks a temptation play, which would also have featured Satan. The best commentary on devils in the Towneley plays is "The Fool in the Wakefield Plays" by Martin Stevens and James Paxson, *Studies in Iconography* 13 (1992, for 1989–90), 48–79.

15 I follow Stephen Spector's division of the N-Town cycle, though others distinguish pageants differently. See, for example, Martin Stevens, *Four Middle English Mystery Plays* (Princeton University Press, 1987), pp. 185–91.

16 Cited by Eamon Duffy, *The Stripping of the Altars: Traditional Religion in England c. 1400–c. 1580* (New Haven: Yale University Press, 1992), p. 358. Hereafter cited as "Duffy" in the text.

17 Gail MacMurray Gibson, *The Theater of Devotion: East Anglian Drama and Society in the Late Middle Ages* (University of Chicago Press, 1989), pp. 72–106.

18 *The York Plays*, ed. Richard Beadle (London: Edward Arnold, 1982), p. 390, lines 154–58.

19 *The Chester Mystery Cycle*, ed. R. M. Lumiansky and David Mills, EETS s.s. 3 (London: Oxford University Press, 1974), p. 201, lines 420–21 and 423–25.

20 Woolf, *English Mystery Plays*, p. 210 and p. 393, n. 83. On the religious significance of wills, see Duffy, *Stripping of the Altars*, pp. 354–57.

21 This stage image is at least as old as the eleventh- or twelfth-century *Sponsus* from St. Martial at Limoges, where the foolish virgins are similarly borne away as the play ends (*The Drama of the Medieval Church*, ed. Karl Young, 2 vols. [Oxford: Clarendon Press, 1933], 2:364). Stephen Spector's note to the N-Town play refers to a Norwich roof boss, printed in M. D. Anderson's *Drama and Imagery in English Medieval Churches* (Cambridge University Press, 1963), plate 11f., depicting a deathbed scene with a devil pulling Herod's soul from his mouth, in a clear iconographical parallel to deathbed scenes from the *Ars Moriendi*, where the soul is depicted as a homunculus ascending from the head of the dying person to join the waiting angels, and the defeated devils writhe in frustrated agony below (see Duffy, *Stripping of the Altars*, plate 119). In the Chester *Antichrist*, a demon physically removes Antichrist's soul from his body as a gift for the devil (435–46/678 SD, 679–82).

22 On devilish avidity, see Barbara Palmer, "The Inhabitants of Hell: Devils," in *The Iconography of Hell*, ed. Clifford Davidson and Thomas H. Seiler (Kalamazoo: Medieval Institute Publications, 1992), p. 25, where devils' weapons are identified as tools of the hunt, the harvest, and the kitchen, suggesting their obsession with hunting, harvesting, and devouring human souls.

23 Duffy, *Stripping of the Altars*, pp. 301–5. For discussion of Chester's Dance of Death, see Stevens, *Four Middle English Mystery Cycles*, pp. 311–12.

24 For specific reflections of the contemporary legal system in York, see Elza Tiner, "*Inventio, Dispositio,* and *Elocutio* in the York Trial Plays" (Ph.D. dissertation, University of Toronto, 1987), pp. 1–78.

25 For a thematic discussion of these charges in their context, see R. H. Nicholson, "The Trial of Christ the Sorcerer in the York Cycle," *Journal of Medieval and Renaissance Studies* 16 (1986), 125–69.

26 Fry, "The Unity of the *Ludus Coventriae,*" *Studies in Philology* 48 (1951), 527–70.

27 Lerud, *Social and Political Dimensions*; Tiner, "*Inventio, Dispositio,* and *Elocutio* in the York Trial Plays"; Lynn Squires, "Legal and Political Aspects of Late Medieval English Drama" (Ph.D. dissertation, University of Washington, 1977); Theodore DeWelles, "The Social and Political Context of the Towneley Cycle" (Ph.D. dissertation, University of Toronto, 1980).

28 R. M. Lumiansky, "Comedy and Theme in the Chester *Harrowing of Hell*" (1960), in *The Chester Mystery Cycle: A Casebook*, ed. Kevin J. Harty (New York and London: Garland Publishing, 1993), pp. 162–70.

29 For some of the sources of this prologue and its relationship to other parts of the N-Town cycle, see Miriam J. Benkovitz, "Some Notes on the 'Prologue of Demon' of *Ludus Coventriae,*" *Modern Language Review* 60 (1945), 78–85.

30 Stephen Spector notes that the description of Satan's costume is so precise as to date it within twenty years – from the mid-1460s to the 1480s (*N-Town Play*, 2:491). For sumptuary satire in drama of the period, see Tony Davenport, "'Lusty fresche galaunts,'" in *Aspects of Early English Drama*, ed. Paula Neuss (Cambridge: D. S. Brewer, 1983), pp. 110–29, and *The Vision of Edmund Leversedge*, ed. W. F. Nijenhuis (Nijmegen: Centrum voor Middeleeuwse Studies, 1991), pp. 40–48.

31 Kathleen M. Ashley, "'Wyt' and 'Wysdam' in N-Town Cycle," *Philological Quarterly* 58 (1979), 121–35, and Stevens, *Four Middle English Mystery Plays*, pp. 213–21.

32 Natalie Zemon Davis, "The Sacred and the Social Body in Sixteenth-Century Lyon," *Past and Present* 90 (1981), 40–70; Mervyn James, "Ritual, Drama and Social Body in the Late Medieval English Town," *Past and Present* 98 (1983), 3–29; Peter Travis, "The Social Body of the Dramatic Christ in Medieval England," in *Early Drama to 1600*, ed. Albert Tricomi, *Acta* 13 (1987 [for 1986]), 18–36; Miri Rubin, *Corpus Christi: The Eucharist in Late Medieval Culture* (Cambridge University Press, 1991), pp. 271–87 et passim.

33 A. P. Rossiter, *English Drama from Early Times to the Elizabethans* (London: Hutchinson's Library, 1950), p. 72.

34 Gibson, *Theater of Devotion*, p. 20.
35 John Bossy, *Christianity in the West 1400–1700* (Oxford University Press, 1987), pp. 84–87; Stephen Spector, "Anti-Semitism and the English Mystery Plays" in Davidson, *Drama in the Middle Ages*, pp. 328–41; James Shapiro, *Shakespeare and the Jews* (New York: Columbia University Press, 1996).
36 Spector, "Anti-Semitism and the English Mystery Plays," pp. 31–32; Gail MacMurray Gibson, "Images of Doubt and Belief: Visual Symbolism in the Middle English Plays of Joseph's Troubles about Mary" (Ph.D. dissertation, University of Virginia, 1975), pp. 120–34.
37 James, "Ritual, Drama and Social Body," pp. 5–10.
38 For conflict between guilds, see Stevens, *Four Middle English Mystery Plays*, pp. 33, 80–82; for conflict during the liturgy, Duffy, *Stripping of the Altars*, pp. 126–29; for competition between guilds and parishes in the York Corpus Christi procession, Anne Higgins, "Streets and Markets" in *A New History of Early English Drama*, ed. John D. Cox and David Scott Kastan, (New York: Columbia University Press, 1997), pp. 77–92.
39 Stevens, *Four Middle English Mystery Cycles*, p. 311.

3 STAGE DEVILS AND SACRAMENTAL COMMUNITY IN NON-CYCLE PLAYS

1 On the Croxton play, see Sarah Beckwith, "Ritual, Church and Theatre: Medieval Dramas of the Sacramental Body," in *Culture and History 1350–1600: Essays on English Communities, Identities and Writing* ed. David Aers (New York and London: Harvester Wheatsheaf, 1992), pp. 65–89.
2 Alfred W. Pollard, ed., *English Miracle Plays, Moralities and Interludes: Specimens of the Pre-Elizabethan Drama* (Oxford: Clarendon Press, 8th edn. rev. 1927), p. lxvii.
3 Bernard Spivack, *Shakespeare and the Allegory of Evil* (New York: Columbia University Press, 1958), p. 130.
4 The proportions of pageants that stage devils to those that do not range from a low of three out of thirty in Towneley (10 percent), to six out of forty-seven in York (12.7 percent), to eleven out of forty-one in N-Town (26.8 percent), to a high of seven out of twenty-four in Chester (34 percent). Spivack's figure of nine out of sixty morality plays that stage devils is equivalent to 15 percent, but the correct figure of eleven out of sixty-one (see note 5) is equivalent to 18 percent.
5 Spivack does not specify the nine plays he refers to, but in his Bibliography of Morality Plays on pp. 483–93, ten of the plays include stage devils (not nine): *All for Money, Castle of Perseverance, Conflict of Conscience, Enough Is as Good as a Feast, Like Will to Like, Lusty Juventus, Mankind, Mary Magdalen* (Digby), *Virtuous and Godly Susanna,* and *Wisdom.* Moreover, the list omits *The Disobedient Child,* presumably because it contains no personified abstractions, though its plot is a straightforward adaptation of the prodigal son story, like many Elizabethan morality plays aimed at the younger generation. Of

these eleven plays, only four are pre-Reformation; one is Edwardian, and six are Elizabethan (using Spivack's own dates).

6 David M. Bevington, *From "Mankind" to Marlowe: Growth of Structure in the Popular Drama of Tudor England* (Cambridge, Mass.: Harvard University Press, 1962), p. 114. Robert Weimann also overgeneralizes about sequential development from mystery cycles to morality plays, in *Shakespeare and the Popular Tradition in the Theater*, ed. Robert Schwartz (Baltimore: Johns Hopkins University Press, 1978), p. 112.

7 Elbert N. S. Thompson, *The English Moral Plays, Transactions of the Connecticut Academy of Arts and Sciences* 14 (1910), 360; Louis B. Wright, "Social Aspects of Some Belated Moralities," *Anglia* 40 (1930), 114.

8 This point is also made by Paul Whitfield White, *Theatre and Reformation: Protestantism, Patronage, and Playing in Tudor England* (Cambridge University Press, 1993), p. 75.

9 Rosemary Woolf, *The English Mystery Plays* (Berkeley and Los Angeles: University of California Press, 1972), p. 239.

10 Robert Potter, *The English Morality Play: Origins, History and Influence of a Dramatic Tradition* (London: Routledge and Kegan Paul, 1975), p. 7.

11 *Mirk's Festial: A Collection of Homilies*, ed. Theodor Erbe, EETS e.x. 96 (London: Kegan Paul, Trench, Trübner, 1905), p. 131.

12 *Mirk's Festial*, p. 131. The bishop's vision is a commonplace in sermon literature on Easter. See also, for example, *Speculum Sacerdotale*, ed. Edward H. Weatherly, EETS o.s. 200 (London: Oxford University Press, 1936), pp. 123–25.

13 *The Castle of Perseverance*, ed. Mark Eccles, *The Macro Plays*, EETS o.s. 262 (London: Oxford University Press, 1969), lines 279 and 294–95.

14 Bodleian MS. Lyell 30 fol. 49v, quoted by Eamon Duffy, *The Stripping of the Altars* (New Haven: Yale University Press, 1992), p. 249.

15 Alexandra F. Johnston, "The Plays of the Religious Guilds of York: the Creed Play and the Pater Noster Play," *Speculum* 50 (1975), 55–90; quotation from Mirk on p. 78.

16 This social emphasis has invited topical readings. See Milla Riggio, "The Allegory of Feudal Acquisition in *The Castle of Perseverance*" in *Allegory, Myth, and Symbol*, ed. Morton W. Bloomfield (Cambridge, Mass.: Harvard University Press, 1981), pp. 187–208, and S. E. Holbrook, "Covetousness, Contrition, and the Town in the *Castle of Perseverance*," *Fifteenth-Century Studies* 13 (1987), 275–89.

17 St. John's MS. s 35, fol. [a2v], under "Enuye," cited by Duffy, *Stripping of the Altars*, p. 59.

18 For the debate about auspices, see three essays in *The "Wisdom" Symposium*, ed. Milla Riggio (New York: AMS Press, 1986): Milla Riggio, "The Staging of *Wisdom*," pp. 1–17; Gail McMurray Gibson, "The Play of *Wisdom* and the Abbey of St. Edmund," pp. 39–66; Donald C. Baker, "Is *Wisdom* a 'Professional' Play?" pp. 67–86.

19 *Wisdom*, ed. Mark Eccles, *The Macro Plays*, EETS 262 (London: Oxford University Press, 1969), lines 124 and 126.

20 996 SD. Eccles's note identifies the hymn's source and cites its place in the liturgy for Holy Thursday.

21 Only six of the sins are actually specified in the stage directions, probably because of limited access to extras in staging the play. See Bevington, *From "Mankind" to Marlowe*, pp. 124–25.

22 David M. Bevington, *Tudor Drama and Politics: A Critical Approach to Topical Meaning* (Cambridge, Mass.: Harvard University Press, 1968), pp. 28–34. For a different topical reading, see John Marshall, "'Fortune in Worldys Worschyppe': the Satirising of the Suffolks in *Wisdom*," *Medieval English Theatre* 14 (1992), 37–66.

23 *The Towneley Plays*, ed. Martin Stevens and A. C. Cawley, EETS s.s. 13 (Oxford University Press, 1994), Play 13, *Second Shepherds' Play*, lines 51–52. Marshall comments that "even if the playwright [of *Wisdom*] intended to connect the vice of maintenance with the Suffolks he did not do so at the expense of wider understanding or the concentration on religious matters within the play" (p. 46).

24 In her reading of the Croxton *Play of the Sacrament*, Sarah Beckwith argues that sacramental social order existed solely to maintain clerical power, but if this were the case, it is not clear how a play like *Wisdom* could mount a serious *critique* of clerical power and still be focused in the sacraments.

25 Cf. a similar idea in the *Speculum Sacerdotale*: "Yit siche maner of men often tymes yeuen hem to fastyngis and doynge of almes dedes, but here wickyd vicis maketh hem to lese here mede and fruyte of euerlastynge blisse that they schuld haue ther-bi. For what profetteth it a man for to yeue to God his doodis and yeve hym-self to the deuell?" (p. 68).

26 Saul's superiors are unnamed in the Book of Acts, but the playwright of the Digby *St. Paul* apparently misconstrued a phrase in the story to refer to the same high priests who prosecuted Jesus (*The Conversion of St. Paul*, ed. Donald C. Baker, John L. Murphy, Louis B. Hall Jr., in *Late Medieval Religious Plays of Bodleian Mss Digby 133 and E Museo 160*, EETS 283 [Oxford University Press, 1982], p. 195). Still, the misconstruction is felicitous (possibly even deliberate), because it identifies the same source of suffering for early Christians as for Christ.

27 The plays' recent editors identify the style of the handwriting in the interpolation as mid-1550s (p. xviii), while the rest of the manuscript better suits the first quarter of the century (p. xxii). The editors also view the scene as dramatically and thematically relevant to the rest of the play (p. xxix). E. K. Chambers, on the other hand, points to the late addition of devils to this play in support of his observation "that the instinct which made the miracle-plays a joy to the mediaeval burgher is the same instinct which the more primitive peasant satisfied in a score of modes of rudimentary folk-drama," including devil scenes (*The Mediaeval Stage*, 2 vols. [London: Oxford University Press, 1903] 2:148 and 149, n. 1).

28 For further commentary on *Mary Magdalen*, see John D. Cox, "Devils and Vices in English Non-Cycle Plays: Sacrament and Social Body," *Comparative Drama* 30 (1996), 199–200.

29 The N-Town manuscript is being viewed increasingly as a loose collection or anthology, rather than a guild cycle of the sort that is preserved from York and Chester. It is not unreasonable, therefore, to consider the *Assumption of Mary* as a separate saint's play. See Martin Stevens, *Four Middle English Mystery Cycles* (Princeton University Press, 1987), pp. 181–257; Stanley Karhl's review of Stevens' book in *Speculum* 65 (1990), 499–502; Stephen Spector, ed., *The N-Town Play*, EETS s.s. 11, 2 vols. (Oxford University Press, 1991), 2: 537–43; Douglas Sugano, "'This Game Wel Pleyd in Good A-ray': The N-Town Playbooks and East Anglian Games," *Comparative Drama* 28 (1994), 221–34; Alan J. Fletcher, "The N-Town Plays," in *The Cambridge Companion to Medieval English Theatre*, ed. Richard Beadle (Cambridge University Press, 1994), pp. 167–78. The N-Town plays are cited here from Stephen Spector's edition.

30 On female saints, see Eamon Duffy, "Holy Maydens, Holy Wyfes: the Cult of Women Saints in Fifteenth- and Sixteenth-Century England," *Studies in Church History* 23 (1990), 175–96, and Clifford Davidson, "The Digby *Mary Magdalene* and the Magdalene Cult of the Middle Ages," *Annuale Mediaevale* 13 (1972), 70–87.

31 Sister Mary Philippa Coogan, *An Interpretation of the Moral Play, "Mankind"* (Washington, D.C.: Catholic University of America, 1947); Kathleen M. Ashley, "Titivillus and the Battle of Words in *Mankind*," *Annuale Mediaevale* 16 (1975), 128–50.

32 Coogan, *Interpretation of the Moral Play*, pp. 15–16. Walter K. Smart first identified particular ways in which *Mankind* is a Shrovetide play, in "Some Notes on *Mankind*," *Modern Philology* 14 (1916), 45–47.

33 *Mankind*, ed. Mark Eccles, *The Macro Plays*, EETS o.s. 262 (London: Oxford University Press, 1969), line 17.

34 On Mercy as a Dominican friar, see Coogan, *Interpretation of the Moral Play*, pp. 5–6.

35 For discussion of three other early Tudor plays that follow the same pattern, *Mundus et Infans* (1500–22), *Youth* (1513–14), and *Hickscorner* (1513–16), see Cox, "Devils and Vices," pp. 203–8.

36 Woolf remarks that the detractors "seem inhuman figures, like the vice or other evil characters in the morality plays: they show the same enormous zest, witty inventiveness, cold glee, and unmotivated delight in malice" (p. 176).

37 *The Trial of Mary and Joseph*, ed. Stephen Spector, *The N-Town Play*, EETS s.s. 11, 2 vols. (Oxford University Press, 1991), lines 44–54.

38 Henry Medwall, *Nature*, ed. Alan H. Nelson, *The Plays of Henry Medwall* (Cambridge: D. S. Brewer; Totowa: Rowman and Littlefield, 1980), 1.138–40.

39 John Skelton, *Magnificence*, ed. Paula Neuss, Revels Plays (Manchester University Press; Baltimore: Johns Hopkins University Press, 1980), lines 19–21.

40 For an argument that politics in *Magnificence* are conceived in terms of

Aristotle's *Ethics* (as the title suggests), see Greg Walker, *Plays of Persuasion: Drama and Politics at the Court of Henry VIII* (Cambridge University Press, 1991), pp. 76–88.

41 *Saint Mary Magdelen*, ed. Donald C. Baker, John L. Murphy, Louis B. Hall Jr., in *Late Medieval Religious Plays*, line 394.

4 STAGE DEVILS AND EARLY SOCIAL SATIRE

1 Quoted by Tony Davenport, "'Lusty fresche galaunts,'" in *Aspects of Early English Drama*, ed. Paula Neuss (Cambridge: D. S. Brewer, 1983), p. 115.

2 *The Castle of Perseverance*, ed. Mark Eccles, *The Macro Plays*, EETS o.s. 262 (London: Oxford University Press, 1969), lines 209 and 1057.

3 Superbia mentions "crakows" on his shoes (1059), and Eccles comments that "the word seems to have been current only from about 1382 to about 1425" (p. 191). For similar precise social observation in the costume of the N-Town Lucifer, see chapter 2, n. 30.

4 These carefully developed courtly details are difficult to reconcile with Robert Weimann's thesis that devils and vices originated in folk figures whose hallmark was their accessibility to commoners. Satan and his courtly cohorts in *Castle* are among the earliest of stage devils, yet they appear on various scaffold stages, not in the *platea*, and their direct address is rhetorically ornate, threatening, and abusive, not colloquial, inviting, and confidential. See *Shakespeare and the Popular Tradition in the Theater*, ed. Robert Schwartz (Baltimore: Johns Hopkins University Press, 1978), pp. 6–11, 30–33, 73–85 et passim.

5 See, for example, *The Towneley Plays*, ed. Martin Stephens and A. C. Cawley, 2 vols., EETS s.s. 13 (Oxford University Press, 1994), *Judgment*, lines 343–48, 355, 391–94, 417–22, 452–81, 618, 672–73, 736–37, and *The Chester Mystery Plays*, ed. R. M. Lumiansky and David Mills, EETS s.s. 3 (London: Oxford University Press, 1974), *Judgment*, lines 17–24, 117–20, 149–53, 277–80, 462, 477–80, 622, 637–44.

6 *Saint Mary Magdalen*, ed. Donald C. Baker, John L. Murphy, Louis B. Hall Jr., in *The Late Medieval Religious Plays of Bodleian Mss Digby 133 and E Museo 160*, EETS o.s. 283 (Oxford University Press, 1982), line 550.

7 Weimann ignores this speech form from the *sedes* in *Mary Magdalen*; the folk fool elements that he identifies in this play are associated with the boy Hawkyn, not with devils (pp. 79, 139, 141).

8 Quoted by Eamon Duffy, *The Stripping of the Altars: Traditional Religion in England c. 1400–1580* (New Haven: Yale University Press, 1992), pp. 340–41.

9 Henry Medwall, *Nature*, ed. Alan H. Nelson, *The Plays of Henry Medwall* (Cambridge: D. S. Brewer; Totowa: Rowman and Littlefield, 1980), 1.767–70.

10 David M. Bevington, "'Blake and wyght, fowll and fayer': Stage Picture in *Wisdom*," in *The Wisdom Symposium*, ed. Milla Cozart Riggio (New York: AMS Press, 1986), pp. 18–38.

11 John D. Cox, *Shakespeare and the Dramaturgy of Power* (Princeton University Press, 1989), pp. 22–40.

12 *Wisdom*, ed. Mark Eccles, *The Macro Plays*, EETS o.s. 262 (London: Oxford University Press, 1969), lines 103–4.

13 *Mankind*, ed. Mark Eccles, *The Macro Plays*, EETS o.s. 262 (London: Oxford University Press, 1969), lines 670–71.

14 This point is an unacknowledged difficulty for Weimann's argument that the vices of *Mankind* are the champions of commoners against ecclesiastical and class oppression (pp. 112–20). He ignores the coat-cutting episode in his discussion of the play.

15 John Mirk, *Festial*, ed. Theodor Erbe, EETS e.s. 96 (London: Kegan Paul, Trench, Trübner, 1905), p. 150.

16 *Dives and Pauper*, ed. Priscilla Heath Barnum, EETS o.s. 275 (London: Oxford University Press, 1976), vol. 1, part 1, p. 152.

17 *The York Plays*, ed. Richard Beadle (London: Edward Arnold, 1982), line 120.

18 This instance of demonic direct address from the *platea* refutes Weimann's argument (above, n. 4) that vices and devils use familiar audience address to turn the hearts and minds of commoners against their social betters, since the superiors that Detractio plots against are other devils, not God, angels, or human authorities.

19 This common player's gulling of a courtly auditor closely reproduces the social dynamics of an exchange attributed to Richard Tarlton on the Elizabethan stage, almost 100 years later. See Andrew Gurr, *Playgoing in Shakespeare's London* (Cambridge University Press, 1987), pp. 125–26. The exchange in *Nature* does not fit Weimann's description of vices' direct address to the audience as "the comic concurrence of audience and actor" (p. 258). If "conflict" were substituted for "concurrence," the phrase would be more appropriate. A similar conflict occurs later with Worldly Affection (510–24), leading to a quarrel with Gluttony.

20 Timothy Fry, "The Unity of the *Ludus Coventriae*," *Studies in Philology* 68 (1951) 527–70. See also Alan Nelson, "The Temptation of Christ; or, The Temptation of Satan," in *Medieval English Drama*, ed. Jerome Taylor and Alan Nelson (University of Chicago Press, 1972), pp. 218–29.

21 In *Family, Sex, and Marriage in England 1500–1800* (London: Weidenfeld and Nicolson, 1977), Lawrence Stone points out that "friend" connoted an aristocratic ally or retainer (p. 97). Covetise also presents himself as "thi best frende" to Humanum Genus in *Castle* (2430), and the aristocratic context is unmistakable when he adds that he is "a frend ryth fre [*noble*]" (2474).

22 Nelson, ed., *Plays of Henry Medwall*, pp. 15–16.

23 N. W. Bawcutt, " 'Policy,' Machiavellianism, and the Earlier Tudor Drama," *English Literary Renaissance* 1 (1971), 195–209.

24 Bernard Spivack cites this passage in his section on dissimulation in the morality play, *Shakespeare and the Allegory of Evil* (New York: Columbia University Press, 1958), p. 156, but in spite of such strong indications of mutual influence between mystery and morality plays, he leaves in place his generalizations about sequential development from one to the other.

25 Morton W. Bloomfield, *The Seven Deadly Sins* ([East Lansing]: Michigan State College Press, 1952), pp. 96, 217, 219, 226.

26 Ann Wierum, "'Actors' and 'Play Acting' in the Morality Tradition," *Renaissance Drama* n.s. 3 (1970), 200.

27 This point is also made by David DeVries, "The Vice Figure in Middle English Morality Plays," in *Fools and Jesters in Literature, Art, and History* ed. Vicki Janik (Westport: Greenwood Press, 1998), pp. 471–84. Despite his title, however, DeVries does not discuss the Vice per se, who enters the picture only midway through the reign of Henry VIII.

28 E. K. Chambers, *The Mediaeval Stage*, 2 vols. (London: Oxford University Press, 1903), 2:203–4, refuting L. W. Cushman, *The Devil and the Vice in English Dramatic Literature before Shakespeare* (Halle: Max Niemeyer, 1900), p. 67. Cushman was more sympathetic than Chambers to continuity between the Vice and earlier personified vices. See also Francis Hugh Mares, "The Origins of the Figure Called 'the Vice' in Tudor Drama," *Huntington Library Quarterly* 22 (1958–59), 11–29; and Peter Happé, "The Vice and the Folk-Drama," *Folklore* 75 (1964), 161–93, and "'The Vice' and the Popular Theatre, 1547–80," in *Poetry and Drama 1570–1700*, ed. Antony Coleman and Antony Hammond (London and New York: Methuen, 1981), pp. 13–31. Happé has also published a useful bibliography in "The Vice: a Checklist and Annotated Bibliography," *Research Opportunities in Renaissance Drama* 22 (1979), 17–35.

29 For other examples, see Martin Stevens and James Paxson, "The Fool in the Wakefield Cycle," *Studies in Iconography* 13 (1992, for 1989–90), 48–79, and Martin Stevens, "Herod as Carnival King in the Medieval Drama," *Mediaevalia* 18 (1995, for 1992), 43–61, where Stevens argues that the cycles test their society against a moral order they affirm (p. 43). Stevens sees "spiritual values" as a formative "social force" – a very different view from the evolutionary assumption that "spiritual values" are other-worldly and were therefore eventually replaced in drama by secular social concerns.

30 *Mundus et Infans, Six Anonymous Plays, 1500–1537*, ed. John S. Farmer (1905; New York: Barnes and Noble, 1966), p. 180.

31 Robert C. Jones, "Dangerous Sport: the Audience's Engagement with Vice in the Moral Interludes," *Renaissance Drama* n.s. 6 (1973), 45–64. A similar point is made by J. A. B. Somerset, "'Fair is Foul and Foul is Fair': Vice-Comedy's Development and Theatrical Effects," in *The Elizabethan Theatre*, ed. G. R. Hibbard (Hamden, Conn.: Archon Books, 1975), pp. 54–75.

32 The most extended discussion of morality-play techniques in the mystery plays is by Hans Jürgen Diller, *The Middle English Mystery Play* (Cambridge University Press, 1992), pp. 148–54. See also E. K. Chambers, *English Literature at the Close of the Middle Ages* (Oxford: Clarendon Press, 1945), p. 51; Rosemary Woolf, *The English Mystery Plays* (Berkeley and Los Angeles: University of California Press, 1972), p. 239; Martin Stevens, *Four Middle English Mystery Cycles* (Princeton University Press, 1987), p. 200.

33 *N-Town Play*, ed. Spector, Play 31, lines 38–41.

34 Heywood may not have needed French farce to make such an abstraction. "Vice" was virtually equivalent to "juggler" in contemporary usage, as the Edwardian play *Jack Juggler* indicates. See *Three Tudor Classical Interludes*, ed. Marie Axton (Cambridge: D. S. Brewer, 1982), pp. 15–20, and Paul Whitfield White, *Theatre and Reformation* (Cambridge University Press, 1993), pp. 126–27. Greg Walker also suggests that for Heywood, "the term 'vice' seems to refer more to the style of acting required by the role than to the character's moral function within the play," though he finds a certain amount of moral ambiguity in the "vices" of both *A Play of the Weather* and *The Play of Love* (*Plays of Persuasion: Drama and Politics at the Court of Henry VIII* [Cambridge University Press, 1991], pp. 142–43).

35 For a complete list of the twenty-two plays that use the label "the Vice," see Mares, "Origins," p. 12.

36 Nathaniel Woodes, *The Conflict of Conscience*, ed. Norman Davis and F. P. Wilson (Oxford: The Malone Society, 1952), marginal dialogue printed beside line 391. The hopelessly ignorant Moros (the Fool) in *The Longer thou Livest the More Fool Thou Art* also identifies himself with knavery, when he complains that he has difficulty learning his alphabet: "I can no further then K for a knaue." W. Wager, *The longer thou Liuest, the more fool thou art*, ed. A. Brandl, *Shakespeare Jahrbuch* 36 (1900), 1–64, line 715.

37 Bernard Spivack, *Shakespeare and the Allegory of Evil*, pp. 140–47; David M. Bevington, *From "Mankind" to Marlowe* (Cambridge, Mass.: Harvard University Press, 1962), pp. 122–23.

38 For a thematic exploration of doubling, see John W. Sider, " 'One Man in His Time Plays Many Parts': Authorial Theatrics of Doubling in Early Renaissance Drama," *Studies in Philology* 91 (1994), 359–89.

39 For examples of weeping Vices, see Spivack, *Shakespeare and the Allegory of Evil*, pp. 161–64.

40 *A Tretise of Miraclis Pleying*, ed. Clifford Davidson, EDAMM 19 (Kalamazoo: Medieval Institute Publications, 1993). Davidson summarizes a few other anti-stage works on pp. 7–13. For commentary see Jonas Barish, *The Antitheatrical Prejudice* (Berkeley and Los Angeles: University of California Press, 1981), pp. 66–79.

41 This is not to deny the influence of official measures to repress the Lollards through heresy trials, torture, and execution. My point is simply that Lollardy did not present itself as a popular alternative to traditional religion; as Davidson points out, "the social order envisioned by Lollardy indeed depended upon aristocratic control" (*Tretise of Miraclis Pleying*, p. 124).

5 PROTESTANT DEVILS AND THE NEW COMMUNITY

1 I am indebted for this concept to C. John Sommerville, *The Secularization of Early Modern England* (New York: Oxford University Press, 1992), as explained in chapter 1 above.

2 For a detailed interpretation of Foxe's role in this process, see Huston Diehl,

Staging Reform, Reforming the Stage (Ithaca: Cornell University Press, 1997), pp. 9–66.

3 Eamon Duffy, *The Stripping of the Altars: Traditional Religion c. 1400–1580* (New Haven: Yale University Press, 1992), pp. 356–57.

4 Nicholas Davidson, "Christopher Marlowe and Atheism" in *Christopher Marlowe and the English Renaissance*, ed. Darryll Grantley and Peter Roberts (Aldershot: Scolar Press, 1996), pp. 129–47. Diehl discusses an episode in Foxe's *Acts and Monuments* as designed to "empower the skeptic" (*Staging Reform*, pp. 28–31), yet Foxe was hardly an atheist.

5 John Bale, *Johan Baptystes Preachynge*, ed. Peter Happé, *The Complete Plays of John Bale*, 2 vols. (Cambridge: D. S. Brewer, 1986), lines 19–23. *The Temptation of Our Lord* and *King Johan* are cited from the same edition.

6 Happé points out that the French *mystères* also depict Satan as a hermit (2: 150–51), and Skelton stages Cloaked Collusion as a priest, so even this detail is not necessarily a dead giveaway of Bale's reformed perspective.

7 For Bale's attack on confession, see Greg Walker, *Plays of Persuasion: Drama and Politics at the Court of Henry VIII* (Cambridge University Press, 1991), pp. 210–14.

8 On the accuracy of Bale's rendering of traditional ritual, see Edwin Shepherd Miller, "The Roman Rite in Bale's *King John*," *PMLA* 64 (1949), 802–22.

9 R. Wever, *An Interlude called Lusty Juuentus*, ed. J. M. Nosworthy, Malone Society Reprints (Oxford: Malone Society, 1971), lines 61 and 370.

10 W. Wager, *The longer thou Liuest, the more fool thou art*, ed. A. Brandl, *Shakespeare Jahrbuch* 36 (1900), 1–64, lines 164–65.

11 Confusion is not identified as a devil in the casting list or in speech prefixes, and he does not act like a devil, but he may have been staged as one nonetheless, because he is described as entering "*with an ill-favored visure and all things beside ill-favored*" (1806 SD); Moros requests Confusion to carry him off to hell on his back (1853–54); and a sixteenth-century handwritten note in an early edition of *Longer* identifies Confusion as "the devilles messenger." The last observation is made by T. W. Craik, who notes that a devil is named "Confusion" in R. Robinson's *The Rewarde of Wickednesse* (1574), *The Tudor Interlude* (Leicester University Press, 1958), p. 132, n. 6.

12 Thomas Ingelend, *The Disobedient Child* (London: Tudor Facsimile Texts, 1908), sig. Fi (no line numbers). Other examples appear in Thomas Garter, *The Comedy of the moste vertuous and Godlye Susanna*, ed. W. W. Greg, Malone Society Reprints (Oxford: Malone Society, 1936), lines 70, 82, 215, and Ulpian Fulwell, *Like Will to Like* (London: Tudor Facsimile Texts, 1909), sig. Aiii (no line numbers).

13 A late revival of this early Protestant custom appears at the end of Shakespeare's *2 Henry IV*, when the Epilogue kneels to pray for Queen Elizabeth. This gesture may be an appeal for nostalgic Protestant sympathy, in view of what *1 Henry IV* had done to Sir John Oldcastle.

14 *The Chester Mystery Cycle*, ed. R. M. Lumiansky and David Mills, EETS s.s. 3

(London: Oxford University Press, 1974), Play XXIII The Diars Playe, *The Coming of Antichrist* (87–88).

15 Michael Sherbrook, "The Fall of Religious Houses," in *Tudor Treatises*, ed. A. G. Dickens, *Yorkshire Archaeological Society Record Series* 125 (1959), 124–25.

16 Quoted from Bale's *Acts of English Votaries* by Leslie Fairfield, *John Bale, Mythmaker for the English Reformation* (West Lafayette: Purdue University Press, 1976), p. 87.

17 Ritchie D. Kenall, *The Drama of Dissent: The Radical Poetics of Nonconformity, 1380–1590* (Chapel Hill: University of North Carolina Press, 1986), pp. 90–131; David Scott Kastan, "'Holy Wurdes' and 'Slypper Wit': John Bale's *King Johan* and the Poetics of Propaganda," in *Rethinking the Henrician Era*, ed. Peter C. Herman (Urbana and Chicago: University of Illinois Press, 1992), pp. 247–68; Andrew Hadfield, *Literature, Politics and National Identity: Reformation to Renaissance* (Cambridge University Press, 1994), pp. 66–72.

18 On Bale and the formation of national identity, see Peter Womack, "Imagining Communities: Theatres and the English Nation in the Sixteenth Century," in *Culture and History, 1350–1600*, ed. David Aers (New York and London: Harvester, 1992), pp. 91–145, and Richard Helgerson, *Forms of Nationhood: The Elizabethan Writing of England* (University of Chicago Press, 1992), pp. 247–68. Both Womack and Helgerson evoke Benedict Anderson's concept of a nation as an "imagined community" to explicate Bale's and Foxe's thinking about nascent nationhood. For a broader and more complex view, see Patrick Collinson, *The Birthpangs of Protestant England* (London: Macmillan, 1988), pp. 1–27.

19 John Foxe, *Acts and Monuments*, 2 vols. (1583), 2:1495.

20 John King, *English Reformation Literature* (Princeton University Press, 1982), p. 191.

21 In the 1583 edition, the woodcuts are presented together on a series of pages (1:783–91).

22 For contentious use of apocalyptic arguments like Foxe's, on both sides of the religious divide, see Stuart Clark, *Thinking with Demons: The Idea of Witchcraft in Early Modern Europe* (Oxford: Clarendon Press, 1997), pp. 335–62.

23 William Haller, *Foxe's Book of Martyrs and the Elect Nation* (London: Jonathan Cape, 1963), pp. 121–25.

24 On Foxe's depiction of commoners as martyrs, see Helgerson, *Forms of Nationhood*, pp. 247–68. Foxe's conception of Elizabeth as suffering Protestant is dramatized in Thomas Heywood's *1 If You Know Not Me You Know Nobody* (1604), as Kathleen E. McLuskie points out in *Dekker and Heywood: Professional Dramatists* (London: St. Martin's Press, 1994), pp. 41–46.

25 Examples include *The Longer Thou Livest, Enough Is as Good as a Feast, Like Will to Like, All for Money*.

26 Collinson, *Birthpangs*, pp. 102–12.

27 *Philargyrie of greate Britayne*, ed. John N. King, *English Literary Renaissance* 10 (1980), 46–75 (citation from pp. 50–51).

28 T. Lupton, *A Moral and Pitiful Comedie, Intituled, All for Money*, ed. Ernst Vogel, *Jahrbuch der deutschen Shakespeare-Geselschaft* 40 (1904), 129–86, lines 123–26.

29 For discussion of two other plays that fit this pattern – T. Lupton's *All for Money* (1559–77) and W. Wager's *Enough Is as Good as a Feast* (1559–70) – see John D. Cox, "Stage Devils in English Reformation Plays," *Comparative Drama* 32 (1998), 102–5.

30 Nathaniel Woodes, *The Conflict of Conscience*, ed. Herbert Davis and F. P. Wilson, Malone Society Reprints (Oxford University Press, 1952), Prologue, lines 43–47.

31 Leslie M. Oliver, "John Foxe and *The Conflict of Conscience*," *Review of English Studies* 25 (1949), 1–9.

32 *The Castle of Perseverance*, ed. Mark Eccles, *The Macro Plays*, EETS o.s. 262 (London: Oxford University Press, 1969), lines 607–8.

33 *Shakespeare and the Allegory of Evil* (New York: Columbia University Press, 1958), p. 131. For a less tendentious view, see Peter Happé, "The Devil in the Interludes," *Medieval English Theatre* 11 (1989), 42–56.

34 For other examples, see Happé, "The Devil in the Interludes," 48.

35 George Wapull, *The Tyde taryeth no Man*, ed. Ernst Rühl, *Shakespeare Jahrbuch* 43 (1907), 1–52, lines 126–40.

36 Susan Brigden, "Youth and the English Reformation," *Past and Present* 95 (1982), 38–67; Paul Whitfield White, *Theatre and Reformation: Protestantism, Patronage and Playing in Tudor England* (Cambridge University Press, 1993), pp. 109–29; and Howard B. Norland, *Drama in Early Tudor Britain 1485–1558* (Lincoln: University of Nebraska Press, 1995), pp. 149–60.

37 *Processus Satanae*, ed. W. W. Greg, Malone Society Collections, vol. 2, pt. 3 (Oxford University Press, 1931), pp. 239–50.

38 Bing Bills, "The 'Suppression Theory' and the English Corpus Christi Plays: a Re-Examination," *Theatre Journal* 32 (1980), 157–68.

39 Ronald Hutton, *The Rise and Fall of Merry England* (Oxford University Press, 1994), pp. 227–62. For a similar argument, but approached from another angle, see Judith Maltby, *Prayer Book and People in Elizabethan and Early Stuart England* (Cambridge University Press, 1998). Maltby reports, for example, that "as late as 1647, 3,000 soldiers in the parliamentary army were reported to be using the Prayer Book," which was a central element of liturgical continuity with traditional religion (p. 28).

6 THE DEVILS OF *DR. FAUSTUS*

1 Harold G. Gardiner, *Mysteries' End* (New Haven: Yale University Press, 1947). For secularization in other aspects of English life, see C. John Sommerville, *The Secularization of Early Modern England* (Oxford University Press, 1992).

2 On the Red Lion, see Janet Loengard, "An Elizabethan Lawsuit: John Brayne, his Carpenter, and the Building of the Red Lion Theater," *Shakespeare Quarterly* 34 (1982), 91–118.

3 This difference was recognized by contemporaries, as Kathleen E. McLuskie points out in "The Poets' Royal Exchange: Patronage and Commerce in Early Modern Drama," *Yearbook of English Studies* 21 (1991), 53–62.

4 Paul Whitfield White, *Theatre and Reformation: Protestantism, Patronage and Playing in Tudor England* (Cambridge University Press, 1993), pp. 163–66.

5 *Forms of Nationhood: The Elizabethan Writing of England* (University of Chicago Press, 1992), p. 200. Helgerson's contrast between an innovative "authors' theatre" and a traditional "players' theatre," however, is overstated and misses the point about what happened to dramatic authorship in the 1580s and '90s.

6 James Shapiro, *Rival Playwrights: Marlowe, Jonson, Shakespeare* (New York: Columbia University Press, 1991), p. 9.

7 Stuart Clark, *Thinking with Demons: The Idea of Witchcraft in Early Modern Europe* (Oxford: Clarendon Press, 1997).

8 Most recent editors are inclined to date the A-text in 1588–89, including David Bevington and Eric Rasmussen, eds., *Doctor Faustus A- and B-texts* (1604, 1616), Revels Plays (Manchester University Press, 1993), pp. 1–3, whose edition of the A-text I have cited. In addition to reasons given in their introduction, Bevington and Rasmussen point out that Marlowe's allusion to the "Prince of Parma" and "the fiery keel at Antwerp's bridge" suggests composition in early 1588, because it refers to a Dutch attempt to destroy a bridge with fireships in April, rather than to Parma's participation in the much more impressive and memorable Armada in the following July and August (1.1.98 n.). The likelihood that the allusion was penned before August, 1588, is increased by the fact that fireships were also used against the Armada in that month. See Garrett Mattingly, *The Armada* (Boston: Houghton Mifflin, 1959), pp. 316–17, 324–26.

9 Harry Levin, *The Overreacher* (Cambridge, Mass.: Harvard University Press, 1952).

10 Charles Nicholl, *The Reckoning* (New York: Harcourt Brace, 1992), pp. 5–9.

11 On the Cambridge curriculum when Marlowe was in residence there as a student, see John Bakeless, *The Tragical History of Christopher Marlowe*, 2 vols. (Cambridge, Mass.: Harvard University Press, 1942) 1:56–61. On Augustine in particular, see Douglas Cole, *Suffering and Evil in the Plays of Christopher Marlowe* (Princeton University Press, 1962), pp. 194–95. In Appendix D, "Libido," of *The Overreacher*, Levin outlines the history of *libido dominandi*. Despite allusions to Augustine's *Confessions*, however, Levin omits Augustine's contribution and attributes the phrase to Pascal (p. 202), who almost certainly learned it from *The City of God*. Augustine first uses the phrase in the preface to Book 1; his influential account of Lucifer's fall is in Books 11 and 12.

12 *Faustus*, ed. Bevington and Rasmussen, Pro. 22 n.

13 Paul Kocher makes the same point about *Tamburlaine* in *Christopher Marlowe* (Chapel Hill: University of North Carolina Press, 1946), p. 71, and later compares "Jove" of the earlier play to the God of *Faustus* (p. 118).

14 *Hero and Leander*, ed. C. F. Tucker Brooke, *The Works of Christopher Marlowe*

(Oxford: Clarendon Press, 1910), i. 143–48. I have used this edition in quoting works by Marlowe other than *Dr. Faustus*.

15 Edward Snow, "Marlowe's *Dr. Faustus* and the Ends of Desire," in *Two Renaissance Mythmakers* (Baltimore: Johns Hopkins University Press, 1977), pp. 70–110, also sees Faustus' repeated midnight invocation, "Come, Mephistopheles" (2.1.26–29) as erotic (p. 72). Constance Kuriyama first noticed the gender switch in Faustus' hyperbolic descriptions (*Hammer or Anvil* [New Brunswick, N.J.: Rutgers University Press, 1984], pp. 119, 123), and her explanation is neither that the wit is mimetic nor intentionally heterodox, but that it is a subconscious expression of Marlowe's own sexually ambivalent imagination. See also Nicholas Davidson, "Christopher Marlowe and Atheism" in *Christopher Marlowe and the English Renaissance*, ed. Darryll Grantley and Peter Roberts (Aldershot: Scolar Press, 1996), pp. 141–42.

16 C. L. Barber argues that *Dr. Faustus* depends for its effect on a lively sense of blasphemy, as an angry way of acknowledging the power of the sacred, "'The form of Faustus' fortunes, good or bad,'" *TDR* 8 (1964): 92–119. Barber cites Mephistopheles' lines about the beauty of Lucifer as an example of language which condemns its users "by the logic of a situation larger than they are" (p. 99). He is referring to Lucifer's pre-fallen happiness, not to the gender switch, but in context it also depends on blasphemy for its effect.

17 Huston Diehl sees God's absence as a reflection of Calvinistic iconoclasm and resistance to ritual in the 1580s, in *Staging Reform, Reforming the Stage* (Ithaca: Cornell University Press, 1997), pp. 73–81. Still, as part of a traditional opposition in *Dr. Faustus*, stage devils are themselves visible remnants of sacred culture, and the ritual of invoking the devil is as potent as any staged miracle.

18 Several critics have noticed differences between the Old Man in the A and B versions of *Dr. Faustus*, and Leah Marcus argues that the A version is closer to militant Protestantism than the B version, in *Unediting the Renaissance* (London and New York: Routledge, 1996), pp. 47–51 (citing other references). My point is that either version compromises the oppositional clarity of militant Protestantism by identifying the Old Man as just another contestant in a pervasive cosmic struggle for mastery. Marcus anticipates this point, observing that the devil's championing of Protestant policy "massively undercuts the 'official' ideology of the play" (p. 61).

19 On the Protestant response to peasant demands for social justice, see Stephen Greenblatt, "Murdering Peasants: Status, Genre, and the Representation of Rebellion," in *Learning to Curse* (New York: Routledge, 1990), pp. 99–130.

20 T. McAlindon, *Dr. Faustus Divine in Show* (New York: Twayne Publishers, 1994), pp. 45–61.

21 On Marlowe's adaptation of morality-play conventions, see David M. Bevington, *From "Mankind" to Marlowe* (Cambridge, Mass.: Harvard University Press, 1962), pp. 199–262.

22 McAlindon sees Mephistopheles as "an entirely original kind of devil" whose early behavior "is totally at variance with both his intentions and his conduct as shown later" (p. 38), but this underestimates the sophistication of Marlowe's devil and ignores Mephistopheles' important aside, quoted in the text below.

23 This point is well made by T. McAlindon, "*Doctor Faustus*: the Predestination Theory," *English Studies* 76 (1995), 215–16.

24 Coburn Freer, "Lies and Lying in *The Jew of Malta*," in *"A Poet and a Filthy Play-maker": New Essays on Christopher Marlowe*, ed. Kenneth Friedenreich, Roma Gill, and Constance Kuriyama (New York: AMS Press, 1988), pp. 143–65, especially the following: "When a majority of characters in a play lie to each other and themselves, their verbal behavior will not only shape the action but will also give that action a multitude of meanings, some of them inevitably contradictory" (p. 145).

25 According to a contemporary Cambridge regulation: "no man, unless he were a doctor, should wear any hood lined with silk upon his gown . . . [nor] wear any stuff in the outward part of his gown but woolen cloth of black, puke, London brown, or other sad color" (*Dr. Faustus*, 1.1.92 n.).

26 George Puttenham, *The Arte of English Poetrie*, ed. Gladys Willcock and Alice Walker (Cambridge University Press, 1936), p. 186. On the social and political commitments of the courtesy tradition (of which Puttenham's work is a Tudor culmination), see Frank Whigham, *Ambition and Privilege: The Social Tropes of Elizabethan Courtesy Theory* (Berkeley and Los Angeles: University of California Press, 1984).

27 See chapter 4 above, and N. W. Bawcutt, " 'Policy,' Machiavellianism, and the Earlier Tudor Drama," *English Literary Renaissance* 1 (1971), 195–209.

28 This section was complete when I encountered a similar idea in Judith Weil, "'Full Possession': Service and Slavery in *Doctor Faustus*," in Paul Whitfield White, ed., *Marlowe, History, and Sexuality* (New York: AMS Press, 1998), pp. 143–54.

29 The best study of Elizabethan espionage is Nicholl's *The Reckoning*, to which I am principally indebted.

30 "The Confession of Richard Baines Priest and Late Stvdent of the Colledge of Rhemes" in *A True Report of the Apprehension of John Nicols* (Rheims, 1583), sig. 24v–27. This English translation of Baines' confession was discovered at about the same time by Nicholl (*Reckoning*, p. 127) and by Roy Kendall, who has published a modern English translation of the Latin original, as well as of Baines' oral confession, "Richard Baines and Christopher Marlowe's Milieu," *English Literary Renaissance* 24 (1994), 507–52. I am grateful to Anna-Lisa Cox for assistance in obtaining a copy of Baines' published confession from the Cambridge University Library.

31 Kendall argues that Baines seems to have turned Marlowe to skepticism in the first place, and that the opinions Baines ascribed to Marlowe in 1593 were likely close to his own.

32 The quoted lines are from *The Chester Mystery Cycle*, ed. R. M. Lumiansky

and David Mills, EETS s.s. 3 (London: Oxford University Press, 1974), *The Last Judgment*, lines 477–78.

33 On Marlowe's familiarity with Elizabethan confidence tricksters, see Nicholl, *The Reckoning*, pp. 22–34. Another university wit, Robert Greene, published a number of "coney-catching" pamphlets in the early 1590s, purporting to warn readers about the methods of petty thieves and confidence tricksters, but the genre was well established when Greene added to it. For examples see *Cony-Catchers and Bawdy Baskets*, ed. Gamini Salgado (Harmondsworth, Middlesex: Penguin, 1972).

34 The now classic materialist reading of *Dr. Faustus* is Jonathan Dollimore's, in *Radical Tragedy* (University of Chicago Press, 1984), pp. 109–19.

35 All but one of these references were collected by E. K. Chambers, *The Elizabethan Stage*, 4 vols. (Oxford: Clarendon Press, 1923), 3:423–24. For the other reference (also dated to 1594), see Eric Rasmussen, "*The Black Book* and the Date of *Doctor Faustus*," *Notes and Queries* 235, n.s. 37 (1990), 168–70.

36 *Three Tudor Classical Interludes*, ed. Marie Axton (Cambridge: D. S. Brewer, 1982), and White, *Theatre and Reformation*, pp. 126–29.

37 Nicholl, *The Reckoning*, p. 205. Both Nicholl and Kendall suggest that Fineux may have been turned to skepticism by Marlowe.

7 REACTING TO MARLOWE

1 My assertion about the precedence of *Dr. Faustus* assumes that it was performed before Greene's *Friar Bacon and Friar Bungay*. See chapter 6, n. 8.

2 Peter Berek, "*Tamburlaine*'s Weak Sons: Imitation as Interpretation before 1593," *Renaissance Drama* n.s. 13 (1982), 55–82.

3 Edward hates the church because it opposes his love for Gaveston, but his lines nonetheless appeal strongly to Elizabethan Protestant feeling. *The Tragedie of Edward the Second*, ed. C. F. Tucker Brooke, *The Works of Christopher Marlowe* (Oxford: Clarendon Press, 1910), lines 391–99.

4 *Doctor Faustus A- and B-texts (1604, 1616)*, ed. David Bevington and Eric Rasmussen, Revels Plays (Manchester University Press, 1993), A-Text, 1.156.

5 Waldo F. McNeir, "Traditional Elements in the Character of Greene's *Friar Bacon*," *Studies in Philology* 45 (1948), 172–79. See also, *Friar Bacon and Friar Bungay*, ed. Daniel Seltzer (Lincoln: University of Nebraska Press, 1963), pp. xii–xiii. I have cited this edition by scene and line number.

6 Frank Towne also emphasizes Bacon's repentance in arguing that the friar renounces black magic, "'White Magic' in *Friar Bacon and Friar Bungay*," *Modern Language Notes* 67 (1952), 9–13.

7 Albert Wertheim, "The Presentation of Sin in *Friar Bacon and Friar Bungay*, *Criticism* 16 (1974), 273–86.

8 Kurt Tetzeli von Rosador makes the same point, though in a different way, in "The Sacralizing Sign: Religion and Magic in Bale, Greene, and the Early Shakespeare," *Yearbook of English Studies* 23 (1993), 30–45.

9 William Empson, *Some Versions of Pastoral* (Norfolk, Conn.: New Directions, n.d. [1950]), pp. 31–34.

10 Caxton records the story, along with Dunstan's quarrel with King Edwin "for his synful lyuyng" and Dunstan's promotion to archbishop of Canterbury by King Edgar, *The Golden Legend of Master William Caxton Done Anew* (Hammersmith: Kelmscott Press, 1892), pp. 496–97. See also Nigel Ramsay and Margaret Sparks, *The Image of Saint Dunstan* (Canterbury: The Dunstan Millennium Committee, 1988), p. 20. Seven of the fourteen pre-Reformation portraits of St. Dunstan in this book depict a victory over the devil. Ramsay and Sparks point out that Dunstan was especially revered by both Henry VI and Henry VII because of his closeness to kings as a royal counselor (p. 33), which is the role he also plays in *Knack to Know a Knave*.

11 Holinshed reports some of the episodes in *Knack*, but Holinshed is also skeptical and derisive. An equally reverential treatment of Dunstan appears in *Grim the Collier of Croydon* (c. 1600), ed. William M. Baillie, in *A Choice Ternary of English Plays* (Binghamton: Medieval and Renaissance Texts and Studies, 1984), pp. 171–321. *Grim* even follows *The Golden Legend* in commending Dunstan's veracity by citing the Rood of Dovercourt's approval of it (1.2.29–30). For commentary on Foxe's condemnation of the Rood, see Huston Diehl, *Staging Reform, Reforming the Stage* (Ithaca: Cornell University Press, 1997), pp. 26–28.

12 *A Knack to Know a Knave* (1592), ed. W. Carew Hazlitt and Robert Dodsley, *A Select Collection of Old English Plays*, 8 vols. (London: Reeves and Turner, 1874), 6:564–65. Cited by page number.

13 Mary G. M. Adkins, "The Genesis of Dramatic Satire against the Puritan, as Illustrated in *A Knack to Know a Knave*," *Review of English Studies* 22 (1946), 81–95.

14 Anthony Fletcher, *Tudor Rebellions*, 3rd edn. (Harlow, Essex: Longman, 1983), p. 114.

15 *The Merry Devil of Edmonton*, ed. William Amos Abrams (Durham: Duke University Press, 1942), pp. 3–13. Abrams's edition is cited here.

16 The quoted terms are used repeatedly in the play to describe Fabell's actions and their effect. See 1.2.54, 1.3.20 and 133, 5.1.93, 212, 247, and 248.

17 Lawrence Stone, *Family, Sex, and Marriage in England 1500–1800* (New York: Harper and Row, 1977), pp. 85–119 and 325–404.

18 Andrew Gurr argues that several plays from rival repertories in the 1590s stage competing views of romantic love and parental decision as the prelude to marriage, "Intertextuality at Windsor," *Shakespeare Quarterly* 38 (1988), 189–200. See also G. R. Hibbard, "Love, Marriage and Money in Shakespeare's Theatre and Shakespeare's England," *Elizabethan Theatre VI* (Hamden, Conn.: Shoe String Press, 1977), pp. 134–55.

19 This association, at least as old as classical Latin elegy, is virtually continuous in English poetry from the fourteenth century, when it appears both in Chaucer and in *Gawain and the Greeen Knight*. The anti-feminism of the image (with its suggestions of violence and rape) is unmistakable, but in context

the boisterous subplot of *Merry Devil* is more closely linked to popular rituals such as the charivari than to literary misogyny.

20 J. Woodfall Ebsworth, ed., *The Roxburghe Ballads*, 9 vols. (Hertford: Stephen Austin and Sons, 1889), 6:378. The following quotation is from the same source, 6:384. I am grateful to Russ MacDonald for assistance in finding these ballads.

21 Though Maurice Charney does not mention Joan in "The Voice of Marlowe's Tamburlaine in Early Shakespeare," *Comparative Drama* 31 (1997), 213–23, his conclusion that Shakespeare's echoes of Tamburlaine are parodic applies to her as much as to other characters.

22 *Narrative and Dramatic Sources of Shakespeare*, ed. Geoffrey Bullough, 8 vols. (New York: Columbia University Press, 1966), 3:56–58, 75–76. See also Richard F. Hardin, "Chronicles and Mythmaking in Shakespeare's Joan of Arc," *Shakespeare Survey* 42 (1990), 25–35.

23 David Riggs also sees Joan and Talbot "as two sides of a complex statement about aristocratic values" in response to Tamburlaine, but his interest is in classical rhetorical theory, not in the two playwrights' native dramatic heritage, *Shakespeare's Heroical Histories* (Cambridge, Mass.: Harvard University Press, 1971), pp. 100–13.

24 Coppélia Kahn understands Talbot to be interpreting his son's death as punishment for overweening ambition, in *Man's Estate: Masculine Identity in Shakespeare* (Berkeley and Los Angeles: University of California Press, 1981), pp. 53–54, but "pride" meant more than "overweening ambition" for Shakespeare. The *OED* cites this passage from *1 Henry VI* under "pride" *sb.*[1] 9.a, "The best, highest, most excellent or flourishing state condition; the prime; the flower."

25 Peter Womack argues that Shakespeare's history plays helped to shape a distinctive English national identity, "Imagining Communities: Theatres and the English Nation in the Sixteenth Century," in *Culture and History 1350–1600*, ed. David Aers (New York and London: Harvester Wheatsheaf, 1992), pp. 91–145.

26 On Joan as an "antitype," "grotesque inversion," and "parody" of Talbot, see Edward I. Berry, *Patterns of Decay: Shakespeare's Early Histories* (Charlottesville: University Press of Virginia, 1975), pp. 1–28.

27 Shakespeare's way of imagining Joan manifestly caricatures and demeans female independence and assertiveness, and it has elicited a great deal of comment, summarized in John D. Cox, "Devils and Power in Marlowe and Shakespeare," *Yearbook of English Studies* 23 (1993), n. 21.

28 I have argued in another context that Shakespeare's histories are shaped by what the young playwright saw in the struggles for power at the late Elizabethan court, *Shakespeare and the Dramaturgy of Power* (Princeton University Press, 1989), pp. 82–127.

29 Berry comments incisively on the "narrowly political and ethical" concerns of *1 Henry VI* (*Patterns of Decay*, p. 15). I would add that a similar narrowness of concern is characteristic of all Shakespeare's histories, in contrast to the tragedies.

30　Bullough, *Narrative and Dramatic Sources*, 3:102.
31　See, for example, Michael Hattaway, "Rebellion, Class Consciousness, and Shakespeare's *2 Henry VI*," *Cahiers Elisabethains* 33 (1988), 13–20; Annabel Patterson, *Shakespeare and the Popular Voice* (Oxford: Basil Blackwell, 1989), pp. 31–51; Richard Helgerson, *Forms of Nationhood: The Elizabethan Writing of England* (University of Chicago Press, 1992), pp. 195–245; Womack, "Imagining Communities," pp. 91–145; William C. Carroll, *Fat King, Lean Beggar: Representations of Poverty in the Age of Shakespeare* (Ithaca, N.Y.: Cornell University Press, 1996), pp. 127–57.
32　Bernard Spivack, *Shakespeare and the Allegory of Evil* (New York: Columbia University Press, 1958).
33　See chapter 4, above.
34　Compare Nichol Newfangle, for example: "Now three knaves are gone, and I am left alone, / Myself here to solace." Ulpian Fulwell, *Like Will to Like*, ed. J. A. B. Somerset, *Four Tudor Interludes* (London: Athlone Press; New York: Humanities Press, 1974), lines 566–68.

8　THE DEVIL AND THE SACRED ON THE SHAKESPEAREAN STAGE: THEATRE AND BELIEF

1　Andrew Gurr, *The Shakespearean Stage 1574–1642*, 3rd edn. (Cambridge University Press, 1992).
2　See Appendix. The count includes "fiends," "spirits," and "furies," and actors playing another character disguised in devil costume who is mistaken for a devil.
3　Stephen Greenblatt, "Shakespeare and the Exorcists," *Shakespearean Negotiations* (Berkeley and Los Angeles: University of California Press, 1988), p. 109.
4　Jonas Barish, *The Antitheatrical Prejudice* (Berkeley and Los Angeles: University of California Press, 1981), pp. 66–190.
5　John Darrel, *The Triall of Maist. Dorrell* (1599): "[Atheism] is confirmed by denying dispossession . . . . If neither possession, nor witchcraft, (contrary to that hath bene so longe generally and confidently affirmed) why should we thinke that there are Divels? If no Divels, no God," pp. 7–8, cited Greenblatt, *Shakespearean Negotiations*, p. 104; Henry More, *An antidote against atheisme* (1653): "a contemptuous misbelief of such like Narrations concerning *Spirits*, and an endeavour of making them all ridiculous and incredible, is a dangerous Prelude to *Atheisme* it self . . . For assuredly that Saying was nothing so true in Politicks, *No Bishop, no King*; as this is in Metaphysicks, *No Spirit, no God*," cited Stuart Clark, *Thinking with Demons: The Idea of Witchcraft in Early Modern Europe* (Oxford: Clarendon Press, 1997), p. 164. Continuity between Protestant and Catholic thinking on demonology is documented by Clark, *Thinking with Demons*, pp. 526–45.
6　For details about these stories, see chapter 6 above, n. 35.
7　*The playe called the foure PP.* (London: William Middleton, n.d. [1544?]), ed. L. M. Clopper (Malone Society, 1984), lines 948–49.

8 *A Trve and Fearfvll Vexaction of One Alexander Nyndge* . . . Written by His Owne
   Brother Edward Nyndge, 2nd edn. (Imprinted at London, for W.B., 1616),
   sig. B. The first edition was published in 1573.

9 Gareth Roberts, "Necromantic Books: Christopher Marlowe, *Doctor Faustus*
   and Agrippa of Nettesheim," in *Christopher Marlowe and the English
   Renaissance*, ed. Darryll Grantley and Peter Roberts (Aldershot: Scolar Press,
   1996), p. 149.

10 John Cotta, *The triall of witch-craft* (1616), quoted James Sharpe, *Instruments of
   Darkness: Witchcraft in Early Modern England* (Philadelphia: University of
   Pennsylvania Press, 1997), p. 83.

11 Clark, *Thinking with Demons*, p. 167.

12 The unpublished account of Foxe's dispossession is discussed by Keith
   Thomas, *Religion and the Decline of Magic* (New York: Charles Scribner's Sons,
   1971), pp. 481–82. Thomas calls Foxe a "Puritan," but the label seems
   designed to support Thomas' point that dispossession was associated only
   with extreme belief. Historically that indeed became true, for reasons
   detailed below, but it was not necessarily true in 1571, and Foxe was no more
   a Puritan than Bale.

13 Reginald Scot, *The discouerie of witchcraft* (Imprinted at London by William
   Brome, 1584). Scot's ambivalent skepticism about devils is manifest in his
   concluding "Discourse vpon diuels and spirits" (pp. 489–560), which is
   omitted from most modern editions.

14 Quoted by Clark, *Thinking with Demons*, p. 306. Whiston was no eccentric; if
   anything, he represented the majority of scientific opinion in the early eighteenth century. For parallel views, see Clark, pp. 294–311.

15 Greenblatt, "Shakespeare and the Exorcists." The relevance of the debate
   about exorcism to *King Lear* was recognized simultaneously by John L.
   Murphy in *Darkness and Devils: Exorcism and "King Lear"* (Athens, Ohio: Ohio
   University Press, 1984), though Murphy's argument is anticipated by Peter
   Milward, S.J., *Shakespeare's Religious Background* (Bloomington: Indiana
   University Press, 1973), pp. 53–54. Some aspects of Greenblatt's essay are
   corrected by F. W. Brownlow's introduction to his edition of Harsnett,
   Shakespeare, Harsnett, and the Devils of Denham (Newark: University of Delaware
   Press, 1993), pp. 49–131.

16 Clifford Geertz, "Religion as a Cultural System," in *The Interpretation of
   Cultures* (New York: Basic Books, 1973), p. 99. Huston Diehl also cites this
   passage in an argument for continuing religious vitality in seventeenth-
   century drama that parallels mine in certain ways. See *Staging Reform,
   Reforming the Stage* (Ithaca: Cornell University Press, 1997), pp. 3–4.

17 On the continuing identification of dispossession with religious dissenters,
   see Michael MacDonald, "Religion, Social Change, and Psychological
   Healing in England, 1600–1800," in *The Church and Healing*, ed. W. L. Sheils
   (Oxford: Blackwell, 1982), pp. 101–25. MacDonald argues that dispossession
   and other "religious therapies" for psychological distress "were rejected
   by the governing elite of the eighteenth century because of religious

controversy, social antagonisms, and cultural change, rather than scientific progress" (p. 102). In other words, the English church's late sixteenth-century stand against dispossession remained the principal reason for continuing to resist it, as an instance of religious enthusiasm, well into the eighteenth century. See also Ian Bostridge, *Witchcraft and Its Transformations c. 1650–c. 1750* (Oxford: Clarendon Press, 1997), pp. 55–65.

18 *The Puritan Widow*, ed. C. F. Tucker Brooke in *The Shakespeare Apocrypha* (Oxford: Clarendon Press, 1908), 4.2.

19 George Lyman Kittredge, *Witchcraft in Old and New England* (1929; rpt. New York: Russell and Russell, 1956), pp. 281–90.

20 For topical readings of *Devil Is an Ass*, see Leah Marcus, *The Politics of Mirth* (University of Chicago Press, 1986), pp. 85–105, and Robert C. Evans, "Contemporary Contexts of Jonson's *The Devil Is an Ass*," *Comparative Drama* 26 (1992), 140–76.

21 Ben Jonson, *The Devil Is an Ass*, Revels Edition, ed. Peter Happé (Manchester University Press, 1994), 5.3.6. Happé cites the parallels with Harsnett. For similar parallels in *Volpone*, see *Ben Jonson*, ed. C. H. Herford and Percy and Evelyn Simpson, 11 vols. (Oxford: Clarendon Press, 1925–52), 9:731–32.

22 Rainer Pineas, "The Morality Vice in *Volpone*," *Discourse* 5 (1962), 451–59.

23 *Volpone*, ed. Alvin B. Kernan (New Haven: Yale University Press, 1962), 5.3.46.

24 The quotation is from *Volpone*, p. 30. For more on Jonson's debt to traditional Vice comedy in *Volpone*, see Alan C. Dessen, *Jonson's Moral Comedy* (Evanston: Northwestern University Press, 1971), pp. 70–104.

25 Happé comments on Jonson's debt to Dekker in *Devil Is an Ass*, pp. 30–32.

26 Cyrus Hoy quotes an allusion to Friar Rush in *Gammer Gurton's Needle* (1553), so the motif is an old one. Hoy's comments about it appear in his *Introductions, Notes, and Commentaries to texts in 'The Dramatic Works of Thomas Dekker' edited by Fredson Bowers*, 4 vols. (Cambridge University Press, 1980), 3:73–80.

27 Ben Jonson, *The Masque of Queens*, ed. Stephen Orgel, in *Ben Jonson: The Complete Masques* (New Haven and London: Yale University Press, 1969), line 87 n., line 59 n. Almost certainly in imitation of Jonson, William Davenant also includes a "Devill in the shape of a Goat" in his masque *Luminalia* (1637).

28 On the oppositional significance of "preposterous," see Clark, *Thinking with Demons*, pp. 43–93. For its significance in Shakespeare, see Patricia Parker, *Shakespeare from the Margins* (University of Chicago Press, 1996), pp. 20–55.

29 Ben Jonson, *Chlorida*, ed. Stephen Orgel, in *Ben Jonson: The Complete Masques* (New Haven and London: Yale University Press, 1969), lines 95–96.

30 Greenblatt remarks that Harsnett was attempting to wipe out "pockets of rivalrous charisma" to the English church (*Shakespearean Negotiations*, p. 96). On early modern monarchs as "charismatic" leaders, in Max Weber's term, see Clark, *Thinking with Demons*, pp. 582–87. He discusses the celebration of such leadership in court festivals on pp. 647–53.

31 Sebastien Michaëlis, *The admirable historie of the possession and conversion of a penitent woman*, trans. W. B. (London, 1613), quoted Clark, *Thinking with Demons*, p. 568.

32 William Davenant, *The Dramatic Works of William Davenant*, ed. James Maidment and W. H. Logan, 5 vols. (Edinburgh: William Paterson; London: Sotheran & Co., 1872), 1:290. This edition does not number the lines.

33 For a parallel, see the stage direction in *The Birth of Merlin*, ed. Joanna Udall (London: Modern Humanities Research Association, 1991): "*Enter the Devil in mans habit, richly attir'd, his feet and his head horrid*" (3.1.141).

34 The play was first published in 1662, but it is manifestly earlier than that. Though its auspices and its precise date are unknown, a reasonable guess is that it was in the public theatre repertoire in the first decade of the seventeenth century (Udall, ed., pp. 11 and 19).

35 Nathan Field, *A Woman Is a Weathercock*, ed. William Peery, *The Plays of Nathan Field* (Austin: University of Texas Press, 1950). For allusions to *The Spanish Tragedy*, see 1.1.44–45 and 1.2.34off.; to *Hamlet*, 3.2.71–230, and to playmaking, 2.1.273–77; 3.1.116–18; 3.2.148–51; 4.3 (where Pendant and Wagtail stage a play-within-the-play), 5.2 (where Scudmore dances in disguise at a masque in order to contact Bellafront and elope with her) and 5.2.230–31. The concluding play-within-the-play, where action takes place that is significant for the play itself, may be another allusion to the *The Spanish Tragedy*.

36 John Fletcher, *Monsieur Thomas*, ed. Hans Walter Gabler, in *The Dramatic Works in the Beaumont and Fletcher Canon*, ed. Fredson Bowers, 10 vols. (Cambridge University Press, 1966–96), vol. 4, 3.3.92 SD.

37 See 1.3.92–96, 109; 2.2.52–53; 3.1.266–69; 4.2.188–89; 5.1.3–4, 43–48, 59–62; 5.10.18–28; and 5.11.47.

38 John Fletcher, *The Chances*, ed. George Walton Williams, in *The Dramatic Works in the Beaumont and Fletcher Canon*, ed. Fredson Bowers, 10 vols. (Cambridge University Press, 1966–96), vol. 4, 5.1.2 and 5 and 5.3.16. Vechio's explanation is at 5.3.166–77.

39 Scot, *Discoverie*, XIII.13, "Of priuate confederacie, and of Brandons pigeon" (pp. 308–9). Brandon poisons a pigeon, places it strategically on a rooftop, then pretends to effect its death by means of a spell at the time he knows the poison will accomplish its purpose.

40 G. E. Bentley's observation, cited in Williams, ed., *The Chances*, in *Dramatic Works*, ed. Bowers 4:543.

41 J. C., *The Two Merry Milkmaids*, ed. G. Harold Metz (New York and London: Garland Publishing, 1979), 1.1.75.

42 For other metadramatic passages in the play, see 2.1.144, 3.1.114–16, 3.1.140–42, 4.1.160–63, 4.3.435ff. (an imitation of Volpone's feigned sickness), 4.3.613–19, and 4.3.717–18.

43 Metz, ed. *Two Merry Milkmaids*, pp. xxxviii–xlvii.

44 Clark, *Thinking with Demons*, p. 211.

45 Scot affirms New Testament miracles in chapter 14 of "A Discourse vpon

diuels and Spirits" (pp. 512–13). On Scot's ambivalence, see Sydney Anglo, "Reginald Scot's *Discoverie of Witchcraft:* Scepticism and Sadduceeism," in *The Damned Art: Essays in the Literature of Witchcraft* ed. Sydney Anglo (London: Routledge and Kegan Paul, 1977), pp. 106–39.

9 TRADITIONAL MORALITY AND MAGICAL THINKING

1 For an incisive materialist reading of commercial relations in London plays, see Douglas Bruster, *Drama and Market in the Age of Shakespeare* (Cambridge University Press, 1992). Bruster's interpretation is qualified by a careful investigation of social relationships among players themselves by Kathleen E. McLuskie and Felicity Dunsworth, "Patronage and the Economics of Theater," in *A New History of Early English Drama*, ed. John D. Cox and David Scott Kastan (New York: Columbia University Press, 1997), pp. 423–40.

2 On continuity and discontinuity in the rituals of social life, see David Cressy, *Birth, Marriage, and Death: Ritual, Religion, and the Life-Cycle in Tudor and Stuart England* (Oxford University Press, 1997).

3 James Knowles, "The Spectacle of the Realm: Civic Consciousness, Rhetoric and Ritual in Early Modern London" in *Theatre and Government under the Early Stuarts*, ed. J. R. Mylryne and Margaret Shewring (Cambridge University Press, 1993), p. 162.

4 Four sermons were written for Rogation Week and included among the homilies appointed to be read by Queen Elizabeth. None of them alludes to the cleansing of fields; instead, the second one sternly warns against recourse to "charms, witchcrafts, and other delusions of the devil" as means to "corporal health" – a concern on both sides of the Catholic/Protestant divide, as Clark points out in *Thinking with Demons: The Idea of Witchcraft in Early Modern Europe* (Oxford: Clarendon Press, 1997), pp. 457–71. The quotation is from *Certain Sermons or Homilies*, 3rd American Edition, from the Last English Edition (Philadelphia: George and Wayne, 1844), p. 429.

5 George Herbert, *Works*, ed. F. E. Hutchinson (Oxford: Clarendon Press, 1967), p. 284.

6 Knowles, "Spectacle," p. 163.

7 F. J. Drake-Carnell, *Old English Customs and Ceremonies* (New York: Charles Scribner's Sons; London: B. T. Batsford, 1938), p. 32 (with photographs). For more recent information, see Charles Kightly, *The Customs and Ceremonies of Britain* (London: Thames and Hudson, 1986), pp. 48–50.

8 Thomas Dekker, *A Nights Conjuring* (1607), ed. Larry M. Robbins (The Hague: Mouton, 1974), p. 84.

9 Thomas Dekker, *If This Be Not a Good Play, the Devil Is in It* (1611–12), ed. Fredson Bowers, in *The Dramatic Works of Thomas Dekker*, 4 vols. (Cambridge University Press, 1953–61), 2.1.180–81.

10 Robert Grams Hunter, *Shakespeare and the Comedy of Forgiveness* (New York: Columbia University Press, 1965).

11 William C. Carroll, *Fat King, Lean Beggar* (Ithaca and London: Cornell University Press, 1996). None of Dekker's plays discussed here is included in Carroll's account.

12 Callousness toward beggars is similarly rejected in another Dekker play, co-written with Philip Massinger, *The Virgin Martyr*, ed. Bowers, in *Dramatic Works of Thomas Dekker*, 2.1.62–64, 2.1.136–38, and 3.3.205–10.

13 Kathleen E. McLuskie, *Dekker and Heywood: Professional Dramatists* (Manchester University Press, 1994), p. 41.

14 Louise George Clubb, "*The Virgin Martyr* and the *Tragedia Sacra*," *Renaissance Drama* 7 (1964), 103–26.

15 Julia Gaspar, "The Sources of *The Virgin Martyr*," *Review of English Studies* n.s. 42 (1991), 17–31.

16 On Foxe and iconoclasm, see Huston Diehl, *Staging Reform, Reforming the Stage* (Ithaca: Cornell University Press, 1997), pp. 9–39.

17 The pamphlet is reprinted in Etta Soiref Onat's edition of *The Witch of Edmonton* (New York and London: Garland Publishing, 1980), pp. 381–400.

18 Michael Hattaway points out that the playwrights invented Sawyer's indigent plight; her social status is not identified by Goodcole. "Women and Witchcraft: the Case of 'The Witch of Edmonton,'" *Trivium* 20 (1985), 49–68.

19 *The Witch of Edmonton*, ed. Bowers, in *Dramatic Works of Thomas Dekker*, 1.1.62–63.

20 Sawyer talks to Tom about bewitching Anne to death in 4.1.166–71. The question is not whether she "really" killed Anne, because the play raises no doubt about her and Tom's ability to accomplish such a task.

21 Sawyer's defense of witches as exploited poor people derives ultimately from Scot, *Discoverie*, Epistle to the Readers (sig. Biv), but it was frequently repeated. See Clark, *Thinking with Demons*, pp. 517–18.

22 Arthus C. Kirsch, *Jacobean Dramatic Perspectives* (Charlottesville: University Press of Virginia, 1972), pp. 83–85.

23 John Webster, *The White Devil*, ed. John Russell Brown, 2nd edn., Revels Plays (London: Methuen, 1966), 5.3.179.

24 Thomas Middleton, *A Mad World, My Masters*, ed. Michael Taylor (Oxford University Press, 1995), 4.2.37. Taylor briefly discusses the demonic imagery of Middleton's city comedies (pp. xi–xii). *A Mad World, My Masters* was written two years after the canons of 1604 forbade exorcism and dispossession, and it is contemporary with the explicit satire of Puritans in *The Puritan Widow*.

25 Arthur F. Marotti, "The Method of the Madness of *A Mad World, My Masters*," *Tennessee Studies in Literature* 15 (1970), 99–108.

26 Thomas Middleton, *Michaelmas Term*, ed. Richard Levin (Lincoln: University of Nebraska Press, 1966), Ind. 3–4.

27 *The Book of Common Prayer 1559*, ed. John E. Booty (Charlottesville: University Press of Virginia, for the Folger Shakespeare Library, 1976), p. 273. Dekker echoes the same passage in *If This Be Not*: "They feare not sattin nor all his workes" (4.2.112).

28 Anne Barton, *Ben Jonson, Dramatist* (Cambridge University Press, 1984), p. 229.

29 Robert Davenport, *A New Trick to Cheat the Devil*, ed. A. H. Bullen, Old English Plays, n.s. vol. III (London and Redhill: Hansard Publishing Union, 1890), 4.2, p. 258, my emphasis. Cited by act, scene, and page number. For other suggestions that Changeable is really Slightall's guardian angel in devil's disguise, see 4.2, pp. 257–58.

30 W. P. Ker's brief appendix to Bullen's edition outlines the sources of *New Trick*'s subplot (pp. 337–40). The play has received little critical attention.

31 Margot Heinemann, *Puritanism and Theatre: Thomas Middleton and Opposition Drama under the Early Stuarts* (Cambridge University Press, 1980), pp. 226–29, and Akiko Kusunoki, "'Their Testament at Their Apron-strings': the Representation of Puritan Women in Early-Seventeenth-Century England," in *Gloriana's Face: Women, Public and Private, in the English Renaissance*, ed. S. P. Cerasano and Marion Wynne-Davies (New York: Harvester Wheatsheaf, 1992), pp. 185–204.

32 Barton, *Ben Jonson*, p. 224.

33 Most influential, in dealing with historical English culture, is Keith Thomas, *Religion and the Decline of Magic* (New York: Charles Scribner's Sons, 1971), pp. 469–77.

34 Clark, *Thinking with Demons*, p. 138.

35 For efforts to resist popular magic, both before and after the Reformation, see Eamon Duffy, *The Stripping of the Altars* (New Haven: Yale University Press, 1992), pp. 207–98, and Clark, *Thinking with Demons*, pp. 457–525.

36 Onat, ed., *The Witch of Edmonton*, pp. 382–83.

37 Thomas Heywood, *The Silver Age*, in *The Dramatic Works of Thomas Heywood*, 6 vols. (London: John Pearson, 1874), 3:123. Cited by page number.

38 In *The Scythe of Saturn* (Urbana and Chicago: University of Illinois Press, 1994), Linda Woodbridge observes that prognostication is the most common kind of magic in Shakespeare's plays (p. 6), but the focus of her discussion lies elsewhere.

39 Scot, *Discoverie*, Books VIII–XII. In these books, Scot demystifies a succession of Hebrew words that were thought to describe various kinds of magical language, in order to support his argument that miracles, oracles, and prophecies had ceased with the apostolic age.

40 *Bussy D'Ambois: A Tragedie*, ed. G. Blakemore Evans and Thomas L. Berger, *The Plays of George Chapman. The Tragedies* (Cambridge: D. S. Brewer, 1987), 5.2.61. Quotations are from the quarto of 1641, "Being much corrected and amended by the Author before his death" (title page).

41 The quotation is from the title page in *The Dramatic Works of Richard Brome*, 3 vols. (London: John Pearson, 1873), 3:453. Cited by act and page number.

42 *The Atheist's Tragedy*, ed. George Parfitt (Cambridge University Press, 1978), (3.2.20 SD).

43 Houston Diehl, "'Reduce Thy Understanding to Thine Eye': Seeing and Interpreting in *The Atheist's Tragedy*," *Studies in Philology* 78 (1981), 47–60.

44 Though Tourneur's play has no devils, the relationship between its plots is morally oppositional, as in many devil plays. See Richard Levin, "The Subplot of *The Atheist's Tragedy*," *Huntington Library Quarterly* 29 (1965), 17–33.

45 Lewes Lavater, *Of Ghostes and Spirites Walking by Nyght* (1572), ed. J. Dover Wilson and May Yardley (Oxford University Press, for the Shakespeare Association, 1929), chapter titles from the Table of Chapters. This is a translation of the Latin work by a Lutheran pastor, Ludwig Lavater, *De spectris, lemuribus et magnis atque infolitis fragoribus* (1570). Wilson published the Elizabethan translation in a modern edition because he was so impressed with its relevance to the Shakespearean stage, especially *Hamlet*.

10 NEW DIRECTIONS

1 Henslowe attributes *The Devil and His Dame* to Haughton, *Henslowe's Diary*, ed. R. A. Foakes and R. T. Rickert (Cambridge University Press, 1963), p. 134. The subtitle of the Restoration play is *The Devil and His Dame*, and it is manifestly a play from the 1590s rather than the 1660s. William M. Baillie offers detailed commentary on the play's origin and date in his edition, which is cited here from *A Choice Ternary of English Plays* (Binghamton: Medieval and Renaissance Texts and Studies, 1984).

2 Barnes' debt to Marlowe is detailed by C. H. Herford, *Studies in the Literary Relations of England and Germany in the Sixteenth Century* (Cambridge University Press, 1886), pp. 188–203, and by Jim C. Pogue in his edition of *The Devil's Charter* (New York: Garland, 1980), pp. 18–22.

3 G. K. Hunter, "English Folly and Italian Vice," in *Dramatic Identities and Cultural Tradition* (New York: Barnes and Noble, 1978), pp. 103–32. Mark Eccles pointed out Barnes' debt to Machiavelli's *Discorsi* in the original Italian in "Barnabe Barnes," *Thomas Lodge and Other Elizabethans*, ed. Charles J. Sisson (Cambridge, Mass.: Harvard University Press, 1933), p. 238.

4 For further development of this argument, see John D. Cox, "Stage Devilry in Two King's Men Plays of 1606," *Modern Language Review* 93 (1998), 934–47.

5 Robert Daborne's lost play, *Machiavel and the Devil*, may be another devil play in the category of Machiavelli's influence, but nothing is known about it except that it was associated with the Lady Elizabeth's Men in 1613.

6 Thomas Heywood, *The Silver Age*, in *The Dramatic Works of Thomas Heywood*, 6 vols. (London: John Pearson, 1874), vol. 3, 159 SD. Contrast the firing of hell's scaffold in the Digby *Mary Magdalen*, where it functions morally to suggest hell's self-defeating strategies, as noted above in chapter 4.

7 Scot identifies the pagan gods as devils in chapter 20 of his "Discourse vpon diuels and spirits," *The discouerie of witchcraft* (Imprinted at London by William Brome, 1584), pp. 521–23.

8 This is not to say that the play as a whole is incoherent. See Ellen R. Belton, "'A Plaine and Direct Course': the Unity of Thomas Heywood's *Ages*," *Philological Quarterly* 56 (1977), 169–82.

9 Christopher Marlowe, *Dr. Faustus*, ed. David M. Bevington and Eric Rasmussen, Revels Edition (Manchester University Press, 1995), A-Text, 1.3.26.

10 *Bussy D'Ambois: A Tragedie*, ed. G. Blakemore Evans and Thomas L. Berger, *The Plays of George Chapman. The Tragedies* (Cambridge: D. S. Brewer, 1987), 4.2.24. Quotations are from the quarto of 1641.

11 Nicholas Brooke's edition of the play is misleading in this regard, translating Chapman's stage direction (*Surgit Spiritus [Behemoth] cum suis* [5.3.54]) as "The Spirit [Behemoth] springs up with his [Devils]," *Bussy D'Ambois*, Revels Edition (London: Methuen, 1964), 5.2.51. Brooke similarly substitutes "devils" for Chapman's "spirits" in the stage direction at 4.2.60.

12 Millar Maclure, *George Chapman: A Critical Study* (University of Toronto Press, 1966), pp. 32–45.

13 Maclure, *George Chapman*, p. 152. The play is cited here from *The Plays of George Chapman. The Tragedies*, ed. G. Blakemore Evans and Thomas L. Berger (Cambridge: D. S. Brewer, 1987).

14 Allen Bergson, "Stoicism Achieved: Cato in Chapman's *Tragedy of Caesar and Pompey*," *Studies in English Literature 1500–1900* 17 (1977), 295–302.

15 The classical allusion is identified by T. M. Parrott, *The Tragedies of George Chapman*, 2 vols. (New York: Russell and Russell, 1961), 2:167.

16 Paradoxically, as it turns out, Shakespeare had substituted ghosts for the devils of his source, Hall's *Union* (following the Croyland Chronicle and Polydore Vergil), probably in conformity to Senecan expectation.

17 Thomas Goffe, *The Courageous Turk*, ed. Susan Gushee O'Malley (New York and London: Garland Publishing, 1979), 5.3.26 SD.

18 Nathan Field, *A Woman Is a Weathercock*, ed. William Peery, *The Plays of Nathan Field* (Austin: University of Texas Press, 1950), 5.2.71.

19 Peter F. Mullany argues that Fletcher's influence also makes *The Virgin Martyr* merely witty, rendering its traditional elements superficial and parodic, in "Religion in Massinger and Dekker's *The Virgin Martyr*," *Komos* 2 (1970), 89–97. Contrast between *The Virgin Martyr* and *The Prophetess* makes clear how much more serious the earlier play is.

20 John Fletcher and Philip Massinger, *The Prophetess*, ed. George Walton Williams, in *The Dramatic Works in the Beaumont and Fletcher Canon*, ed. Fredson Bowers, 10 vols. (Cambridge University Press, 1966–96), vol. 9.

21 John Suckling, *The Goblins*, ed. L. A. Beaurline, *The Works of Sir John Suckling: The Plays* (Oxford: Clarendon Press, 1971), 1.1.113–30.

22 John Dryden "Preface to the Enchanted Island," *Five Restoration Adaptations of Shakespeare*, ed. Christopher Spence (Urbana: University of Illinois Press, 1965), pp. 111–12.

23 James Shirley, *St. Patrick for Ireland*, ed. John P. Turner (New York: Garland, 1979), pp. 33–45.

24 For references, see 1.1.223–24, 2.2.0 SD, 2.2.74, 3.2.130, 4.1.179.

25 Quoted from Pepys' diary in Cyrus Hoy, *Introductions, Notes, and Commentaries to texts in "The Dramatic Works of Thomas Dekker" edited by Fredson Bowers*, 4 vols. (Cambridge University Press, 1980), 3:193.

26 *The Chester Mystery Cycle*, ed. R. M. Lumiansky and David Mills, EETS s.s. 3
    (London: Oxford University Press, 1974), *The Last Judgment*, lines 477–78.
27 Mark Koch, "The Desanctification of the Beggar in Rogue Pamphlets of
    the English Renaissance," in *The Work of Dissimilitude*, ed. David Allen and
    Robert White (Newark: University of Delaware Press; London: Associated
    University Presses, 1992), pp. 91–104.
28 For more detail about Dekker's view in a Foucauldian analysis of anti-indi-
    gent literature, see William C. Carroll, *Fat King, Lean Beggar: Representations of
    Poverty in the Age of Shakespeare* (Ithaca: Cornell University Press, 1996).
29 John Marston, *Histriomastix*, in *The School of Shakespeare*, ed. Richard
    Simpson, 2 vols. (London: Chatto and Windus, 1878), 2.1.281ff.
30 Thomas Lodge and Robert Greene, *A Looking Glass for London and England*,
    ed. George Alan Clugston (New York and London: Garland Publishing,
    1980), G2ᵛ–G3. The ruffians have an earlier scene with Adam at Bᵛ–B2ᵛ.
31 *A Pleasant Comedy Called Wily Beguilde* (1606) (Tudor Facsimile Texts, 1912;
    reprinted New York: AMS, 1970), p. 60.
32 *The Two Noble Ladies*, ed. Rebecca G. Rhoads, Malone Society Reprints
    (Oxford University Press, 1930), lines 3.3.1111–12. Act and scene divisions
    are in the manuscript, which the editor transcribed, adding through-line
    numbering.
33 Stoic advice also appears in 2.3.698–99, 703–4, 720–22, and 3.3.1050ff.
34 *Microcosmus A Morall Maske*, ed. A. H. Bullen, *The Works of Thomas Nabbes*, 2
    vols. (London: Wyman & Sons, 1887), 2:159–218.

Index